SOLUTIONS MANUAL TO ACCOMPANY

THE ANALYSIS AND USE OF FINANCIAL STATEMENTS

GERALD I. WHITE, CFA
Grace & White, Inc

ASHWINPAUL C. SONDHI, Ph.D.
Columbia Business School
Columbia University

DOV FRIED, Ph.D.
Stern School of Business
New York University

JOHN WILEY & SONS, INC

New York   •   Chichester   •   Brisbane   •   Toronto   •   Singapore

CONTENTS

ERRATA FOR FIRST PRINTING

Page 559:

11B: (i)   should be "deferred tax <u>assets</u>"

    (ii)   should be "deferred tax <u>asset</u>"

    (iii) should be "deferred tax <u>asset</u>"

Page 619:

Problem 5, line 2: 2014 should be <u>2004</u>

Part D should read:

    D.   Discuss two reasons why Derek might choose to refinance its 8% debt at a higher interest rate.

Page 621:

Problem 9, line 3: add the words <u>(on the lessee)</u> after "effects of this choice"

Page 742:

Problem 2B, line 1, should read <u>10P-1</u> (delete A)

Problem 4A, line 2, "transfers" should be <u>retains</u>
             line 3, "retains" should be <u>transfers</u>

Page 756:

Problem 7, table, add line after Current assets:

        Total assets   6454.3   6176.5

Problem 8, line 1, "data" should be <u>debt</u>

Page 834:

Add to the end of the footnote:

> The Company sold its 28 percent ownership interst in Baruch-Foster Corporation and recognized a $1 million gain in the first quarter of 1991 [included in income from investments].

Page 926:

Exhibit 12P-2, add line to table after "Stockholders' equity:"

> Sales 29000 10550

Page 930:

Problem 4B(iii), replace "at the close" with <u>on the first day</u>

Page 931:

Problem 5, line 5, add: <u>Roadway's 1991 revenues were $3177 million.</u>

Page 1005:

Problem 12, line 2, add:

> The effect of exchange rate changes on cash for 1991 was $(2,075,000); inventories at October 31, 1990 and 1991 were $59,762,000 and $51,777,000 respectively.

Problem 12C(ii), 1992 should be 199<u>1</u>

Page 1145:

Problem C, line 3, replace "beginning' with <u>end</u>

Page 1146:

Problem C should be <u>D</u>

Problem D should be <u>E</u>

Chapter 1 - Solutions

1. (i)   Need to decide whether standards are meant to primarily serve
         preparers (provide flexibility), auditors (easy to audit) or users
         (provide information). The standards would also be a function of
         expected or planned growth in capital markets, the extent of private
         and government participation in the standard setting process, and
         the degree of foreign investment sought by the government.

    (ii) Relevance indicates that financial statements provide information
         useful for decision making, even at the cost of precision.
         Reliability requires that financial data be verifiable even if less
         relevant. The degree of emphasis placed on relevance versus
         reliability will depend on decisions made in (i) above.

    (iii) Comparability would argue for a single accounting standard for all
         similar situations. For example, one method for inventories and one
         depreciation method for all firms. The standard setters must also
         decide whether to allow different treatment across industries for
         similar economic events, e.g., reporting for certain short-term
         investments in the United States differs across industrial,
         insurance, and banking firms.

    (iv) Political factors relate to whether financial reporting should serve
         governmental aims, for example promoting certain economic decisions.
         Legal factors would include whether financial reporting should
         conform to tax reporting. Cultural factors would include historic
         accounting methods in China and whether the country wants to emulate
         Western accounting standards or develop another model.

2. Short-term lenders are concerned primarily with liquidity. Accounting
    standards would focus primarily on near-term cash flows and might include
    cash flow forecasting.

    Long-term equity investors are primarily concerned with the earning
    power of the firm. Income measurement would be the focus of standards for
    such users.

    Tax authorities are concerned with the generation of revenue.
    Accounting standards might limit the ability of firms to shift income from
    one period to another and place stricter controls on the amount and timing
    of deductible expenditures.

    Corporate managers seek to control their reported earnings, to cast
    the best possible light on their stewardship. Accounting standards set by
    managers would be highly flexible, with little supplementary information
    and footnote disclosure.

3. The matching principle states that revenues should be matched with the expenses incurred to generate them. As the revenues and required expenditures may be incurred in different accounting periods, accrual accounting is required to recognize them in the same period.

4. The going concern assumption states that the enterprise will continue operating in a normal fashion. This assumption permits financial statements to record assets and liabilities based on the cash flows that they will generate as the firm operates. If this assumption were absent, all assets and liabilities would have to be evaluated on a liquidation basis. Accrual accounting could not be used, as the assumption that expenditures would produce future revenues could no longer be made.

5. Public companies must provide current investors with detailed financial statements, mandated by the FASB and the SEC. Because of SEC requirements, annual and quarterly financial data are publicly available to potential investors as well as current ones. Private companies do not prepare audited financial data in many cases. When financial statements are prepared, they will lack certain SEC-mandated data (such as the management discussion and analysis). In addition, these statements may not be made available to potential investors.

6. All public companies in the United States are required to issue financial statements whose form and content are determined by the FASB after much public debate. The SEC oversees this process and supplements these standards with additional disclosure requirements. U. S. GAAP has an investor and user orientation and it provides for detailed disclosures. Financial statements issued by non-U.S. firms follow local accounting standards, often with limited disclosures. These standards are often developed from legal and political requirements and do not have the same investor protection objective as in the United States.

7. The FASB sets accounting standards for all audited financial statements prepared under U.S. GAAP. The SEC has jurisdiction over all public companies. Given the overlapping jurisdiction, the SEC generally relies on the FASB to set standards but supplements those standards with additional disclosure requirements deemed necessary to inform and protect investors in public companies.

8. The balance sheet includes only those economic events that qualify as assets and liabilities. As accounting standards define, in effect, assets and liabilities they determine which economic events are accounted for and which are ignored. Events ignored (such as many contracts) are excluded from the process of preparing financial statements. The recognition rules also influence managers' decisions regarding the form of contractual agreements used to acquire assets and incur liabilities, thereby affecting the preparation of financial statements.

9. Liabilities represent the assets of the firm funded by trade and financial creditors. Equity represents the permanent capital of the firm, and is the residual after all liabilities have been satisfied. Thus the distinction between liabilities and equity is the difference between prior claims and permanent capital. Misclassification will over- or understate the firm's reported debt and the degree of leverage or financial risk affecting the equity holders.

10. Historical cost is more reliable as it is measured by reference to past transactions. Market values are less reliable as they may require assumptions and estimates. However, general inflation and specific price changes make historical costs less useful (relevant) as time passes. Market values always have relevance as they represent the current value of the firm's resources. The nature of the markets (liquidity, volatility, and transparency) affects the reliability of the values reported.

11. Contra accounts are deductions from asset or liability accounts that accumulate valuation or other adjustments (such as accumulated depreciation) and reduce the asset or liability account to its "net" amount. Adjunct accounts are reported separately; examples are valuation adjustments in equity and bond premium.

12. A. Revenues and expenses result from the firm's operating activities; gains and losses result from valuation and other non-operating events. The latter are peripheral to the normal activities of the firm and, therefore, should be separated for analytic purposes.

    B. Comprehensive income includes all changes in equity other than transactions with stockholders. It encompasses operating earnings and "non-recurring" items as well as valuation adjustments and the cumulative effect of accounting changes. Comprehensive income could serve as a bridge between "income from continuing operations" (most useful for earnings forecasting) and the net change in stockholders' equity (excluding transactions with owners).

13. Recurring income refers to income from continuing operations, the best measure of the operating profits of the firm for that time period, and therefore the best base for forecasting. Non-recurring items are unusual or infrequent in nature, and usually result from non-operating factors. Extraordinary items are both unusual in nature and infrequent in occurrence, and are even less useful as an indicator of the firm's profitability.

14. The classification of cash flows into three categories highlights their differing natures. Cash from operations reports the cash generated or used by the firm's operating activities. Cash for investment measures the outflow for investments in capacity, for acquisitions, or for long-term investments. Cash from financing indicates the source (debt or equity) of any financing required by the firm as well as distributions to preferred and common stockholders.

    These classifications should be viewed over time as indicators of the firm's liquidity and solvency. The relationship among these classifications is especially important.

15. Footnotes are an integral part of the financial statements and are included in the audit. They supply detail that supplements financial statement data. Supplementary schedules may be included with the financial statements (e.g. oil and gas disclosures) but may not be audited.

16. The Management Discussion and Analysis is intended to explain changes in reported income statement, balance sheet, and cash flow items and therefore help financial statement users to interpret these financial

statements. The MD&A should discuss trends, including those expected to continue in the future. This discussion should aid the prediction of future cash flows and earnings.

17. (i)   The opinion should report any changes in accounting principles used and refer to the footnote providing additional information on the change.

     (ii)   Changes in accounting estimates are not reported by the auditor.

     (iii) The auditor's report must describe uncertainties if they are material to the firm's financial position.

     (iv)   While the auditor's opinion provides reasonable assurance that there are no material errors in the financial statements, it is not a guarantee against error or even fraud.

18. A.   Deere changed its accounting method for income taxes, adopting SFAS 109 in fiscal 1992. The argument for including a reference to the change in the auditor's report is that accounting changes reduce the comparability of financial statements as different methods are used in different years. The argument against reporting the change is that there was no material effect in the year of the change.

     B.   While the effect of SFAS 109 may not have been material in fiscal 1992, the new standard may affect reported net income in future years.

19. The preparer gathers financial data, chooses accounting principles and estimates, and assembles the data into financial statements using those methods and estimates. The auditor examines the financial statements for errors, and checks that the accounting methods and assumptions are permissible under GAAP and whether they have been applied consistently over time.

20. Companies generally prepare financial statements using the accounting principles of their home country. When selling securities in a foreign jurisdiction, they may be required to prepare supplementary financial statements using the accounting standards of that country. The cost and inconvenience of this extra work may dissuade the firm from selling securities in that country, thus depriving that country's investors of the opportunity to invest.

     On the other hand, investors must choose between that firm's securities and those of home country firms using local accounting principles. If the foreign firm uses different accounting principles, investors may make poor investment decisions because of their inability to separate real differences between firms from differences caused by alternative accounting principles.

21. A. Because the probability of loss is so low (less than one in ten thousand), Bonnywill will report no loss. If a fire occurs, the firm will then accrue the estimated loss.

    B. An alternative method would accrue the expected value of the loss, computed by multiplying the number of units sold by the expected loss per unit. The result would be 10,000 x .00009 x $100,000 = $90,000.

22. A. For firm A the probability of loss is remote (.3%) so that no liability should be recognized. If an accident occurs, the firm would recognize a liability equal to the expected loss.

    B. Firm B expects to have 10 workers' compensation claims each year (10,000/1,000) with a loss of $10,000 per claim. Thus firm B should accrue $100,000 per year. The difference from firm A is that the employee population is large enough to make the loss predictable.

23. A. "Discontinued operations" refers to a segment of the firm which has been (or will be) sold or closed down. The advantage of segregating the results of such operations is that reported sales and earnings become a more reliable indicator of future results (which will exclude those of the discontinued operations). On the other hand, segregating these results sweeps management errors under the rug as the results of discontinued operations are often ignored by financial statement users.

    B. When only a portion of a segment is discontinued, it may not be possible to segregate the sales, expenses, assets, and liabilities of those operations from those of the remainder of the segment (which will continue to operate). As a result, the operating results of the discontinued portion of the business will disappear from the financial statements but the assets and liabilities will remain as will the operations of the remaining segment.

    Analysis of the firm is helped because the financial statements report how management has performed given all of the assets under its control. If some operations are discontinued, management should be able to find replacement business. On the other hand, sales and expense comparisons are hampered by the disappearance of part of the segment's operations. If the gross margin of the discontinued portion of the segment is very different from that of the rest of the segment, unadjusted operating results will not be a good basis for forecasting.

Chapter 1A - Solutions

1.   Accounting Entries

(1) Inventory	$ 881	
Accounts payable		$ 881
(2) Accounts receivable	1,265	
Income summary (sales revenue)		1,265
(3) Income summary (depreciation expense)	10	
Accumulated depreciation		10
(4) Income summary (interest expense)	19	
Cash		19
(5) (a) Cash	65	
Short-term debt		65
(b) Long-term debt	2	
Cash		2
(6) Cash	5	
Common stock		5
(7) Cash	1,210	
Accounts receivable		1,210
(8) Income summary (COGS)	843	
Inventory		843
(9) (a) Income summary (income tax expense)	33	
Income tax payable		33
(b) Income tax payable	19	
Cash		19
(10) Retained earnings*	21	
Cash		21
(11) Property, plant, and equipment	17	
Cash		17
(12) Common stock	14	
Cash		14
(13) Income summary (operating expense)	320	
Cash		320
(14) Accounts payable	867	
Cash		867
(Close) Income summary	40	
Retained earnings		40

*The declaration of dividends would be recorded as a debit to retained earnings and a credit to dividends payable which would be debited when paid.

T-Accounts

Cash

	34		
(7)	1,210	19	(4)
		19	(9b)
		320	(13)
		867	(14)
		17	(11)
(5a)	65	2	(5b)
(6)	5	21	(10)
		14	(12)
	35		

Accounts Receivable

	365		
(2)	1,265	1,210	(7)
	420		

Inventory

	227		
(1)	881	843	(8)
	265		

Property, Plant and Equipment

	120	
(11)	17	
	137	

Accumulated Depreciation

		40
		10 (3)
		50

Income Summary

(3)	10	1,265	(2)
(4)	19		
(8)	843		
(9a)	33		
(13)	320		
Close	40		

Accounts Payable

		104	
(14)	867	881	(1)
		118	

Taxes Payable

		81	
(9b)	19	33	(9a)
		95	

Short-term Debt			Long-term Debt	
	181			48
	65 (5a)		(5b) 2	
	246			46

Common Stock			Retained Earnings	
	81			211
(12) 14	5 (6)		(10) 21	40 close
	72			230

Balance Sheet

Cash	$ 35	Accounts payable	$ 118
Accounts receivable	420	Income tax payable	95
Inventory	265	Short-term debt	246
Current assets	$ 720	Current liabilities	459
		Long-term debt	46
Property, plant, & equipment	137	Total liabilities	$ 505
Accumulated depr.	(50)	Common stock	72
	87	Retained earnings	230
Total assets	$ 807	Total equities	$ 807

Income Statement

Sales		$ 1,265
Expenses:		
Cost of goods sold	$ 843	
Operating expense	320	
Depreciation	10	
Interest	19	
Tax	33	(1,225)
Net income		$ 40

Statement of Cash Flows

Cash from operations:
Collections from customers $ 1,210

Payments for:
Inventory	$ 867	
Operating expense	320	
Interest	19	
Taxes	19	(1,225)

                                                              $ (15)

Cash for investments:
Purchase of property   (17)

Cash from financing:
Short-term debt	$ 65	
Long-term debt	(2)	
Common stock	(9)	
Dividends paid	(21)	33
Change in cash		$ 1

Indirect Calculation of Cash from Operations

Net income	$ 40	
Depreciation	10	$ 50

Changes in operating accounts:
Increase in accounts receivable	$(55)	
Increase in inventory	(38)	
Increase in accounts payable	14	
Increase in income tax payable	14	(65)
		$(15)

2.
Sales	$ 75,000	(2)
COGS	(25,000)	(1 & 2)
Rent	(3,000)	(3)
Wages	(5,000)	(4)
Net income	$ 42,000	
Dividends	(7,000)	(6)
Balance in retained earnings	$ 35,000	

NOTE: Item (5) common stock issuance does not affect retained earnings.

3.
Revenues:	Sales	$ 130,000	(1)
	Consulting	20,000	(6)
	Total	$ 150,000	
Expenses:	Cost-of-goods-sold	$ (80,000)	(1)
	Depreciation	(7,000)	(3)
	Rent	(8,000)	(7)
	Net income	$ 55,000	
	Change in retained earnings	(24,000)	(8)
	Dividends declared	$ 31,000)	

Items (2) and (4) are ignored as these costs are first capitalized as inventory and then "flow" to expense as part of cost of goods sold.

4.
	Cash balance 1991	$ 2,000,000	(5)
+	Cash from operations	600,000	(1)
+	Issuance of notes	100,000	(2) & (3)
−	Dividends paid	(80,000)	(6)
	Cash balance 1992	$ 2,620,000	

5. A.   Cost of goods sold = $80,000 ($100,000/1.25).

Since inventory decreased by $60,000, purchases were $20,000.

Since accounts payable decreased by $30,000, payments must have been $50,000.

B.   Since net income was $12,000 and retained earnings increased by only $10,000, dividends declared must have been $2,000. Since dividends payable decreased by $8,000 with new dividends of $2,000, dividends paid must have been $10,000.

C.   Change in property less change in accumulated depreciation = $(50,000).

Therefore change in property = $(50,000) + $(40,000) = $(90,000). $90,000 must be the cost of assets disposed of during the year.

Change in accumulated depreciation = depreciation expense less accumulated depreciation of assets disposed of during the year.

$(40,000) = $30,000 − ?

Accumulated depreciation of assets disposed of = $70,000

6. **T-Accounts**
   ($ thousands)

Cash			
	80		
(1)	225	100	(2)
		20	(3)
		50	(4)
		15	(5)
(J)	10		
(6)	10	20	(7)
	120		

Accounts Receivable				Inventory	
	55				75	
(A)	250	225 (1)	(C)	110	95 (D)
	80				90	

Prepaid Rent			
	5		
(5)	15	20	(B)
	0		

Property, Plant & Equipment			
	100		
		20	(J)
	80		

Accumulated Depreciation			
		30	
(J)	10	10	(I)
		30	

Income Summary			
(B)	20	250	(A)
(D)	95		
(E)	30		
(F)	60		
(I)	10		
(H)	35		

Accounts Payable			
		55	
(2)	100	110	(C)
		65	

Taxes Payable			
		40	
(3)	20	30	(E)
		50	

Wages Payable			
		0	
(4)	50	60	(F)
		10	

Dividends Payable			
		30	
(7)	20	30	(G)
		40	

Common Stock			
		90	
		10	(6)
		100	

Retained Earnings			
		70	
(G)	30	35	(H)
		75	

A. 1. Dividends declared (G) = $30,000

2. Inventory purchased (C) = $110,000

3. Monthly rent = $20,000 (B)/12 = $1,667

4.   Cash receipts from customers (1) = $225,000

5.   Income (H) = $35,000

6.   Cash from operations ((1)-(2)-(3)-(4)-(5)) = $40,000

7.   Original cost of PP&E sold (J) = $20,000

B. | | |
|---|---:|
| Sales | $250,000 |
| Cost of goods sold | (95,000) |
| Wage expense | (60,000) |
| Rent expense | (20,000) |
| Depreciation expense | (10,000) |
| Income tax expense | (30,000) |
| Net income | $ 35,000 |

7.   **T-Accounts**
      ($ thousands)

Cash

	185		
(K)	152	80	(2)
		2	(5)
		70	(B)
		20	(D)
		20	(E)
(G)	20	55	(F)
(H)	10		
	120		

Accounts Receivable

	80		
(J)	222	152	(K)
	150		

Inventory

	120		
(A)	60	100	(1)
	80		

Property, Plant and Equipment

	180	
(E)	20	
	200	

Accumulated Depreciation

	40	
	10	(4)
	50	

Income Summary			
(1)	100	222	(J)
(2)	80		
(3)	60		
(4)	10		
(5)	2		
		30	(I)

Accounts Payable					Rent Payable			
		120					0	
(B)	70	60	(A)		(D)	20	60	(3)
		110					40	

Bond Payable					Dividends Payable			
		20					5	
		10	(H)		(F)	55	50	(6)
		30					0	

Common Stock					Retained Earnings			
		200					180	
		20	(G)		(6)	50		
					(I)	30		
		220					100	

A. 1. Inventory purchased (A) = $60,000

2. Dividends paid (F) = $55,000

3. Additions to property, plant, and equipment (E) = $20,000

4. Net loss (I) = $(30,000)

5. Sales revenue (J) = $222,000

6. Monthly rent (3) = $60,000/12 = $5000

7. Interest rate (2) = $2000/$20,000 = 10%

B. Cash from operations
       From customers $152,000
       For inventory   (70,000)
       For wages   (80,000)
       For rent   (20,000)
       For interest   (2,000)
                                              $(20,000)

    Cash for investment (increase in PP&E)   (20,000)

    Cash for financing:
       Stock issue $ 20,000
       Bond issue   10,000
       Dividends paid   (55,000)
                                              (25,000)

    Change in cash $(65,000)

8. **T-Accounts**
    ($ thousands)

		Cash		
	101			
(B)	191	120	(D)	
		40	(E)	
		12	(F)	
		13	(L)	
(J)	13	25	(7)	
(G)	20	12	(8)	
(H)	10			
	113			

Accounts Receivable					Allowance for Doubtful Accounts			
	70						3	
(1)	200	4	(A)		(A)	4	2	(2)
		191	(B)					
	75						1	

Inventory					Prepaid Rent			
	50					3		
(C)	100	90	(3)				3	(K)
	60					0		

Property, Plant and Equipment			
(7)	100 25	15	(J)
	110		

Accumulated Depreciation			
(J)	1	30 1	(6)
		30	

Income Summary			
(2)	2	200	(1)
(3)	90		
(4)	30		
(5)	12		
(6)	1		
(I)	42		
(J)	1		
(K)	22		

Merchandise Accounts Payable			
(D)	120	40 100	(C)
		20	

Services Accounts Payable			
(E)	40	50 30	(4)
		40	

Rent Payable			
(L)	13	0 19	(K)
		6	

Interest Payable			
(F)	12	1 12	(5)
		1	

Long-Term Debt			
		100 20	(G)
		120	

Common Stock			
		80 10	(H)
		90	

Retained Earnings			
(8)	12	20 42	(I)
		50	

```
Cash from operations:
    From customers          $191,000
    For inventory           (120,000)
    For services             (40,000)
    For rent                 (13,000)
    For interest             (12,000)
                                             $   6,000

Cash for investment:
    Purchase of PP&E         $(25,000)
    Sale of PP&E               13,000
                                              (12,000)

Cash from financing:
    Stock issue              $ 10,000
    Debt issue                 20,000
    Dividends paid            (12,000)
                                               18,000

Change in cash                               $  12,000
```

Chapter 2 - Solutions

1. A. When the product is a commodity with a known price and liquid market.

    B. When collection is assured because the risk of non-payment can be estimated.

    C. When collection is uncertain because the risk of non-payment cannot be estimated.

2. A. (i) Terry can recognize revenue as long as collection is assured (it can estimate bad debts).

        (ii) Terry cannot recognize revenue until the return period has passed and it is possible to determine actual sales.

    B. Early recognition of sale results in the overstatement of accounts receivable, the understatement of inventory (that should not have been considered sold), and the overstatement of retained earnings (as income has been recognized too soon).

3. A. Under the completed contract method, reported earnings are more volatile because all recognition is delayed until completion. As a result, net income occurs only in periods when projects are completed, and depends on the number and profitability of projects completed in each period.

    B. With many contracts, some averaging occurs so that the volatility of firm results is not as great (although it is still greater than under the percentage of completion method).

    C. When a firm has relatively few projects and uses the completed contract method, reported revenues and net income are highly variable. The volatility makes forecasting extremely difficult. With a greater number of contracts, volatility is reduced, and forecasting is easier. The percentage of completion method, by reporting revenues and net income as earned over the life of the project, provides better data regarding the operations of the firm. However, reported cash flows are not affected by the choice of accounting method.

4. (i) Under the completed contract method, no revenues or cost-of-goods-sold are recognized until completion; both are lower during the project but higher during the period when completion takes place. Their trend is highly volatile. Under the percentage of completion

method, revenues and COGS are recognized as projects progress; they are higher during the project but lower at completion. The trend will reflect the overall level of activity and will be less volatile.

(ii)   Earnings recognition follows the same pattern as revenue recognition, as explained in (i), assuming that estimates of project profitability prove to be accurate. Under the percentage of completion method, revised estimates of profitability increase the volatility of income as the past over- or underaccrual of income must be offset in the period of revision.

(iii) No difference between methods; operating cash flows are not affected by the choice of accounting method.

(iv)   Accounts receivable will always be higher under the percentage of completion method, as that method recognizes revenue sooner, creating accounts receivable. Total current assets will also be higher as the higher level of accounts receivable under the percentage of completion method more than offsets the higher level of inventory under the completed contract method. Long-term assets are not affected by the choice of method.

5.   (All data in $ millions)

A.

	19X5	19X6	19X7	Total
Revenue*	$2.75	$4.40	$3.85	$11.00
Profit*	.25	.40	.35	1.00
CFO	(.50)	(.50)	2.00	1.00

*For each year James recognizes both revenue and profit based on the percentage of the tunnel completed as measured by costs incurred.

B.

Revenue*	---	---	$11.00	$11.00
Profit*	---	---	1.00	1.00
CFO	(.50)	(.50)	2.00	1.00

*Under the completed contract method, all revenue and income recognition takes place at completion of the tunnel in 19X7. CFO is identical, however.

C.   Revenue is unaffected by the change unless completion is measured by reference to cost. Profit, however, must be recalculated. Estimated total profit is now zero. As James recognized $.25 of profit in 19X5, it must recognize a *loss* of $.25 in 19X6 in order to bring the cumulative profit to zero.

   If completion is measured by cost incurred, then cumulative revenue (through 19X6) will now be $6.50 million (equal to cost incurred). As $2.75 million of revenue was recognized in 19X5, only $3.75 million ($6.50 - $2.75) can be recognized in 19X6. Note that, while *cumulative* results are correct, revenues and profit may not reflect the operating results for either 19X5 or 19X6.

D.   The completed contract method has the advantage of delaying recognition of revenue and profit until all risk has been eliminated. The disadvantage is that, under normal circumstances, the performance of the firm is understated.

The percentage of completion method has the advantage of reporting revenues and profits as earned. The disadvantage is the risk of surprise if estimates must be revised during the project.

6.   A. (i) and (ii)

19X0: Revenue = 20% x $6 million = $1.2 million

Costs incurred = 20% x $4.5 million = $.9 million.

(Income recognized is $.3 million difference.)

19X1: Revenue = 60% x $6 million = $3.6 - $1.2 = $2.4 million

Costs incurred (cumulative) = 60% x $4.8 million = $2.88 million. As 19X0 recognition was $.9 million, 19X1 recognition must be $ 1.98 million ($2.88 - $0.9).

(Income recognized is $.42 million difference, making cumulative recognition $.72 million for two years.)

B.   There should be no effect; expenditures that do not contribute to the completion of the project do not affect revenue or income under the percentage of completion method.

7.   A.

	Able	Baker	Charlie	David
Sales	$ 170,000[1]	$ 160,000[2]	$ 100,000	$ 50,000[3]
COGS	85,000	80,000	50,000	25,000
Net Income	$ 85,000	$ 80,000	$ 50,000	$ 25,000

[1]Sales = goods shipped + inventory + backorders, all measured at selling price.
[2]Sales = goods shipped + inventory
[3]Cash collected = sales - accounts receivable

B. and C.   CFO and cash balances will be identical; revenue and net income differences reflect only the choice of accounting method, not any economic differences among the companies.

8.   A.   The pattern of income and revenue recognition are identical. Therefore, the answers to A(i) and A(ii) are identical. To maximize the present value of the bonus, you should prefer the method that

recognizes revenue (and income) earlier. Thus, you should prefer the percentage of completion method to the completed contract method.

The pattern of recognition is (1/2, 1/4, 1/4) for the percentage of completion method and (1/3, 1/3, 1/3) for the installment method. Since on a cumulative basis, the percentage of completion method (1/2, 3/4, 1) dominates the installment method (1/3, 2/3, 1) it is preferred.

All three methods show identical CFO patterns and you should be indifferent under the third bonus criterion.

B.   Over the project's life all three methods generate identical total revenue, income, and CFO. Since payment is made at completion, you are indifferent.

9.   A.   Projects for which work was done in previous years were completed in 1991 and revenue was recognized. Under the percentage of completion method, revenue for those projects was recognized in 1990 and prior years. Apparently completions were larger in 1991 than in 1990. However, revenue recognized in 1991 under the percentage of completion method was less than revenue under that method for 1990.

B.   Similar to A, projects begun pre-1989 were completed in 1989-1991. The fact that the completed contract shows more revenue may be a signal that current business was declining.

C.   **Completed Contract Method**

	1989	1990	1991
Sales	$ 100,436	$ 79,865	$ 98,747
COGS	83,884	64,211	76,872
Gross Margin	$ 16,552	$ 15,654	$ 21,875
Percent	16.48%	19.60%	22.15%

Percentage of Completion Method

	1989	1990	1991
Sales	$ 95,974	$ 92,160	$ 89,309
COGS	79,473	74,203	69,225
Gross Margin	$ 16,501	$ 17,957	$ 20,084
Percent	17.19%	19.48%	22.49%

Gross Margin is improving over time indicating that the "markup" on recent projects is higher. The percentage of completion method picks this up earlier as it recognizes profits from more recent projects sooner. Thus, the profit margin under this method is higher (except for 1990 when the difference is marginal.)

D. Changing to the percentage of completion method should increase Newcor's accounts receivable (faster revenue recognition) but decrease inventory and customer advances. The result will increase the current ratio and change turnover ratios for these accounts.

E. The change in method should have no effect on the cash flow statement. All of the affected accounts are operating in nature and the changes will cancel out. Cash from operations will reflect only the actual cash flows associated with this business.

F. Some accounting changes do affect the classification of reported cash flows. Such effects occur when a change in method affects balance sheet accounts whose changes receive different cash flow classification. An example would be the capitalization of interest, which shifts interest from operating cash flow to investing cash flow.

10. A.

	19X0	19X1	19X2	19X3	19X4	19X5
Sales	$ ---	$ 140	$ 150	$ 165	$ 175	$ 195
Bad debt expense	---	7	7	8	10	10
Net receivables	30	40	50	60	75	95
Cash collections[1]	$ ---	$ 123	$ 133	$ 147	$ 150	$ 165

[1]Sales - bad debt expense - increase in net receivables

B. The bad debt provision does not seem to be adequate. From 19x1 - 19X5 sales increased by approximately 40%, while net receivables more than doubled, indicating that collections have been lagging. The ratios calculated below also indicate the problem. While bad debt expense has remained fairly constant at 5% of sales over the 5 year period, net receivables as a percentage of sales have increased from 29% to 49%; cash collections relative to sales have declined. Other possible explanations for these data are that stated payment terms have lengthened or that Stengel has allowed customers to delay payment.

Bad debt expense/sales	5.0%	4.7%	4.9%	5.7%	5.1%
Net receivables/sales	28.6	33.3	36.4	42.8	48.7
Cash collections/sales	87.9	88.7	89.1	85.7	84.611.

11. A.   **Palomba Pizza Stores**
          Statement of Cash Flows
          Year Ended December 31, 1991

Cash Flows from Operating Activities:		
Cash Collections from Customers	$ 250,000	
Cash Payments to Suppliers	(85,000)	
Cash Payments for Salaries	(45,000)	
Cash Payments for Interest	(10,000)	
Net Cash from Operating Activities		$ 110,000
Cash Flows from Investing Activities:		
Sales of Equipment	38,000	
Purchase of Equipment	(30,000)	
Purchase of Land	(14,000)	
Net Cash for Investing Activities		$ (6,000)
Cash Flows from Financing Activities:		
Retirement of Common Stock	(25,000)	
Payment of Dividends	(35,000)	
Net Cash for Financing Activities		$ (60,000)
Net Increase in Cash		$ 44,000
Cash at Beginning of Year		50,000
Cash at End of Year		$ 94,000

B.   Cash Flow from Operations (CFO) measures the liquidity of operations, in addition to profitability. If used as a measure of performance, CFO is less subject to distortion than the net income figure. Analysts use the CFO as check on the quality of reported earnings, although it is not a substitute for net income. Companies with high net income and low CFO may be using income recognition techniques that are suspect. The ability of a firm to generate cash from operations on a consistent basis is one indication of the financial health of the firm. Analysts search for trends in CFO to indicate future cash conditions and potential liquidity or solvency problems.

Cash Flow from Investing Activities (CFI) is an indication of how the firm is investing its excess cash. The analyst must consider the ability of the firm to continue to grow and CFI is a good indication of the attitude of management in this area. Analysis of this component of total cash flow indicates the capital expenditures made by management to maintain and expand productive capacity. Decreasing CFI may be a forecast of slower future growth.

Cash Flow from Financing (CFF) indicates the sources of financing for the firm. For firms that require external sources of financing (either borrowing or equity financing) it communicates management's preferences regarding financial leverage. Debt financing indicates future cash requirements for principal and interest payments. Equity financing will cause future earnings per share dilution.

For firms whose operating cash flow exceeds investment needs, CFF indicates whether that excess is used to repay debt, pay (or increase) cash dividends, or repurchase outstanding shares.

C.   Cash payments for interest should be classified as CFF for purposes of analysis. This classification separates the effect of financial leverage decisions from operating results. It also facilitates the comparison of Palomba with other firms whose financial leverage differs.

D.   The change in cash has no analytic significance. The change in cash (and hence, the cash balance at the end of the year) is a product of management decisions regarding financing. For example, the firm can show a large cash balance by drawing on bank lines just prior to year end.

12.   **Niagara Company**
       Statement of Cash Flows 19X2

Cash Collections	$ 980		[Sales – Δ A/C Receivable]
Cash Inputs	(670)		[COGS + Δ Inventory
Cash Expenses	(75)		[S & G Exp – Δ A/C Payable[1]]
Cash Interest Paid	(40)		[Int. Expense – Δ Int. Pay.]
Income Taxes Paid	(30)		[Income Tax Exp. – Δ Deferred
Cash from Operations		$ 165	Tax]
Purchase of Fixed Assets	(150)		[Depreciation Expense + Δ
Cash Used for Investing		(150)	Fixed Assets (net)]
Increase in LT Debt	50		
Decrease in Notes Pay.	(25)		
Dividends Paid	(30)		[Net Income – Δ Retained
Cash Used for Financing		(5)	Earnings]
Net Change in Cash		$ 10	
Cash Balance 12/31/X1		50	
Cash Balance 12/31/X2		$ 60	

[1]Can also be used to calculate cash inputs, decreasing that outflow to $645 while increasing cash expenses to $100.

13.   A.   **G Company**
              Income Statement, 19X4 ($ thousands)

Sales	$ 3,841	[receipts from customers + increase in accounts receivable]
COGS + Operating Expenses[1]	3,651	[payments – increase in inventory + increase in accounts payable]
Depreciation	15	[increase in accumulated depreciation]
Interest	41	[payments]
Taxes	42	[payment + increase in tax payable]
Net Income	$ 92	[check = change in retained earnings as there are no dividends]

[1]Note that these two cannot be calculated separately from the information available.

B.   **M Company**
       Cash Receipts and Disbursements, 19X4 ($ thousands)

Cash receipts from:		
Customers	$ 1,807	[Sales - increase in receivables]
Issue of stock	3	[Increase in account]
Short-term debt	62	[Increase in liability]
Long-term debt	96	[Increase in liability]
Total	$ 1,968	
Cash disbursements for:		
COGS/operating exp.	$ 1,843	[COGS + operating expense + increase in inventory + decrease in accounts payable]
Taxes	3	[Expense - increase in tax payable]
Interest	51	[Expense]
Total	$ 1,952	
Change in cash	$ 16	

NOTE: This is not a true receipts and disbursements schedule as it shows certain amounts (e.g., debt) on a net basis rather than gross. Such schedules (and cash flow statements) prepared from published data can only show some amounts net, unless supplementary data is available.

C.   The cash flow statements are presented together with the income statement for comparison purposes in answering Part D.

M Company--Statement of Cash Flows
($ thousands)

	19X0	19X1	19X2	19X3	19X4
CFO:					
From customers	$ 1,165	$ 1,210	$ 1,327	$ 1,587	$ 1,807
Less outlays for:					
COGS/Op. Exp.	1,130	1,187	1,326	1,672	1,843
Interest	15	19	16	21	51
Taxes	23	19	9	9	3
	$ (3)	$ (15)	$ (24)	$ (115)	$ (90)
CFI:					
PP&E purchase	(14)	(17)	(37)	(30)	(33)
CFF:					
Issue of stock	5	5	8	3	3
Short-term debt	64	65	--	153	62
Long-term debt	--	--	100	--	96
Dividends	(20)	(21)	(21)	(21)	(22)
Repurchase of stock	(22)	(14)	--	(10)	--
Repayment of LT debt	(2)	(2)	(3)	--	--
Repayment of ST debt	--	--	(8)	--	--
	$ 25	$ 33	$ 76	$ 125	$ 139
Change in Cash	$ 8	$ 1	$ 15	$ (20)	$ 16

M Company--Income Statement
($ thousands)

	19X0	19X1	19X2	19X3	19X4
Sales	$ 1,220	$ 1,265	$ 1,384	$ 1,655	$ 1,861
COGS	818	843	931	1,125	1,277
Operating exp.	298	320	363	434	504
Depreciation	9	10	11	12	14
Interest	15	19	16	21	51
Taxes	38	33	27	26	6
Total	$ 1,178	$ 1,225	$ 1,348	$ 1,852	$ 1,852
Net Income	$ 42	$ 40	$ 36	$ 37	$ 9

G Company--Statement of Cash Flows
($ thousands)

	19X0	19X1	19X2	19X3	19X4
CFO:					
From customers	$ 1,110	$ 1,659	$ 2,163	$ 2,809	$ 3,679
Disbursements:					
COGS/Op. Exp.	1,214	1,702	1,702	2,895	3,778
Interest	11	13	23	29	41
Taxes	13	15	16	29	35
CFO	$ (128)	$ (71)	$ (93)	$ (144)	$ (175)
CFI:					
PP&E purchase	---	---	(20)	(10)	---
CFF:					
Issue of stock	10	---	5	45	30
Short-term debt	80	52	91	3	60
Long-term debt	40	23	20	125	50
CFF	$ 130	$ 75	$ 116	$ 173	$ 140
Change in Cash	$ 2	$ 4	$ 3	$ 19	$ 35

G Company--Income Statement
($ thousands)

	19X0	19X1	19X2	19X3	19X4
Sales	$ 1,339	$ 1,731	$ 2,261	$ 2,939	$ 3,841
COGS	1,039	1,334	1,743	2,267	---
Operating exp.	243	312	398	524	3,651
Depreciation	10	10	12	14	15
Interest	11	13	23	29	41
Taxes	13	20	27	31	42
Total	$ 1,316	$ 1,689	$ 2,203	$ 2,865	$ 3,749
Net Income	$ 23	$ 42	$ 58	$ 74	$ 92

D. Both companies are credit risks. Although both are profitable, their CFO is increasingly negative. If current trends continue they face possible insolvency. However, before rejecting both loans outright, it is important to know whether CFO and income differ because the companies are doing poorly or because they are growing too fast.

Both companies increased sales over the 5 year period; Company M by 50%, Company G by more than 300%. Are these sales real (will cash collections materialize)? If they are "growing too fast", it may be advisable to make the loan but also to force the company to curtail its growth until CFO catches up. One way to verify whether the gap is the result of sales to poor credit risks is to check if the growth in receivables is "proportional" to the sales growth. Similar checks can be made for the growth in inventories and payables. In this case, the inventory of M company has doubled from 19X0 to 19X4 while COGS increased by only 56%. The inventory increase would be one area to investigate further.

There is a significant difference in the investment pattern of the two companies. Company M has made purchases of PPE each year, while Company G has made little net investment in PPE over the period. Yet Company G has grown much faster. Does this reflect the nature of the business (Company G is much less capital intensive) or has Company G used off balance sheet financing techniques?

The cash from financing patterns of the two companies also differ. Both tripled their total debt over the period and increased the ratio of total debt to equity. Given Company M's slower growth (in sales and equity), its debt burden has grown much more rapidly. Despite this, Company M has continued to pay dividends and repurchase stock. Company G has not paid dividends and has issued new equity. These two factors account for its larger increase in equity from 19X0 to 19X4.

Based only on the financial data provided, G looks like the better credit risk. Its sales and income are growing rapidly, while M's income is stable to declining on modestly growing sales. Unless further investigation changes the insights discussed here, you should prefer to lend to Company G.

14. A. **Mercantile Stores**
    Cash Flow from Operations, Direct Method
    Year Ended January 31, 1992
    ($ thousands)

Net sales	$ 2,442,425	
Δ in accounts receivable	11,172	
Cash collections		$ 2,453,597
Cost of goods sold	(1,720,947)	
Depreciation expense[1]	70,607	
Δ in inventories	11,898	
Δ in accounts payable	(1,698)	
Merchandise purchases		(1,640,140)
Selling and admin. expense	(546,682)	
Δ in other current assets		
Δ in other current	669	
liabilities	(1,751)	
Δ in accrued payroll	(2,147)	
Unidentified changes[2]	(3,601)	
Cash operating expense		(553,512)
Interest expense	(23,390)	
Δ in accrued interest[3]	(7)	
Interest paid		(23,397)
Interest income	4,511	
Other income	30,485	
Undistributed equity		
income[4]	(931)	
Cash other income		34,065
Income tax expense	(72,363)	
Δ in (3X) deferred income	$ 198	
tax (c/a)		
Δ in (3X) deferred income	697	
tax (ltl)		
Subtotal deferred taxes	$ 895	
Δ in (3X) accrued income		
tax (c/1)	(273)	
Income tax paid[5]		(71,741)
Cash Flow from Operations		$ 198,872

---

[1]As depreciation, a nonoperating expense, is not separately identified in the income statement, it must be removed. We assume that it is entirely included in cost of goods sold.

[2]Some of the "adjustments to reconcile" in the indirect method cash flow statement cannot be derived from the financial data provided. Some of the adjustments in the direct method statement (note 3, for example) are not shown in the indirect method statement. Yet both must produce the same cash flow from operations. These problems require a "plug" figure that is the "net" of all of these items:

The direct method cash flow statement follows the approach and format of Exhibit 2-3. The objective is to use the indirect method statement, as well as income statement and balance sheet data, to obtain a direct method statement that is as accurate as possible.

B. While the direct method statement for one year can provide only limited insight into cash flow relationships, there is some benefit. For example, compare the ratios of COGS and operating expenses to sales as shown in the income statement with their cash analogues:

	% Sales		% Collections
Cost of goods sold	70.5%	Merchandise purchases	66.8%
Selling and admin.	22.4	Cash operating expense	22.6

While depreciation expense accounts for most of the difference between the ratios, purchases are a lower percent (although collections exceed sales) as Mercantile controlled inventories to cope with recessionary conditions.

The direct method cash flow statement also permits the comparison of income statement accruals and their cash analogues (e.g., cost-of-goods sold and merchandise purchases). Both short- and long-term divergences may convey information about the impact of accounting choices and economic events. For example, an excess of merchandise purchases over COGS may indicate (if short-term) disappointing sales or purchases in anticipation of future orders. If long-term, the excess may indicate obsolete or excessive inventory.

Given more than one year of data, the direct method statement should facilitate analysis by providing comparisons (such as those above) not available from the indirect cash flow statement.

15. A. As Castle had no non-U.S. operations prior to the acquisition of Norton, balance sheet changes that differ from the corresponding cash flows must be the result of the acquisition of Norton. This relationship allows us to deduce the assets and liabilities of Norton that Castle acquired ($ thousands):

---

[2]Continued from previous page:

Shown in indirect method statement:		
Pensions	$ (4,256)	
Other working capital changes	(2,854)	
Subtotal		$ (7,110)
Shown in direct method statement:		
Accrued payroll	(2,147)	
Income tax accruals (net)	(273)	
Subtotal		(3,509)
Difference: unidentified changes (plug)		$ (3,601)

[3]The supplemental cash flow information discloses interest paid; the difference from interest expense must be an undisclosed accrual.

[4]This represents Mercantile's share of earnings not received as dividends; equity earnings (see Chapter 11) are assumed to be part of other income.

[5]Computed income taxes paid equal the amounts disclosed in the supplemental cash flow information; no adjustment is required.

	Balance Sheet – Change	Cash Flow Change	= Difference
Accounts receivable	$ (2,025) –	$ (3,818) =	$ 1,793
Inventories	17,594 –	13,592 =	4,002
Accounts payable	(8,605) –	(11,709) =	3,104

B. Similar to A, the fixed assets of Norton acquired must be the discrepancy between the balance sheet change and the cash flows. Because we must account for depreciation and asset sales, both of which reduce the carrying amount of fixed assets, the calculations are more complex ($ thousands):

Balance sheet change	$ 9,490
Depreciation expense	5,215
Basis of assets sold[1]	17
Assets acquired	$14,722
Less: capital expenditures[2]	(13,390)
Equals: Norton assets	$ 1,332

[1]The cash flow statement reports that the proceeds from assets sold were $34 and the gain was $17, indicating that the cost basis of assets sold was $17 ($34-$17). See Chapter 6 for further analysis of the fixed asset account of Castle.
[2]From the cash flow statement.

C. (i) While net income almost vanished in 1991, Castle reduced both accounts receivable and inventories during the year (lower receivables reflect lower sales). While lower payables offset part of these declines, nondebt current accounts fell by more than $20 million in 1991, in contrast to a rise of nearly $25 million in 1990. As a result, cash from operations swung from an outflow of nearly $15 million in 1990 to an inflow of $25 million for 1991.

(ii) The acquisition of Norton in 1990 increased Castle's inventories and accounts receivable, as shown in part A. The purchase of these assets was reflected in cash from investing activities. If the 1991 reduction included Norton assets acquired in 1990, then 1991 cash from operations is inflated. These assets were not acquired through operations and their sale distorts the trend of cash from operations.

16. A. This part of the question requires an understanding of SFAS 95, which governs the preparation of the Statement of Cash Flows. SFAS 95 permits use of either the direct or indirect method. As an initial step under either method, the effect of the Kraft acquisition must be removed as follows:

Balance Sheet Changes

	As Reported 1987	As Reported 1988	Total Change 1987–1988	Less Kraft	Adjusted Change
Receivables	$ 2,065	$ 2,222	$ 157	$ 758	$ (601)
Inventory	4,154	5,384	1,230	1,232	(2)
PPE	6,582	8,648	2,066	1,740	326
Goodwill	4,052	15,071	11,019	10,361	658
ST debt	1,440	1,259	(181)	700	(881)
A/C Payable	791	1,777	986	578	408
Accrued li- abilities	2,277	3,848	1,571	530	1,041
LT debt	6,293	17,122	10,829	900	9,929

Transactional Analysis Worksheet
($ Millions)

Revenues	$ 31,742		
Decrease in receivables	601		
Cash collections		$ 32,343	
Cost of goods sold	(12,156)		
Decrease in inventory	2		
Increase in accounts payable	408		
Cash inputs		(11,746)	
Selling & admin. expense	(14,410)		
Increase in accrued liabilities	1,041		
Cash expenses		(13,369)	
Income tax expense	(1,390)		
Increase in income taxes payable	362		
Decrease in deferred income taxes	(325)		
Income taxes paid		(1,353)	
Interest expense		(670)	
Cash flow--operating activities		$ 5,205	
Depreciation expense	$ (654)		
Increase in net PPE	(326)		
Cash invested in PPE		$ (980)	
Goodwill amortization	(125)		
Increase in goodwill	(658		
Goodwill purchased		(783)	
Decrease in investments		405	
Acquisition of Kraft		(11,383)	
Cash flow--investing activities		$(12,741)	
Dividends declared	$ (941)		
Increase in dividends payable	47		
Dividends paid		$ (894)	
Decrease in stockholders' equity (repurchase)*		(540)	
Net change in short-term debt		(881)	
Net change in long-term debt		9,929	
Cash flow--financing activities		$ 7,614	
			$ 78
Increase in cash and equivalents			

*The net issuance or repurchase of equity is computed by reconciling the stockholders' equity account:

Reconciliation of Stockholders' Equity

12/31/87 Balance	$ 6,823
1988 Net income	2,337
Dividend declared	(941)
Total	$ 8,219
12/31/88 Balance	(7,679)
Decrease in stockholders' equity (repurchase)	$ 540

If the "indirect method" is utilized, the following presentation is appropriate:

Philip Morris Companies, Inc.
Worksheet for Statement of Cash Flows
Year Ended December 31, 1988
($ Millions)

Cash flows from operating activities:			
Net income	$ 2,337		
Adjustments to cash basis:			
Depreciation expense	654		
Amortization of goodwill	125		
Decrease in accounts receivable	601		
Decrease in inventory	2		
Decrease in deferred taxes	(325)		
Increase in accounts payable	408		
Increase in accrued liabilities	1,041		
Increase in income taxes payable	362		
Net cash flow--operating activities		$ 5,205	
Cash flows from investing activities:			
Increase in PPE (before depreciation)	$ (980)		
Increase in goodwill (before amort.)	(783)		
Decrease in investments	405		
Acquisition of Kraft	(11,383)		
Net cash used by investing activities		(12,741)	
Cash flows from financing activities:			
Decrease in short-term debt	$ (881)		
Increase in long-term debt	9,929		
Decrease in stockholders' equity			
(repurchase)	(540)		
Dividends declared	(941)		
Increase in dividends payable	47		
Net cash provided by financing activities		7,614	
Net increase in cash		$ 78	
Supplementary disclosure of cash flow information:			
Interest paid during year		$ 670	
Income taxes paid during year		$ 1,353	
Schedule of noncash investing and financing activities:			$---

B. The simplest calculation would be operating cash flow less capital expenditures: $5205 - 980 = $4225 million. But many variations are possible.

    The more important part of the question is the connection between free cash flow and future earnings and financial condition. Possible uses of free cash flow include:

    1) Repayment of debt resulting in lower interest cost and higher earnings. This also reduces debt ratios and improves interest coverage, possibly lending to higher debt ratings.

2)   Repurchase of equity may raise earnings per share and (if repurchased below stated book value or real value per share) increase these.

3)   Acquisitions (such as Kraft) that may provide future growth, better diversification, lower risk, etc.

4)   Expenditures to fund internal growth through capital spending, research and development, new product costs, etc.

C.   If the acquired inventories and receivables are sold the proceeds will be reported as cash flow from operations (CFO). As their acquisition was reported as cash used for investment, CFO will be inflated. This will occur if Kraft reduces its required level of inventories and receivables because of operating changes (such as changes in product lines or credit terms) or the use of financing techniques that remove these assets from the balance sheet.

17. A. **Hertz Corp. ($ millions)**

	1989	1990	1991
Reported cash flow from operations	$ (117)	$ 92	$ 286
Add back: purchases of equipment	3,003	4,024	4,016
Subtract: sales of equipment	(2,354)	(3,434)	(3,784)
Adjusted cash flow from operations	$ 532	$ 682	$ 518

B.   As reported, cash flow from operations shows steady improvement over the period 1989-1991, changing from a negative to a positive amount. After adjustment, the trend is eliminated; cash flow from operations is lower in 1991 than in either 1989 and 1990. The improvement in reported cash flow from operations was the result of reducing Hertz's net investment in rental equipment.

C.

	1989	1990	1991
Reported cash flow for investing	$ (133)	$ (79)	$ (72)
Subtract: purchases of equipment	(3,003)	(4,024)	(4,016)
Add back: sales of equipment	2,354	3,434	3,784
Adjusted cash flow for investing	$ (782)	$ (669)	$ (304)

D.   Reported cash flow for investing shows little change over the three year period. After reclassification of equipment purchases and sales, cash flow for investing drops by more than half in 1991.

After reclassification it reflects the sharp drop in net car and truck purchases in that year.

E. Free cash flow can be defined as cash flow from operations less investment required to maintain productive capacity. If we assume that Hertz's investments are solely to maintain existing capacity, then free cash flow equals cash flow from operations less cash flow for investing:

	1989	1990	1991
Reported cash flow from operations	$ (117)	$ 92	$ 286
Less: reported cash flow for investing	(133)	(79)	(72)
Equals: free cash flow	$ (250)	$ 13	$ 214

Note that reclassification of purchases and sales of revenue equipment has no effect on free cash flow:

	1989	1990	1991
Adjusted cash flow from operations	$ 532	$ 682	$ 518
Less: adjusted cash flow for investing	(782)	(669)	(304)
Equals: free cash flow	$ (250)	$ 13	$ 214

Thus by defining free cash flow in a manner which subtracts out all expenditures required to maintain the operating capacity of the firm, whether capitalized or not and regardless of classification, the effects of accounting and reporting differences can be overcome. This solution requires, of course, the identification of the amounts of such items.

F. When equipment is purchased, the full amount is reported as an operating cash outflow. For leased equipment, only the periodic lease payments are reported as operating cash outflows. Thus, for Hertz, leasing increases reported cash flow from operations.

G. When equipment purchases are classified as investing cash flows, then leasing reduces operating cash flows relative to purchases. That is because the outflow connected with purchases (or any other capitalized expenditure) is never classified as an operating outflow. [See Chapter 8 for a detailed analysis of this issue.]

Chapter 3 - Solutions

1.   A.   **Activity Ratios:**

      1.   Inventory turnover = COGS / Average inventory
          = \$8048 / \$1919
          = 4.19X

      2.   Accounts receivable turnover = Sales / Average receivables
          = \$12065 / \$2545
          = 4.74X

      3.   Fixed asset turnover = Sales / Average property
          = \$12065 / \$1304
          = 9.26X

      4.   Total asset turnover = Sales / Average assets
          = \$12065 / \$6425
          = 1.88X

    B.   **Liquidity Ratios:**

      1.   Operating cycle:
          = 365 [1/inventory turnover + 1/receivable turnover]
          = 365 [1/4.19 + 1/4.74]
          = 164.1 days

      2.   Cash cycle:

          Purchases
          = COGS + Increase in accounts payable
          = \$8048 + \$448
          = \$8496

          Number of days payable
          = 365 x Average payables/purchases
          = 365 x \$709/\$8496
          = 30.5 days

          Therefore cash cycle = 164.1 - 30.5 = 133.6 days

      3.   Current ratio:
          = Current assets / Current liabilities
          = \$6360 / \$3945
          = 1.61X

4. Quick ratio:
    = (Cash + Receivables) / Current liabilities
    = $3924 / $3945
    = 0.99X

5. Cash ratio:
    = Cash / Current liabilities
    = $325 / $3945
    = 0.08X

6. Cash from operations to current liabilities:
    = Cash from operations / Current liabilities
    = $(256) / $3945
    = (0.06)X

7. Defensive interval:
    = 365 x [Cash+Receivables] / Projected expenditures
    = 365 x $3924 / $9828
    = 146 days

    Projected expenditures estimated as total costs and expenses
    less depreciation
    = $10,151 - $323 = $9828

C. **Solvency Ratios:**

1. Debt to equity:
    = Debt (nontrade) / Equity
    = $1170 / $3803
    = 0.31

2. Debt to capital:
    = Debt / Capital (debt + equity)
    = $1170 / $4973
    = 0.24

3. Times interest earned:
    = Earnings before interest and tax/interest expense
    = $2337 / $78
    = 29.96X

4. Capital expenditures:
    = Cash from operations / Capital expenditures
    = $(256) / $798
    = (0.32)X

D. **Profitability Ratios:**

1. Gross Margin:
    = (Sales - COGS) / Sales
    = ($12065 - $8048) / $12065
    = 33.3%

2. Operating income to sales
   = Operating income / Sales
   = $2337 / $12065
   = 19.4%

3. Return on sales
   = Net income / Sales
   = $1265 / $12065
   = 10.5%

4. Return on assets
   = (Net income + [Interest expense (1-tax rate)])
     / Average Assets
   = ($1265 + [$78 (1-.44)]) / $6425
   = 20.4%

   Return on assets (pretax)
   = Earnings before interest and taxes / Average assets
   = $2337 / $6425
   = 36.4%

5. Return on equity
   = Net income / Average equity
   = $1265 / $3336
   = 37.9%

2. **Three component disaggregation of ROE:**

	1. Profitability	Net income / Sales	=	10.5 %
x	2. Asset turnover	Sales / Average assets	=	1.88X
x	3. Leverage	Average assets/Average equity	=	1.93X
=	Return on equity	Net income / Average equity	=	37.9 %

Five component model:

	1. Operating margin	EBIT / Sales	=	19.4 %
x	2. Interest burden	Pretax income / EBIT	=	0.97X
x	3. Tax burden	Net income / Pretax income	=	0.56X
x	4. Asset turnover	Sales / Average assets	=	1.88X
x	5. Leverage	Average assets/Average equity	=	1.93X
=	Return on equity	Net income / Average equity	=	37.9 %

3. A. Although ratio analysis has an implicit proportionality assumption, these relationships are not always proportional. When the scale of operations changes dramatically, relationships between variables that hold at one level of operations may not hold at another level. (The asset turnover ratio described in Figure 3-1 is one example.)

   B. (i) Use the average of end of year and end of first quarter assets in denominator, or alternatively, use end of year assets.

      (ii) Use weighted average: .25 x opening assets + .75 closing assets; this matches the numerator that reflects a return on the additional assets for 3/4 of the year.

(iii) Average of opening and closing assets is weighted average.

(iv) Use weighted average: .75 x opening assets + .25 closing assets.

4.   A.   Estimate of 19X5 fixed and variable costs:

S = Sales
F = Fixed costs
V = Variable costs
v = Variable costs as a percentage of sales
TC = Total costs = F + V = F + vS

$$v = \frac{TC(year\ 2) - TC\ (year\ 1)}{S(year\ 2) - S\ (year\ 1)}$$

$$= \frac{\$10151 - \$6403}{\$12065 - \$7570}$$

$$= .833815$$

F = TC - vS
  = $10151 - (.833815 x $12065)
  = $92

B.   Financial Leverage Effect (FLE) = Operating income/net income

19X4: FLE   = $1450/$800   19X5: FLE = $2337/$1265
            =   1.81   =   1.85

     Operating   Leverage   Effect   (OLE)   =   Contribution margin/operating income

19X4: OLE = $1520/$1450   19X5: OLE = $2351/$2337
          =   1.05   =   1.01

where contribution margin is pretax income plus fixed costs ($92 for both years).

     Total Leverage Effect (TLE) = OLE x FLE = Contribution margin/net income

19X4: TLE = $1520/$800   19X5: TLE = $2351/$1265
          =   1.90   =   1.86
          =   1.05 x 1.81   =   1.01 x 1.85

C.   The basic formula used to estimate fixed and variable costs assumes that the underlying relationships are constant. Growth of the magnitude experienced by Chicago requires a fixed-to-variable cost ratio for 19X5 that may be quite different from that based on 19X4 data.

     As a result, the part A estimate of fixed costs is certainly too low. The primary reason is the high growth rate of Chicago during 19X5. A partial solution would be to deduct known fixed costs like depreciation and interest expense from total costs before applying the formula. However, the lack of information about depreciation eliminates this method. All of the problems discussed in Appendix 3-A, including relevant range and the non-linear relationship between costs and output, apply in this case as well.

The calculation of OLE in part B is not meaningful given the inability to estimate variable and fixed cost components. Chicago's operating leverage is surely greater than the OLE calculated. The total leverage effect (TLE) is also understated in the part B computation.

5.

		Method of Calculation
1. Inventory turnover	3.71X	Asset turnover x (COGS/sales) x (assets/inventory)
2. Receivable turn-over	5.65X	Asset turnover x (assets/receivables)
3. Days of inventory Days of receiv. Operating cycle	98 days 65 163 days	365/inventory turnover 365/receivable turnover Total
4. Days of payables	(72) days	365/payables turnover (calculated as 5.06X using COGS instead of purchases)
Cash cycle	91 days	Operating cycle less days of payables
5. Fixed asset turnover	2.67X	Asset turnover divided by (PPE/assets)
6. Cash ratio	0.08X	Cash/current liabilities
7. Quick ratio	0.79X	(Cash + receivables)/Current liabilities
8. Current ratio	1.67X	Current assets/Current liabilities
9. Debt-to-equity	0.60	(Debt payable + long-term debt)/equity
10. Interest coverage	11.0X	Operating income/interest expense
11. EBIT/sales	11.0%	Given directly
12. Sales/assets	0.96	(Asset turnover) Given directly
13. EBIT/assets	10.6%	(EBIT/sales) x (sales/assets)
14. EBT/assets	9.6%	(EBT/sales) x asset turnover
15. Assets/equity	2.50X	Inverse of equity/assets (given)
16. EBT/equity	24.0%	(EBT/assets) x (assets/equity)

6. A.   **Company**   **Industry**

            1   Chemicals and drugs (Monsanto)
            2   Aerospace (Boeing)
            3   Computer software (Altos Computer)
            4   Department stores (J.C. Penney)
            5   Consumer foods (Quaker Oats)
            6   Electric utility (SCEcorp)
            7   Newspaper publishing (Knight Ridder)
            8   Consumer finance (Household Finance)
            9   Airline (AMR Corp.)

    B.   The airline, consumer finance, and electric utility industries are
            service industries. They are characterized by the absence of cost of
            goods sold and inventories. Companies 6, 8, and 9 have the lowest
            ratios (COGS/sales and inventories/total assets). Newspaper
            publishing may also be considered a service industry; we will return
            to this later.

            Company 8 is the consumer finance company. It has a high level
            of debt balanced by a high level of receivables and investments
            (loans and securities). Much of its debt is short-term, reflecting
            the short maturities of its loans. It has almost no fixed assets.
            The ratio of interest expense to revenues is the highest for this
            company.

            Both the electric utility and airline firms would have high
            fixed assets; utilities generally have higher assets (lower asset
            turnover), are more profitable, and have higher debt and interest
            expense. Airlines, on the other hand, have high current liabilities
            for trade payables (payments to suppliers) and for advance ticket
            sales (other current liabilities). *We conclude that company 6 is the
            electric utility and company 9 is the airline.*

            Companies 1, 2, and 3 have high R&D expense, consistent with
            the aerospace, chemicals and drugs, and computer software
            industries. Aerospace would have the highest inventory (low
            inventory turnover). Customer prepayments under long term contracts
            result in lower receivables and large customer advances (other
            current liabilities). *Therefore, company 2 is the aerospace firm.*

            Distinguishing company 1 from 3 is difficult. Computer
            software and drugs are both characterized by high R & D. The
            inclusion of chemicals, however, should lower the intensiveness of
            R&D, suggesting that company 3 is the computer software firm.
            Computer software, lacking manufacturing, is less capital intensive
            than chemicals and drugs and the latter is generally more
            profitable. Further, the chemical industry (being older) should have
            "older" plant (greater proportion depreciated). *Company 1 is,
            therefore, the chemical and drugs firm and company 3 is in the
            computer software industry.*

            Companies 4, 5, and 7 remain. Company 4 has high inventories
            and COGS, the highest receivables relative to assets, and high asset
            turnover, all of which suggest a retailer. It has no R&D, high
            advertising expense, and low pretax profit margins. *Company 4 is the
            department store firm.*

            Company 5 has high net property relative to assets, and the
            highest ratio of advertising to revenues. *Company 5 must be the
            consumer foods company.*

Company 7 is the newspaper publisher. It has very low inventory but high cost of goods sold; inventory is primarily newsprint while cost of goods sold includes the high cost of reporting and production. Company 7 has the highest intangibles (newspapers purchased) and very high pretax profit margins (most newspapers have only indirect competition).

This exercise was intended to show that industries have balance sheet and income statement characteristics that set them apart from others. These characteristics are often used to compare firms within an industry (e.g. advertising as a percentage of sales for consumer goods firms). Summarized data should be used with caution, however. Different firms (even in the same industry) classify identical items differently. Thus the analyst should examine original financial statements to achieve better comparability. Differences among firms may be due to operational or classification differences. When management is available to answer questions, these differences are often useful starting points for obtaining a better understanding of the firm.

7.   A.   (i)   **Brewing Industry compared with the S&P 400:**
The brewing industry's liquidity ratios were marginally lower during the years 1982-1984 with some improvement in 1985-1986. However, the difference may be due to the nature of inventories and the quick ratio bears this out. The brewing industry reported the lowest (best) debt ratios and the ratios improved over the five year period shown. The times interest earned and cash flow ratios were also better. The industry's profitability and return ratios were significantly better than those reported by the S&P 400. The brewing industry appeared to be better off and improving relative to the market.

(ii)   **Anheuser-Busch (BUD) compared with the Brewing Industry:**
BUD presents a mixed picture compared with the brewing industry. Relative improvement in 1985 was short-lived. BUD remained more highly leveraged than the brewing industry, although leverage declined from 1982-1986. BUD's times interest earned ratio prior to 1986 was higher due to the better profitability of its operations, as seen in the profit margin and the return on asset ratios. However, the trend was poor (declining from 12.2 to 9.8) compared to the industry (rising from 7.2 to 11.0) Finally, BUD showed both absolute and relative improvement in its cash flow ratios. Overall, the credit position of BUD was similar to that of the industry, better in some respects but worse in others.

(iii) **Anheuser-Busch (BUD) compared with the S&P 400:**
BUD reported lower liquidity but as pointed out in (i) this may be due to the nature of its inventories. Leverage and interest coverage ratios reflected a significantly stronger position for BUD compared to the market. Cash flow and asset turnover ratios improved for BUD relative to those reported by the industry. BUD's better credit position was augmented by its stronger profitability and return ratios.

8. A.

	19X1	19X2	19X3
Current ratio	2.00X	2.00X	2.00X
Quick ratio	1.20	1.10	1.00
Cash ratio	.40	.30	.25

B. Common size statements would show that cash as a percentage of (current) assets is declining; accounts receivable and inventory are growing. Similarly, current liabilities would show the proportion of (bank) borrowing growing relative to credit granted by suppliers.

C. Although the current ratio has remained constant over the 19X1-19X2 period, its components have not as the quick and cash ratios have deteriorated. The firm's liquidity position has weakened over the period as its current assets are less liquid (more inventory and receivables, less cash). At the same time its debt financing relative to trade credit has grown.

D. The CFO to current liabilities and turnover ratios would be used to measure the length of the operating and cash cycle. We would expect slower turnover and therefore longer operating and cash cycles. Similarly, CFO and the CFO to current liabilities ratio would be expected to decline.

9. A. and B.   The following liquidity, solvency, and profitability ratios can be used to support the conclusions reached in Problem 13 of Chapter 2:

	19X1	19X2	19X3	19X4	19X5
M COMPANY					
Turnover Ratios:					
Inventory	3.60	3.43	3.27	3.17	2.96
Receivables	3.34	3.22	3.09	3.24	3.25
Payables	7.87	7.47	7.76	10.85	12.79
Number of days:					
Inventory	101.29	106.51	111.54	115.02	123.33
Receivables	109.20	113.25	118.00	112.70	112.00
Payables	(46.40)	(48.90)	(47.00)	(33.60)	(28.50)
Cash cycle	164.09	170.86	182.54	194.12	206.83
Current ratio	1.71	1.57	1.75	1.55	1.60
Quick ratio	1.09	0.99	1.11	0.91	0.93
Debt-to-equity	0.78	0.97	1.17	1.60	2.14
Times interest earned	6.33	4.84	4.94	4.00	1.35
Return on equity	0.14	0.13	0.11	0.11	0.03

G COMPANY					
Turnover ratios:					
Inventory	3.43	3.84	3.87	3.84	4.73
Receivables	5.38	6.07	6.11	6.07	6.10
Payables	10.19	10.61	10.52	10.34	12.47
Number of days:					
Inventory	106	95	94	95	77
Receivables	68	60	60	60	60
Payables	(36)	(34)	(35)	(35)	(29)
Cash cycle	138	121	119	120	108
Current ratio	2.23	2.13	1.95	2.29	2.30
Quick ratio	1.07	1.01	0.92	1.08	1.05
Debt-to-equity	0.38	0.49	0.63	0.71	0.74
Times interest earned	4.27	5.77	4.70	4.62	4.27
Return on equity	0.05	0.09	0.11	0.12	0.12

C.   The deterioration in M company's liquidity and financial position can be seen from the cash cycle, which increased to 207 days in 19X5 from 164 days in 19X1. Also see the decline in the current and the quick ratios. M company's debt-to-equity ratio has more than doubled from 0.78 to 2.14, accompanied by a decline in interest coverage from 6.33x to 1.35x. That decline resulted from both the increasing leverage and the decreasing ROE (from .14 in 19X1 to .03 in 19X5).

G company's cash cycle has declined (improved) and its liquidity ratios remained steady. The problem here is the higher leverage and low interest coverage (albeit, a steady 4.27 with modest change during the five years shown). Profitability (ROE) increased from .05 to .12. The substantial growth has been managed well so far but it remains to be seen whether the firm can manage future growth as well.

10. A.   **Tennant Equity Return Components**

		1975	1981	1987
1.	EBIT margin	17.9 %	15.8 %	10.6 %
X 2.	Asset turnover	1.42X	1.72X	1.57X
X 3.	Interest burden	100.0 %	99.7 %	98.6 %
X 4.	Financial leverage	1.32X	1.36X	1.53X
X 5.	Tax retention rate	51.3 %	55.6 %	56.1 %
=	Return on equity	17.2 %	20.6 %	14.1 %

B.   From 1975 to 1981, although the EBIT margin declined, increases in asset turnover coupled with the lower tax burden resulted in increased ROE. An increase in financial leverage also helped, but to a lesser degree than the other factors.

From 1981 to 1987 asset turnover reversed and EBIT margins continued to decline. Financial leverage continued to increase. The dominant factor was the 33 percent decline in EBIT margins. This was due to the increase in selling and general expenses as Tennant's growth rate slowed. Interest burden was a relatively trivial factor and the tax retention rate changed only nominally. The decrease in asset turnover and increase in financial leverage were more meaningful but tended to cancel each other.

Over the entire period (1975-1987) gross margins remained steady. However, selling and general expense as a percentage of net sales rose from 24.8% (1975) to 27.1% (1981) and 32.4% (1987). This 7.8 percentage point increase exceeded the 7.3 percentage point decline in EBIT margins over the 1975-1987 period. Increases in asset turnover, financial leverage, and tax retention offset only a portion of decline in margins. Clearly, rising selling and general expense was the major factor in the decline in Tennant's ROE over the 1975-1987 period.

11. A. **Identification of common-size statements:**

Company C is highly automated with higher gross plant assets ($175,000 versus $65,000). Therefore it would tend to have higher fixed operating costs. As sales drop, COGS as percentage of sales should increase more than for a firm with lower fixed costs. As Company C is more capital intensive it would be expected to have higher debt and (as a percentage of sale) interest costs. *Thus, the second set of common size statements are for Company C. The first set belong to Company L.*

Identification of ratios:

As Company C operates in a JIT inventory environment and has prompt payments and collections, it should have the higher turnover ratios:

Turnover	Company L	Company C
Inventory	6.667	16.667
Receivables	7.409	11.111
Payables	4.444	25.000

Similarly Company C would be expected to have more long term debt as it is more capital intensive. Therefore the debt to capital ratio of .429 (.195) applies to Company C (Company L).

B. **Creation of income statement, Company C, 19X2:**

Since CFO/current liabilities = 5.275 and CFO = $52,750, then current liabilities = $10,000

Since the current ratio (current assets/current liabilities) = 9.475 and current liabilities = $10,000, then current assets = $94,750

Similarly the quick ratio [(cash + receivables)/current liabilities] = 8.875 yields cash + receivables = $88,750 and therefore,

Inventory (19X2) = (current assets less quick assets)
= ($94,750 - $88,750) = $6,000

As there was no change in inventory during 19X2, inventory(19X1) = $6,000

As average inventory = \$6,000 and 19X2 inventory turnover was 16.667,
then COGS(19X2) = 16.667 x \$6,000 = \$100,000

Using COGS and the common size statement for Company C, we can now reconstruct the income statement for 19X2:

Sales	100.00%	$150,000
COGS	66.67%	$ 100,000
SG&A	20.00%	30,000
Interest	4.67%	7,000
Taxes	2.17%	3,250
Total Expense	93.50%	$ 140,250
Net Income	6.50%	$ 9,750

Creation of income statement, Company C, 19X1:

Since sales dropped by 1/6 from 19X1 to 19X2, and sales in 19X2 were \$150,000; sales in 19X1 were \$180,000. This amount and the common size income statement for 19X1 can be used to prepare the income statement for 19X1:

Sales	100.00%	$180,000
COGS	58.33%	$ 105,000
SG&A	17.78%	32,000
Interest	3.89%	7,000
Taxes	5.00%	9,000
Total Expense	85.00%	$ 153,000
Net Income	15.00%	$ 27,000

Creation of income statement, Company L, 19X2:

This follows the methodology used for Company C.

Since CFO/current liabilities = .807 and CFO = \$28,250, then current liabilities = \$30,000

Since current ratio = 3.592, and current liabilities = \$30,000, then current assets = \$107,750

Similarly the quick ratio of 3.192 yields quick assets of \$95,750 (3.192 x \$30,000) and therefore inventory(19X2) of \$12,000 (\$107,750 - \$95,750).

As the 19X2 change in inventory was (6,000), inventory(19X1) was \$18,000.

As average inventory = \$15,000 and inventory turnover = 6.667,

COGS (19X2) = 6.667 x \$15,000 = \$100,000

We can now reconstruct the income statement for 19X2:

Sales	100.00%	$150,000
COGS	66.67%	$ 100,000
SG&A	20.00%	30,000
Interest	2.00%	3,000
Taxes	2.83%	4,250
Total Expense	91.50%	$ 137,250
Net Income	8.50%	$ 12,750

Creation of income statement, Company L, 19X1:

Since sales dropped by 1/6, sales in 19X1 were $180,000. The income statement for 19X1 is:

Sales	100.00%	$180,000
COGS	63.89%	$ 115,000
SG&A	19.44%	35,000
Interest	1.67%	3,000
Taxes	3.75%	6,750
Total Expense	88.75%	$ 159,750
Net Income	11.25%	$ 20,250

C. Interest costs (Company C = $7,000; Company L = $3,000) are fixed for both companies. The breakdowns for COGS and SG&A follow:

Company C: 19X2 sales decreased by $30,000, COGS decreased by $5,000, and SG&A decreased by $2,000. Therefore, variable costs as a percentage of sales are:

COGS = $5,000/$30,000   =   16.67%
SG&A = $2,000/$30,000   =   6.67
   Total   23.34%

Therefore, (using 19X1 income statement), fixed costs equal

COGS = $105,000 - (.1667 x $180,000)   = $75,000
SG&A = $ 32,000 - (.0667 x $180,000)   = $20,000
   Total $95,000

Company L: 19X2 sales decreased by $30,000, COGS decreased by $15,000, and SG&A decreased by $5,000. Therefore, variable costs as a percentage of sales are:

COGS = $15,000/$30,000   =   50.00%
SG&A = $ 5,000/$30,000   =   16.67%
   Total   66.67%

Therefore, (using 19X1 income statement), fixed costs equal

$$COGS = \$115,000 - (.5000 \times \$180,000) \qquad = \qquad \$25,000$$
$$SG\&A = \$\ 35,000 - (.1667 \times \$180,000) \qquad = \qquad \underline{\$\ 5,000}$$
$$Total \qquad\qquad\qquad\qquad\qquad\qquad\qquad\qquad\qquad \$30,000$$

Taxes are a constant 25% of pretax income.

D. The 19X3 sales forecast is .8 x 19X2 sales = .8 x $150,000 = $120,000 for both companies. Projected income statements for 19X3 follow:

	Company C	Company L
Sales	$ 120,000	$ 120,000
COGS[1]	95,000	85,000
SG&A[2]	28,000	25,000
Interest	7,000	3,000
Total expenses	$ 130,000	$ 113,000
Pretax income	$(10,000)	$ 7,000
Taxes (25%)	2,500	(1,750)
Net income	$ (7,500)	$ 5,250

[1]Company C: $75,000 + (.1667 x $120,000) = $95,000
   Company L: $25,000 + (.5000 x $120,000) = $85,000

[2]Company C: $20,000 + (.0667 x $120,000) = $28,000
   Company L: $ 5,000 + (.1667 x $120,000) = $25,000

E. With higher fixed operating costs and interest costs, Company C has higher operating as well as financial leverage. The effects can be demonstrated by reference to the following schedule that uses 19X2 as its reference point:

	19X1	19X2	19X3
Sales (both)	$180,000	$150,000	$120,000
% change from 19X2	20%	---	(20%)
Net income: Company C	$ 27,000	$ 9,750	$ (7,500)
% change from 19X2	177%	---	(177%)
Net income: Company L	$ 20,250	$ 12,750	$ 5,250
% change from 19X2	59%	---	(59%)

With higher sales in 19X1, the leverage effect works in Company C's favor and its income is higher. However, when sales decline in 19X2 and 19X3, Company L's income is higher as it does not bear the burden of high fixed costs.

Using 19X2 as the base period, (since percentage changes in sales are symmetric to that year) we find that Company C's total leverage effect is 8.85 as a 20% change (higher or lower) in sales results in a 177% change in net income.

3-13

% Change in income = TLE x % change in sales
177% = 8.85 x 20%

Company C's TLE is three times as large as Company L's whose TLE (with a 19X2 base) is only 2.95:

% Change in income = TLE x % change in sales
59% = 2.95 x 20%

NOTE: The components of the TLE, the Operating Leverage Effect (OLE) and Financial Leverage Effect (FLE), can be calculated by converting the 19X2 income statements into the following format (on a pretax basis):

	Company C		Company L	
Sales		$150,000		$150,000
Variable COGS				
and SG&A	(23.33%)	(35,000)	(66.67%)	(100,000)
Contribution		$115,000		$ 50,000
Fixed costs		(95,000)		(30,000)
Operating income		$ 20,000		$ 20,000
Interest		(3,000)		(3,000)
Pretax income		$ 13,000		$ 17,000

As the following breakdown indicates, the OLE is the major contributor to the TLE for both companies and is the primary difference between the two companies as well. The difference in OLE is then further magnified by the difference in FLE:

	Co. C	Co. L
OLE = Contribution/operating income	5.75	2.50
FLE = Operating income/pretax income	1.54	1.18
TLE = OLE x FLE = Contribution/pretax income	8.85	2.95

The calculations can also be done on a posttax basis but that would require "tax effecting" the contribution margin and operating income as well as net income. For example, for Company C, the contribution margin is $86,250 (.75 x $115,000), operating income is $15,000 (.75 x $20,000) and net income is $9,750 (.75 x $13,000).

12. A. Balance Sheet - Company C:

	19X1	19X2
Cash	$ 25,000	$ 76,750
Receivables	15,000	12,000
Inventory	6,000	6,000
Property	175,000	175,000
(Depreciation)	(80,000)	(120,000)
Totals	$141,000	$149,750
Payables	$ 4,000	$ 4,000
S.T.Debt	7,000	6,000
L.T.Debt	60,000	60,000
Equity	70,000	79,750
Totals	$141,000	$149,750

These amounts can be calculated from the data provided as follows:

Property, Plant and Equipment:
Given at $175,000 for 19X2. Since cash for investing is zero, the same level applies to 19X1.

Accounts Receivable:
For 19X2, A/R turnover of 11.1111 and sales of $150,000 imply average receivables of $13,500. Since receivables decreased by $3,000 in 19X2, they must have been $15,000 in 19X1 and $12,000 in 19X2.

Inventory:
From the answer to problem 11-B, Inventory (19X2) = Inventory (19X1) = $6,000

Cash:
Since current assets = $94,750, and cash = current assets less receivables and inventory, then cash (19X2) = $94,750 - $12,000 - $6,000 = $76,750.

Since the 19X2 change in cash = CFO + cash from financing + cash from investment = $52,750 - $1,000 + $0 = $51,750

Then cash (19X1) = $76,750 - $51,750 = $25,000

Accounts Payable:
With no change in inventory and COGS = $100,000, 19X2 purchases must be $100,000.

19X2 accounts payable turnover of 25 and purchases of $100,000 imply an average accounts payable of $4,000. Since there was no 19X2 change in payables, then

A/P (19X1) = A/P (19X2) = $4,000

Short-term debt (S.T.Debt):
Short term debt = Current liabilities - accounts payable

For 19X2, current liabilities of $10,000 imply short term debt of $10,000 - $4,000 = $6,000. Given a decrease of $1000 in 19X2, S.T.Debt (19X1) = $7,000.

Equity:
ROE = 0.13 and net income of $9750 imply average equity = $75,000

Since only change in equity is net income of $9,750, equity (19X1) = $70,000, and equity (19X2) = $79,750.

Long-term Debt (L.T.Debt):
With L.T.Debt/capital of 0.429 and equity of $79,750, L.T.Debt = $60,000.

Accumulated Depreciation:
Total liabilities + equity = $141,000 and $149,750 for 19X1 and 19X2 respectively.

Total assets must be same, yielding accumulated depreciation of $80,000 and $120,000 for those years. The 19X2 increase must be depreciation expense for that year (as no property was sold or retired) of $40,000.

Alternate Method of Calculation:
CFO = income + noncash items + changes in operating assets
$52,750 = $9,750 + noncash items + $3,000

Therefore noncash items (depreciation expense in this case) = $40,000

Balance Sheet - Company L:

	19X1	19X2
Cash	$ 54,500	$ 77,750
Receivables	22,500	18,000
Inventory	18,000	12,000
Property	65,000	65,000
(Depreciation)	(30,000)	(40,000)
Totals	$130,000	$132,750
Payables	$ 23,650	$18,650
S.T.Debt	16,350	11,350
L.T.Debt	20,000	20,000
Equity	70,000	82,750
Totals	$130,000	$132,750

The methodology is the same as for Company C:

Property, Plant and Equipment:
Given at $65,000 for 19X2. Since cash for investing is zero, the same level applies to 19X1.

Accounts Receivable:
For 19X2, A/R turnover of 7.409 and sales of $150,000 imply average A/R = $20,250.

Since A/R decreased by $4,500
A/R (19X1) = $22,500 and A/R (19X2) = $18,000

Inventory:
     From 11-B, inventory (19X2) = $12,000 and inventory (19X1) = $18,000

Cash:
     Since current assets = $107,750, cash (19X2) = $107,750 - $12,000 - $18,000 = $77,750

19X2 change in cash
= CFO + cash from financing + cash from investment
= $28,250 - $3,000 + $0
= $23,250

and cash (19X1) = $77,750 - $23,250 = $54,500

Accounts Payable:
     With inventory change of $(6,000) and COGS of $100,000; purchases = $94,000

For 19X2, accounts payable turnover of 4.444 and purchases of $94,000 imply an average A/P of $21,150. Since the change in A/P was (5,000), A/P (19X1) = $23,650 and A/P (19X2) = $18,650

Short-term Debt:
     Short-term debt = Current liabilities - accounts payable
                     = $30,000 - $18,650 = $11,350

Since S.T.Debt decreased by $5,000 in 19X2, S.T.Debt (19X1) = $16,350

Equity:
     ROE = 0.167 and net income = $12,750, therefore average equity = $76,350.

Since only change in equity is net income of $12,750, equity (19X1) = $70,000, and equity (19X2) = $82,750.

Long-term Debt (L.T.Debt):
     L.T.Debt/capital = 0.195 and equity = $82,750; L.T.Debt = $20,000.

Accumulated Depreciation:
     Total liabilities + equity = $130,000 and $132,750 for 19X1 and 19X2 respectively.

Total assets must be same, yielding accumulated depreciation of $30,000 and $40,000. Change is depreciation expense of $10,000:

Alternate Method of Calculation:
CFO = income + noncash items + changes in operating assets
28,250 = $12,750 + noncash items + $5,500
Therefore noncash depreciation expense = $10,000

B.   **19X3 Forecast Balance Sheet - Company C:**

Cash	$111,650	Accounts payable	$ 4,000
Accounts receivable	9,600	Short-term debt	6,000
Inventory	6,000	Long-term debt	60,000
Property, plant	175,000		
(Depreciation)	(160,000)	Equity	72,250
Total assets	$142,250	Total equities	$142,250

Explanation: Given the JIT environment, and the patterns for 19X1 and 19X2, we assume that inventory and payables stay at the same level even with the decline in sales. These levels are presumably "minimum" working levels. To maintain the receivable turnover ratio of 11.111, accounts receivable (19X3) = $9,600. Assuming no new investments or debt repayment implies a change in cash solely due to cash flow from operations. In 11-D, 19X3 net income was projected at $(7,500).

$$\text{19X3 CFO} = \text{Net income} + \text{depreciation} + \text{change in operating accounts}$$
$$= \$(7,500) + \$40,000 + \$2,400 = \$34,900$$

Therefore cash (19X3) = $76,750 + $34,900 = $111,650.

19X3 Forecast Balance Sheet - Company L:

Cash	$ 96,700	Accounts payable	$ 20,250
Accounts receivable	14,400	Short-term debt	11,350
Inventory	13,500	Long-term debt	20,000
Property, plant	65,000		
(Depreciation)	50,000	Equity	88,000
Total assets	$139,600	Total equities	$139,600

Explanation: For Company L, we assume that all turnover ratios are maintained.

A/R turnover of 7.409 with sales of $120,000 implies average inventory of $16,200. From part A, we have A/R (19X2) = $18,000. Thus A/R (19X3) equals $14,400.

Inventory turnover of 6.667 with COGS of $85,000 (see 11-D) implies average inventory of $12,750. Given inventory (19X2) of $12,000, inventory (19X3) = $13,500.

Purchases = COGS + increase in inventory = $85,000 + $1,500 = $86,500.

With accounts payable turnover of 4.444, average payables = $19,450. Since 19X2 payables are $18,650, A/P for 19X3 = $20,250.

Assuming no new investment or debt repayment implies a change in cash solely due to cash from operations. In 11-D, 19X3 net income was projected at $5,250.

$$\text{CFO} = \text{Net income} + \text{depreciation} + \text{change in operating accounts}$$
$$= \$5,250 + \$10,000 + [\$3,600 + \$(1,500) + \$1,600] = \$18,950$$

Cash (19X3) = $77,750 + $18,950 = $96,700

C.   Although both companies have positive CFO and "seem" to be cash rich, the picture is not as rosy as it appears. CFO does not make

3-18

allowance for the replacement of productive capacity. The fixed assets of both companies are almost fully depreciated and may have to be replaced soon. Also any improvement in sales will require additional working capital, especially for Company L. Thus, cash is not really "excess" as it may be needed for working capital and future capital expenditures to maintain present productive capacity.

13. A. Since there is no debt, ROA and ROE are identical at 10%.

B. ROE = ROA + D/E [ROA - cost of debt] where cost of debt is measured on an after-tax basis. This formula is used to prepare the following table showing the expected ROE at each level of debt:

	{A} Debt/ Equity	{B} Pretax Interest	{C}= .80x{B} After-Tax Interest	10%+[{A}(10%-{C})] ROE
(1)	0.25X	6.0%	4.8%	11.3%
(2)	0.50	8.0	6.4	11.8
(3)	1.00	10.0	8.0	12.0
(4)	1.50	12.0	9.6	10.6
(5)	2.00	15.0	12.0	6.0

C. Detailed calculations for cases (1) and (5):

Case Number	(1)	(5)
Debt Equity	$200,000 800,000	$666,667 333,333
Income before interest and taxes Interest expense Income before tax Tax expense Net income	$125,000 (12,000) $113,000 (22,600) $ 90,400	$ 125,000 (100,000) $ 25,000 (5,000) $ 20,000
ROE	$ 90,400 = 11.3% $800,000	$ 20,000 = 6.0% $333,333

D. Leverage works up to a point. As a firm takes on more debt the interest rate tends to rise (riskiness of debt increases). When the interest rate exceeds the firm's ROA then the benefits of leverage are lost. This trend is accelerated when ROA declines with increasing amounts of investment as more attractive (higher ROA) investments are made first.

In theory, the firm should borrow as long as the expected ROA exceeds the cost of debt. In practice firms place their "hurdle rate" for new investments above the cost of capital to allow for risk. Many investments fail to achieve their expected ROA. When the realized ROA falls short of the cost of debt, the investment reduces ROE.

14. In this problem the debt/equity ratios and cost of debt have to be adjusted to include all the debt (even that which is non-interest bearing).

A. The D/E ratio without any *bank* borrowing is $200,000/$800,000 = .25

   Therefore ROE = 10% + .25[10% - 0] = 12.5%

B. Calculations for the table that follows can be illustrated using case (1) with a D/E ratio of 25% and interest rate of 6%.

   Total assets are $1,000,000 and trade payables equal $200,000. That leaves $800,000 to be divided between bank debt and equity. A D/E ratio of 25% implies bank debt of $160,000 and equity of $640,000.

   The actual D/E ratio (including trade payables) is therefore: $360,000/$640,000 = .56.

   Interest (on bank debt only) at 6% = $9,600. The interest rate on total debt of $360,000 (bank debt + trade payables) can be computed as:
   $9,600/$360,000 = 2.67%

   Therefore, ROE = ROA + D/E [ROA - (1-tax rate)cost of debt]
   = 10% + .56 [10% - .8 x 2.67%] = 14.4%

Data for all five cases follows:

	Stated D/E Ratio	Stated Interest Rate	Bank Loan Amount	Actual D/E Ratio	Actual Interest Rate	ROE
(1)	0.25	6.0%	$ 160,000	0.56	2.67%	14.4%
(2)	0.50	8.0	266,667	0.88	4.57	15.6
(3)	1.00	10.0	400,000	1.50	6.67	17.0
(4)	1.50	12.0	480,000	2.13	8.47	16.9
(5)	2.00	15.0	533,333	2.75	10.91	13.5

C.

Case Number	(1)	(5)
Debt	$160,000	$533,333
Equity	640,000	266,667
Income before interest and taxes	$125,000	$ 125,000
Interest expense	(9,600)	(80,000)
Income before tax	$115,400	$ 45,000
Tax expense	(23,080)	(9,000)
Net income	$ 92,320	$ 36,000
ROE	$ 92,320 = 14.4% $640,000	$ 36,000 = 13.5% $266,667

D.   Trade debt appears to be interest free credit (in fact the cost of credit is often included in the price of the goods sold). The result of such debt is a higher return on equity as the same return is earned on a smaller investment. While the numbers change from problem 13, the conclusion is the same. Leverage enhances returns only when the cost of credit is less than the return on assets. As in problem 13, the highest ROE is earned at a debt/equity ratio of 1.

15.   Sales growth: revenues grew at a 25% compound annual rate from $287 million in 1985 to $865 million in 1990. However, a substantial portion of this increase came in 1987 (from $295 million to $685 million). Sales grew at a less than 9% compound annual rate from 1987 to 1990. Gross margin was stable and averaged 26% over the 1985-1990 period. The explosive growth in net income came in part from cost controls (e.g. S,G&A as a percentage of sales was 20% in 1985 and 17% in 1990). Interest expense declined considerably (1988-1990) after three years of high debt levels. These trends can be seen from the disaggregation of ROE that follows.

The ratios used in the following analysis are based on income before extraordinary items and discontinued operations. 1985 ratios use year end balances; average balances are used for all other years.

Year	Net income Sales	x	Sales ATA	=	Net income ATA	x	Ave.total assets Average equity	= ROE
1985	0.92%	x	2.52X	=	2.31%	x	24.69X	= 57.14%
1986	1.46	x	1.34	=	1.95	x	14.34	= 28.01
1987	2.58	x	1.94	=	4.99	x	7.95	= 39.68
1988	3.59	x	1.94	=	6.95	x	4.24	= 29.43
1989	4.12	x	2.03	=	8.36	x	2.81	= 23.47
1990	4.43	x	2.20	=	9.74	x	2.22	= 21.58

The interesting result shown by the disaggregation is that ROE declined sharply at the same time that profit margins (net income/sales) were rising. The steady decline in equity turnover explains this apparent contradiction. Equity grew from a nominal amount in 1985 (4% of assets) to nearly half of total assets by the end of 1990. Not only did Harley pay nominal if any dividends to stockholders but the firm sold equity as well. (Net income was about $120 million over the 1986-1990 period while equity increased by $194 million.)

Harley is a classic case of deleveraging. Total debt (current + long-term) declined by $138 million, from about $210 million at the end of 1986 to barely $72 million four years later. Thus more than 70% ($138/$194) of the equity increase over the 1986-1990 period was used for debt reduction rather than for investment purposes.

Harley's return on assets did multiply fourfold over the 1985-1990. The firm's 21.58% return on equity in 1990, while very respectable, is far below what it would have been if Harley had remained highly leveraged.

Appendix 3-C - Solutions

1.   A.   The convertible bonds are common equivalents because their effective yield, 5%, was less than two-thirds of the Aa bond rate, 8.5%, at the time of issuance.

The convertible preferred shares are not common equivalents as their effective yield was greater than two thirds of the Aa bond yield (5.5% versus 2/3 of 7.5%) at the issue date.

The options must be included in the computation of primary earnings per share because they are dilutive (the average market price exceeds the exercise price). The number of shares outstanding (primary) is therefore:

Average number of shares actually outstanding	2,500,000
Shares issuable upon bond conversion[*]	400,000
Effect of options	50,000
Total common and common equivalent shares	2,950,000

[*]$12,000,000/$30

Treasury stock method: Proceeds on exercise 200,000 options @ $15 = $3,000,000. At the average price of $20, can repurchase 150,000 shares ($3,000,000/$20). Thus the incremental number of shares is the difference (200,000 less 150,000).

B.

Net income	$ 6,500,000
Less: preferred dividends (70,000 x $4.00 x 1/2)	(140,000)
Plus: interest on bonds assumed converted[*]	360,000
Net income after adjustment	$ 6,720,000

[*]$12 million x 5% x .6 (tax adjustment)

Earnings per common and common equivalent share are:

$6,720,000/2,950,000 = $2.28

C.   For the fully diluted calculation, the convertible preferred shares are assumed to be converted (for the one half year outstanding). In addition, the treasury stock calculation is based on the year end price when it exceeds the average price. The number of shares outstanding (fully diluted) is therefore:

Average number of shares actually outstanding	2,500,000
Shares issuable upon bond conversion[*]	400,000
Shares issuable upon preferred stock conversion[#]	175,000
Effect of options	80,000
Total common and common equivalent shares	3,155,000

[*]$12,000,000/$30
[#]70,000 x 5 x 1/2

Treasury stock method: Proceeds on exercise 200,000 options @ $15 = $3,000,000. At year-end price of $25, can repurchase 120,000 shares ($3,000,000/$25). Thus the net number of shares is the difference (200,000 less 120,000).

D.
Net income	$ 6,500,000
Plus: interest on bonds assumed converted[*]	360,000
Net income after adjustment	$ 6,860,000

[*]$12 million x 5% x .6 (tax adjustment)

Fully diluted earnings per share is:

$6,860,000/3,155,000 = $2.17

E. i. Only the fully diluted calculation would change. At a closing price of $30, only 100,000 shares could be repurchased, resulting in 100,000 net shares outstanding, an increase of 20,000.

ii. There would be no effect. The two thirds rule is applied only at issuance and the classification is not affected by later events.

F. i. Pooling transactions result in the addition of (a) earnings of acquired or merged firm to that of the buyer or surviving firm and (b) all shares issued are assumed to be outstanding for the entire period. If the acquisition had not been made, the primary earnings per share would be:

Primary EPS: net income after adjustment	$ 6,720,000
Less: addition due to pooling	(600,000)
Adjusted primary EPS net income	$ 6,120,000

Primary EPS: total common and common equivalent shares	2,950,000
Less: addition due to pooling	(240,000)
Adjusted primary EPS shares	2,710,000

Adjusted primary EPS is $6,120,000/2,710,000 = $2.26

ii. Assuming a purchase method acquisition, the issued shares are considered outstanding for, and the earnings of the acquired firm are included only for the period following the acquisition. Since the acquisition was made on March 31, 1992, only 3/4ths of the income or $450,000 can be included and the additional equivalent shares are 180,000 (.75 x 240,000).

Adjusted primary EPS net income	$ 6,120,000
Plus: purchase method adjustment	450,000
Readjusted primary EPS net income	$ 6,570,000

Adjusted primary EPS shares	2,710,000
Plus: purchase method adjustment	180,000
Readjusted primary EPS shares	2,890,000

Readjusted primary EPS is $6,570,000/2,890,000 = $2.27

2. A.   The stock dividend shares are considered outstanding for the entire
         year. The additional shares resulting from other securities are
         considered outstanding only for the portion of the year following
         their issue.

         The number of common and common equivalent shares is:
Number outstanding at December 31, 1987	2,000,000
Effect of stock dividend (10%)	200,000
Shares issuable on bond conversion*	1,000,000
Total	3,200,000

              *As effective yield (5%) is less than two-thirds of the
              Aa bond yield (8%) at issue date, the convertible bonds are
              considered common equivalents. The number of shares is
              $10,000,000/$5 or 2,000,000; as the bonds were sold on July 1,
              only half the number of shares is included.

         The warrants are *not* reflected because they are anti-dilutive;
         the exercise price exceeds the average stock price for the period
         outstanding.

    B.   For the fully diluted calculation, the treasury stock method is
         based on the (higher) closing price of Champion shares ($8). At that
         price, the proceeds of exercise (800,000 x $5 = $4,000,000) could
         repurchase 500,000 shares ($4,000,000/$8) resulting in a net
         issuance of 300,000 shares. For one-quarter year, 75,000 shares are
         deemed outstanding. Thus the fully diluted number of shares
         outstanding is:

Number outstanding at December 31, 1987	2,000,000
Effect of stock dividend (10%)	200,000
Shares issuable on bond conversion*	1,000,000
Effect of stock options	75,000
Total	3,275,000

    C.   i.   At a closing price of $10, the treasury stock method would
              result in repurchase of 400,000 shares ($4,000,000/$10) and
              net issuance of 400,000 shares (800,000 less 400,000). For one
              quarter year, the net effect would be 100,000, an increase of
              25,000 from the total in part B. The closing price only
              affects fully diluted EPS.

         ii. At an average price of $8, the warrants are dilutive in the
              primary calculation. The proceeds of exercise ($4,000,000)
              could repurchase 500,000 shares, resulting in a net issuance
              of 300,000 shares. The effect for one quarter year is 75,000
              shares, making the number of common and common equivalent
              shares equal to 3,275,000.

         iii. No effect. The determination of common equivalent
              classification is made at the time of issue and is not changed
              by subsequent events.

    D.   U.K. and Canadian standards require the computation of basic and
         fully diluted EPS. The basic EPS does not include the effect of any
         potentially dilutive securities and the number of shares outstanding
         would be 2,200,000. The numerator (earnings used in the fully

diluted EPS calculation) would be affected since most countries' accounting standards assume that the proceeds on the exercise of warrants are invested, generating a notional return that must be included in the numerator.

Chapter 4 - Solutions

NOTE: The problems in this chapter are designed primarily as a basis for discussion of the issues covered in this chapter. There are no absolutely right/wrong answers. The solutions below should be viewed in that spirit.

1. The FASB view of neutrality is consistent with the classical approach, that takes the position that an "ideal" accounting paradigm can and should be designed disregarding potentially adverse impacts.

    Market-based researchers, however, argue that the costs and benefits of accounting policy setting should be subject to economic analysis. Neutrality as defined in the quotation is therefore *not a desirable objective*. The fact that certain firms would be adversely affected by accounting standards renders the standard non (pareto[*]) optimal. Thus, although the efficacy of an accounting system is measurable by its market impact (information content), that same impact means that it is not possible to use information content to determine accounting policy.

    The "positive" approach argues that *de facto* neutrality is *not a feasible objective*. The accounting standard setting process is influenced by the impact, favorable or unfavorable, that standards have on firms. Firms lobby (in many cases successfully) for or against certain standards precisely for that reason. This is not necessarily bad. Rather it is a "fact of life" and in this view, accounting standards and the standard setting process cannot be determined exogenously of firms' production-investment decisions.

    [*]Pareto optimality is defined as an equilibrium condition where nobody is worse off and at least one participant is better off.

2. A. This question is difficult to answer without knowing the total information set provided by each system in its first report. However, assuming that in other respects they are identical, information system Alpha is a superior system insofar as it provides a better prediction of the second report.

    B. Since, under the Alpha system, the second report would be better known in advance, at the time of its issuance it would contain fewer "surprises" and show less information content. The Gamma system, however, would contain a greater degree of "surprise" and, therefore, show greater information content.

---

[*]Pareto optimality is defined as a condition where a change to a new equilibrium leaves nobody worse off and at least one participant is better off.

C.   The answers to parts A and B point out the problems of focusing only on the market reaction to one report at a specific point in time. Although market reaction may tell us something about the information content of that given report, it does not tell the whole story. Accounting reports may contain information that will only be known at a later point in time (outside the "window" examined). Similarly, nonreaction may be due to knowledge generated by previous information provided by the system (alone or in conjunction with external information sources); the better a system predicts, the less "information" content in subsequent reports.

D.   Ingberman and Sorter viewed accounting systems as part of an overall data base whose purpose is to aid in forecasting the impact on the firm of changes in the firm and the environment. Thus, their view suggests the following "scenario":

1.   Financial statements provide information as to how previous changes in the environment impacted the firm.

2.   A change occurs in the environment. Market participants use their previous knowledge (see #1) to assess the potential impact of that change on the firm. Market reaction occurs at this time.

3.   Subsequent reports update and confirm the extent to which the environmental change affected the firm. A small (or nonexistent) market reaction at the time of issuance of these reports means that most (or all) of the reaction occurred earlier.

4.   The measures of the effects on the firm provided by the subsequent reports are then used to update the database and make projections.

Similar to the situation described by the Alpha and Gamma information systems, Ingberman and Sorter argued that focusing on the specific point in time when a given accounting report is issued may be the wrong way to assess the value of the information provided by accounting reports.

3.   Standard research procedures abstract from (i.e. eliminate) general market conditions to test for (market) reaction specific to a firm or sample of firms. If an accounting standard affects all firms equally, then a test looking for firm-specific reaction will not find anything as the informational impact is (inadvertently) included in "general" market conditions. Even if the standard does not affect all firms, but only a sizeable proportion of them, then standard research designs would be unlikely to find (significant) market reaction. Thus, somewhat paradoxically, the more pervasive the impact of an accounting change the less likely that market reaction will be found. Only if studies are designed to measure the differential effect of such changes on particular firms will a market reaction be found.

Examples of pervasive accounting standards are:
1. Changing prices (SFAS 33[*])
2. Pension plans (SFAS 87)
3. Income taxes (SFAS 96/109)
4. Postretirement benefits (SFAS 106)
   [*]This argument may explain the insignificant results (see Chapter 6) found in studies that examined the impact of SFAS 33.

4. This statement is most consistent with the positive approach to accounting theory. Proponents of the classical and market-based approaches might agree with the descriptive validity of the statement. However, the political process is viewed by classicists as an undesirable 'fact of life' to be overcome and as irrelevant by the market-based proponents. The positive approach, on the other hand, holds that the ramifications and implications of this political process are an essential element in understanding how accounting standards are developed and the motivation of firms in opting for alternative choices.

5. *NOTE: Most, if not all, of the items listed have analytical implications that are independent of financial statements, i.e., they would have to be considered whether or not the firm issued financial statements. We focus here only on the implications of these items in the context of financial statements.*

    1. To the extent that a firm's labor costs are related to profitability, (e.g. profit sharing plans), management may have an incentive to select accounting policies that dampen reported profits. Lower reported profits may also keep down demands for higher wages and benefits. Thus, the analyst should be prepared to "adjust" the firm's reported performance upwards as the firm may have been too conservative.

        Alternatively, if a labor contract is coming up for renewal, and the firm's financial statements show strong performance, then one can expect higher demands from labor, increased probability of a strike, and increased labor costs in the future. (Also see #3.)

    2. Market efficiency is increased by analysts competing to "beat the market." This motivation and the resultant behavior (somewhat paradoxically) leads to information being immediately impounded in prices. If this is true then the degree of efficiency should be (positively) related to the number of analysts covering the firm. Thus, an analyst who wants to uncover and exploit information not recognized by the market should look for firms that are covered by few other analysts. (Also see #4.)

    3. The bonus plan hypothesis is that managers will act to enhance their well being even if it may not be in the firm's best interest. For example, managers may opt for financial reporting methods that increase income if their compensation is directly (or indirectly) tied to the firm's income. Analysts need to be aware of this phenomenon to better understand the effect of this behavior on the firm's reported performance. (Also see #5.)

        More sophisticated manifestations of this behavior include:

        (i) taking a "big bath" in a year when performance is below some threshold anyway, thereby increasing the probability that the threshold level will be achieved in the future.

        (ii) alternatively, if a threshold has been achieved and no further benefit (to managers) accrues from exceeding that threshold, they may engage in income smoothing to "store" income for future years when adverse business conditions make the threshold harder to achieve.

4. (i)   One of the documented anomalies of the efficient market hypothesis is the small firm effect. Small firms tend to earn abnormal positive returns (even after compensating for risk). This phenomenon may be related to item 2, the number of analysts covering the firm as larger firms tend to have more of an analyst following. This argues for more emphasis on the analysis of smaller firms.

          However, there is a cost-benefit tradeoff. An investor with $100 million to invest may have to choose between investing in ten larger firms or 100 smaller firms. The additional return earned on the latter may not compensate for the higher research costs (especially time) and lower liquidity. For a given research effort that results in an additional 1% return, the benefits will differ considerably depending on the size of the firm. The 1% additional return for a firm whose capitalization is $100 million is considerably greater than a 1% return on a firm whose capitalization is only one million dollars. The $10,000 return earned on the latter may not compensate for the research time and money expended.

    (ii) On the other hand, the political cost hypothesis argues that larger firms are more sensitive to certain accounting changes and patterns of income. Analysts should be on the lookout to see if large firms have chosen accounting methods that shield them from political costs.

5. As noted earlier (item 3) managers may have incentives to take actions that enhance their position at the expense of the firm. The incentives for this behavior are reduced when managers are also owners of the firm. Thus, the more a firm is controlled by its owners, the lower the potential effects of agency costs.

6. Companies in the same industry tend to choose similar accounting methods. When a company deviates from these policies, in addition to adjusting for the alternative methods the analyst should ask what motivates these changes and what can be learned about the company's "corporate profile." Do the changes signal a shift in emphasis from one segment (industry) to another?

    Additionally, for firms in certain industries (oil and gas, banking) the political cost hypothesis discussed earlier is a relevant consideration.

6. Assuming the survey is accurate, there are three possible explanations for the results:

    (i)   Firms were not aware of the magnitude of their postretirement health benefits until they were forced to calculate them by the new accounting rule.

    (ii) The mandated balance sheet recognition and disclosure of health care liabilities was directly responsible for their curtailment by firms.

    (iii) There is no direct cause and effect between balance sheet recognition and the curtailment of benefits. The events are only correlated with another.

The first explanation assumes that managers (as well as investors) are "fixated" on annual reports and that managers have no appreciation of actual costs unless and until they are contained in the financial reporting system. Previous research on leases and foreign currency translation suggest that managers do pay more attention to events that they must account for. Similarly, field tests carried out when the health cost disclosure was first introduced indicated that (some) managers had difficulty in complying with the requirements because of a lack of data availability.

Because of this lack of data and the complexity of calculating the present value of these benefits (see Chapter 9) it is possible that some firms had only the haziest idea of the cost of these benefits. Postemployment benefits were often granted to unionized employees as trade offs for current wages, that had to be recognized as expense immediately. Managers had a clear incentive to trade future costs for present costs. [A senior manager of one Fortune 100 company told one of the authors that he thought the benefits would not have been granted if management had known their cost.]

The second explanation is consistent with the "economic consequences" branch of the positive accounting approach. By adversely affecting the company's reported performance, the new accounting standard may impact one or more of the following:

(1) management compensation,
(2) bond covenants on existing debt,
(3) the terms of any new debt,
(4) future labor negotiations, and
(5) internal resource allocation decisions.

All of these factors can have real costs associated with them and may be incentives for management to reduce health care costs.

Somewhat less likely in our opinion, is the possibility that managers reduced their health care costs because they feared the market reaction to the accounting recognition and disclosure. This is not necessarily inconsistent with the efficient market hypothesis as it is possible that even though the market is efficient, managers may not perceive it to be so. However, in this case, prior disclosure requirements (SFAS 81) may have taken some of the surprise out of the actual accounting.

The third explanation is the most likely. Under this view, the benefit curtailments were not caused by new accounting standards. Rather, both events were influenced by the same underlying factor--the explosion of health care costs in recent years. The growth in these costs was a major factor that triggered the FASB project that resulted in new accounting standards. Similarly, the higher costs induced firms to reduce the health care benefits offered to employees. Thus the coincidence of these events is an example of *association and correlation not causation*.

One would not expect to see any market reaction to the survey as companies had already been disclosing the effect of the new standard. As far as reaction to the accounting rule itself and subsequent disclosures, any market reaction observed and its direction (positive or negative) would result from one of three factors:

(1) the disclosure requirement itself,
(2) the curtailment of benefits, or
(3) the level of health care costs.

Under the efficient market hypothesis, *ceteris paribus*, one would not expect to see any market reaction to the rule itself or the subsequent balance sheet disclosures unless the market (analysts) had previously done a poor job of estimating the level of a firm's health care liabilities. Then the actual disclosure may contain surprises ("good" and "bad") triggering market reaction.

Under the "economic consequences" hypothesis one would expect to see market reaction, primarily at the time of the adoption of the new rule. The direction would presumably be negative, unless it is assumed that the market anticipates that the disclosure rule will force firms to curtail future benefits. The curtailment may be perceived as being positive as it lowers future costs.

Under any approach, the results must be understood in the context of rising health care costs. Any results indicating that firms that have a higher burden of health care costs perform poorly relative to firms whose health care costs are not as high may be measuring reaction to rising health care costs rather than to the new accounting and disclosure requirement. This point would be especially relevant if the research did not focus on the period (days) immediately surrounding the new disclosure requirement.

7.   A.   To determine abnormal returns, one must abstract from general market conditions as well as industry factors. Overall market indices rose by 1% to 2%, much less than the increases in Amgen (6.3%) and Deere (5.2%) and, in the opposite direction, the 16.9% decline in Dell. Thus, ignoring industry factors all three firms could be said to exhibit abnormal returns.

When we consider industry factors, the answers become more complicated. As the index for computer stocks increased slightly, it would be safe to argue that the decline in Dell is firm-specific and would qualify as an "abnormal" return. To a lesser extent, a similar argument can be made for Deere as the overall industry index for heavy machinery increased by only 2.9%; Deere's increase was substantially higher. However, this conclusion would depend on Deere's "beta" relative to the industry index. If it was very high then Deere's high return would be considered industry rather than firm related.

For Amgen, it would seem that its increase of 6.3% was industry-specific (rather than firm-specific) as the biotechnology index increased by a similar 5.4%. However, the industry index may itself be affected by firm-specific events (see Part E to this problem). Amgen is a component of the biotechnology index. Thus the change in that index may reflect the firm-specific change in Amgen rather than industry wide factors. To remedy this problem, an industry index without Amgen would have to be constructed and used. Additionally, to the extent that news about one firm provides information about other firms in the industry, it is difficult to argue that the market reaction was not related to Amgen simply because it affected the shares of other firms in the same industry. Similar arguments can, of course, be made for the other industry indices.

B.   The efficient market hypothesis does not hold that the market is omniscient; only that it correctly and rapidly processes available information. If the information about Amgen's earnings was not known earlier, then the negative reaction at the time of the announcement would be totally consistent with the efficient market hypothesis. Only if there existed prior public information,[1] in the form of lower orders for example, that could have permitted the market to anticipate the earnings disappointment, would the lack of anticipation be an example of market inefficiency.

For Dell, the question of market inefficiency seems to be more relevant. Only a month earlier, Dell had hit an all-time high of approximately $50. This raises the first question: how did this happen? What news (seemingly completely contrary to present news about the firm) did the market react to then? Since then, the stock had declined by about 30% prior to February 24. Obviously, the market had wind of the negative news prior to the February 24th announcement. The question now becomes: why wasn't the full reaction immediate? Why did the decline take over a month? To answer these questions, more information would be required as to the pattern of news relating to Dell appearing in the last month.

C.   The existence of abnormal returns would be an indicator of reaction to firm-specific news. Thus, as argued in part A, it appears that Dell's market reaction was related to the news item.

However, the strongest argument can be made for Amgen. The reaction was over a very short time horizon (one half-hour) *after* the normal market close, it immediately followed the release of the news item, and it was in the opposite direction to the stock's movement prior to the news release.

D.   It is difficult to determine the "cause" of the market reaction because there are confounding news items:

(i)   the reduction of the long-term profit goal; and

(ii)   the withdrawal of the stock issue.

Which of these items is "responsible" for the market reaction is difficult if not impossible to determine.

E.   (i)   In this part, we assume that the Amgen effect is not large enough to significantly affect the Biotechnology index.

                The actual change in Amgen occurred after the market closed on February 24. On that day the biotechnology index was positive, and as we argued in part C, Amgen's reaction is surely a result of the news item. However, by using February 25 as the announcement date, when the index was negative, a researcher may erroneously conclude that the reaction was industry related.

---

[1]We are ignoring the strong form of the efficient market hypothesis, that holds that even nonpublic information is reflected in prices as insiders trade on it. In Amgen's case, one would have to know when the insiders became aware of the disappointing earnings expectation and whether they had the time or opportunity to trade on it.

(ii) The evidence about the components of the index clearly indicate that the index was significantly affected by Amgen. The assumption made in (i) does not hold. However, since the index is affected by Amgen, by using the index to abstract industry wide effects, the researcher would erroneously conclude that the Amgen effect was industry related when the correct conclusion was the reverse. The industry effect was caused by Amgen! (Also see discussion earlier for questions 3 and 7A.)

F. One would expect to see little or no market reaction after the financial statements are released as all the information was anticipated by then. The market reaction will depend on how the actual earnings report compares with that expected (not just with prior year earnings).

This does not mean that financial statements in general are irrelevant. As discussed in previous questions (see #2), relevance should not be based on one statement but rather on the whole system of accounting reports. After all, the market reacted to a forecast of a number produced by that system. It is difficult to argue then that financial statements are irrelevant. Moreover, the detailed income statement will contain the components of earnings and may explain why earnings were disappointing (were gross margins too low, was selling expense too high, did research expense increase, did the tax rate rise, etc.). Taken together with the balance sheet (e.g. inventory levels) and cash flow statement (cash from operations) the statements may contain data that help the market forecast future earnings and cash flows. [At times, the market may first react to an earnings release in one direction, then reverse direction when details of the earnings report become available, casting new light on the results.]

G. Changes in production (and demand) ultimately affect profitability. Financial statements are useful in determining how such changes affect profitability. They provide information about a firm's operating and financial leverage, and provide a historical record of how previous changes in volume affected profitability.

8. This question is based on the notion that, as there are market incentives to disclose financial data, market forces will result in rational managers providing such information.

Beaver's approach to the solution of this question is based on the concept of information as an economic good and explores three potential reasons why market forces alone will not provide the "sufficient" or "right amount" of information. The reasons offered attempt to explain why market forces by themselves do not result in the "appropriate" amount of information being produced. These reasons, however, do not necessarily mean that levels of disclosure mandated by regulation result in an optimal amount of information production and disclosure. Beaver's three reasons follow:

(1) An economic commodity will be produced so long as the benefits from the commodity outweigh its production cost (marginal cost equal marginal benefits). This holds so long as those who benefit from a good also bear its cost. Information, however, is a *public good*. Access to it cannot be [and perhaps should not (see (2) below)] be

limited. Thus, there will be some who benefit from disclosure without having to pay for it. Two examples are given:

(i) Competing firms who obtain information from annual reports without bearing the cost of information production; and

(ii) Investors who, based on the information provided, decide *not* to invest in the company. They obtain the benefit without paying any of the cost.

This so-called *free rider problem* reduces the incentive to disclose, as those bearing the cost are not fully compensated.

(2) The second reason is usually couched in terms of equity or fairness. Without regulation, there may be selective disclosure and uneven distribution of information. Some investors will be better informed than others.[2] Regulation is needed to "protect" the uninformed from the informed.

(3) There exists *information asymmetry* as managers are better informed about the firm than investors. Moreover, managers have incentives to suppress (unfavorable) information. As investors know that some firms suppress information but do not know which firms are doing so, they will treat all firms in some "average" fashion. Hence, poorer performing (below average) firms will be priced "too high" and better (above average) firms will be priced "too low". Poorer (better) performing firms will want to offer more (fewer) shares to investors as a result. To combat this, managers of better performing firms may offer warranties on their information (audited statements) and other guarantees to investors to distinguish themselves. The result may be that managers of "better" firms absorb too much risk leading to an inefficient sharing of risk in the economy. Regulation is designed to mitigate this information asymmetry.

9. A. The actual reserve additions should not result in any market reaction, assuming that the market knew about the potential losses. However, the rule change itself could cause market reaction, not so much from the actual requirement to recognize losses, but from the associated *requirement that increased the level of required reserves*. This tightening up would increase the risk of a firm becoming "technically insolvent".

B. This article would probably not result in any market reaction. Any reaction (as described in part A) would occur at the time of the announcement of the rule change itself.

C. Positive accounting theory views a firm and its environment as consisting of a "nexus of contracts". The terms of these contracts, in many cases, are determined by accounting based numbers. RAP rules

---

[2]One can debate, as does Beaver, whether this is inherently unfair. Presumably, those who are better informed have paid for more information. The only thing stopping others from becoming as well informed is their unwillingness to pay (or lack of funds). This may be unfortunate but, as with any other good, it is a fact of life. Should all goods be distributed equally? Certainly some have put forth this argument. Its ramifications are clearly beyond the scope of this text.

are a perfect example of this concept. Regulators set the rules for the contract between the firm and its environment. RAP rules determine not only the amount of profits that regulators (the environment) allow the firm to report but also the terms (net worth requirements) permitting the firm to operate at all.

10. More than five years after the October, 1987 market "crash", there is considerable divergence of opinion regarding the implications of that crash for the Efficient Market Theory (EMT). Detractors of the EMT cite the crash as evidence that the theory is not a good description of financial markets. They argue that there was no significant news prior to the crash, certainly not sufficient news to justify a 25% decline in New York Stock Exchange prices. The market reacted, they contend, to sharp declines experienced the previous two days. Thus panic set in, there was no rationality and a herd instinct took over.

Defenders of the EMT, on the other hand, say that the crash does not invalidate the EMT. Market volatility had increased in the weeks prior to the crash. Then when a sell-of began, the exchanges broke down. The computers could not keep up with the flow of orders and specialists panicked. Thus, institutional factors helped turn a normal decline into a panic.

These arguments are summarized from Christopher Farrell "The 'Efficient Market' was a Good Idea - and Then Came the Crash", *Business Week* (February 22, 1988), page 140.

Chapter 5 - Solutions

1.   A.   Start with the basic inventory relationship (page 332 in text):

$$BI + P = COGS + EI$$

Since opening inventory is zero, both BI and P (purchases) are identical under FIFO and LIFO; the difference in COGS equals the difference in ending inventory. That difference can be computed as follows:

Total purchases in units = (3 x 100,000) + (3 x 125,000)
                                  + (3 x 150,000) + (3 x 200,000)
                                  = 1,725,000

Total sales in units = (6 x 100,000) + (6 x 150,000)
                              = 1,500,000.

Therefore units in ending inventory =
                 1,725,000 − 1,500,000 = 225,000

(i)   Purchases are identical; there is no difference between methods.

(ii)   Closing inventory under FIFO uses the latest costs of $15; under LIFO uses the earliest costs of $25; the difference is $10/unit x 225,000 = $2,250,000 (LIFO higher).

(iii) COGS will be lower under LIFO by $2,250,000, as the total of COGS and ending inventory is identical.

(iv)   As a result of lower COGS, LIFO pretax income will be higher by $2,250,000.

(v)   Income tax expense will be higher under LIFO by

.40 x $2,250,000 = $900,000

(vi)   Net income will be higher under LIFO by

.60 x $2,250,000 = $1,350,000

(vii) Since income tax is higher under LIFO, cash flow is lower by $900,000 (assuming taxes paid in same year).

(viii) From (vii) cash is lower by $900,000 but from (ii) ending inventory is higher by $2,250,000. Therefore, LIFO working capital is higher by $(900,000) + $2,250,000 = $1,350,000

The problem illustrates that, when prices are declining, LIFO results in higher inventory and higher net income than FIFO. This solution would, however, be modified in practice as all inventory must be reported at the lower of cost or market. Thus inventory would have to be written down to market value for financial reporting purposes (but not for tax).

B. If all inventory units were liquidated, FIFO and LIFO would be identical in all respects.

2. A. This problem tests the interrelationships among accounting methods and differentiates between the flow of units and the flow of costs. Keep in mind that some factors are affected by the choice of accounting method but others are not.

Opening inventory (in this problem), purchases, and actual inventory turnover are not a function of accounting method. *Actual* turnover is based on units while *reported* turnover is based on dollars and is affected by the choice of accounting method. Thus the accounting method can only approximate the actual turnover.

Opening inventory is $500 for all methods. Since the firm replenishes inventory every month, its *actual* inventory turnover is 12. Thus, in units, its cost of goods sold is 12 times its inventory level. That is, 12 months of inventory were sold; one month remains.

The solution begins with the weighted average method:

Cost-of-goods sold = units sold x average cost = $12,000

As closing inventory = units in inventory x average cost, and, units sold are 12 times units in inventory; then closing inventory equals $1,000.

We can now solve for purchases:

Opening Inventory + Purchases = COGS   + Closing Inventory
    $500   +   ?   = $12,000 + $1,000

Therefore, purchases equal $12,500.

Reported turnover is COGS/Average Inventory = $12,000/$750 = 16.

Under the LIFO method:

Since inventory in units does not change:

Closing Inventory = Opening Inventory = $500

Therefore, Cost of Goods Sold = Purchases = $12,500

Reported turnover is COGS/Average Inventory = $12,500/$500 = 25.

Under the FIFO method:

First, note that under the weighted average method, closing inventory is greater than opening inventory. As cost changes were only in one direction, they must have gone up during the year. Therefore, use of FIFO must result in higher net income (lower COGS) and higher income taxes. Since the cash flow difference is $400 (all attributable to taxes), the income/COGS difference must be $1000. Therefore, $COGS_{FIFO}$ is $11,500 and Closing Inventory is $1,500.

Reported Turnover is COGS/Average Inventory = $11,500/$1,000 = 11.5.

The completed table is:

	FIFO	Weighted Average	LIFO
Opening Inventory	$ 500	$ 500	$ 500
Purchases	12,500	12,500	12,500
Cost of Goods Sold	11,500	12,000	12,500
Closing Inventory	1,500	1,000	500
Inventory Turnover (Reported)	11.5X	16.0X	25.0X
Inventory Turnover (Actual)	12.0X	12.0X	12.0X

B. Reported turnover under the FIFO method most closely approximates the actual physical turnover whereas LIFO is farthest away. It is interesting to note that the weighted average method, using COGS/closing inventory (rather than average inventory) yields the actual turnover of 12.

C. The choice of method will affect reported income, income taxes paid, and (therefore) the change in cash. The LIFO method will report the lowest net income but highest cash flow from operations (because of lower tax payments). Neither cash for investment nor cash for financing are affected. Thus LIFO will report the highest net cash flow. The FIFO method will report the lower cash from operations and, therefore, the lowest net cash flow. The average cost method will be halfway between the other two methods.

3. A. The first step is to obtain FIFO cost-of-goods-sold:

Pretax income = sales - COGS - other expenses

$5,000 = $25,000 - COGS - $12,000

Solving: COGS = $8,000

Purchases are equal to COGS + Closing Inventory
= $8,000 + $10,000 = $18,000.

The key to this problem is to distinguish between the flow of units and the flow of costs. Purchases are independent of the accounting method used.

Since half the units were sold, half remain in inventory. Under LIFO, therefore, the cost allocated to inventory and COGS will be the reverse of those allocated under FIFO. That is, under LIFO, COGS = $10,000 and Closing Inventory = $8,000.

Under the weighted average method, as total purchases equal $18,000, the allocation between COGS and closing inventory will be equal: COGS = Closing Inventory = $9,000.

The rest of the table can now be filled in by recalling that CFO is a function of purchases, not COGS.

	FIFO	Weighted Average	LIFO
Sales	$25,000	$25,000	$25,000
Cost of Goods Sold	8,000	9,000	10,000
Other Expenses	12,000	12,000	12,000
Pretax Income	5,000	4,000	3,000
Taxes	2,000	1,600	1,200
Net Income	3,000	2,400	1,800
Dividends Paid	1,500	1,200	900
Retained Earnings	1,500	1,200	900
Cash from Operations[1]	(7,000)	(6,600)	(6,200)
Cash Balance[2]	1,500	2,200	2,900
Closing Inventory	10,000	9,000	8,000
Purchases	18,000	18,000	18,000

[1]Cash from Operations = Sales – Other Expenses – Purchases – Tax Expense.

[2]Cash Balance = $10,000 + Cash from Operations – Dividends Paid

B.   **M & J Company**
Balance Sheet, December 31, 19X0

	FIFO	Weighted Average	LIFO
Cash	$ 1,500	$ 2,200	$ 2,900
Inventory	10,000	9,000	8,000
Total Assets	$ 11,500	$ 11,200	$ 10,900
Common Stock	$ 10,000	$ 10,000	$ 10,000
Retained Earnings	1,500	1,200	900
Total Equities	$ 11,500	$ 11,200	$ 10,900

C.   The advantages of LIFO are that it results in the highest cash flow (by reducing income taxes) and it measures net income by matching the cost of sales with most recent costs to replace inventory sold. The disadvantage of LIFO is that inventory on the balance sheet is understated.

Note the lower dividend payment under LIFO. This is an advantage in the sense that dividends are not based on earnings inflated by unrealized holding gains. LIFO produces the highest cash balance because of the combination of lower income tax and lower dividends. As inflation can strain the financing capacity of the firm, LIFO is doubly beneficial.

The advantage of FIFO is that inventory is measured at most recent costs. Its disadvantages are the reduced cash flow and overstatement of reported income.

Average cost has the disadvantage of misreporting both the balance sheet inventory and net income. Income taxes are higher than under the LIFO method (but lower than under FIFO). The "advantage" of average cost is that it is "less wrong" than LIFO on the balance sheet and "less wrong" than FIFO on the income statement.

4. The last sentence in the statement is patently absurd. The accounting method for inventory should have nothing to do with a company's pricing strategy. Pricing should be based on current market conditions. Companies that ignore the cost of replacing inventory when setting prices will suffer from poor cash flows and, in some cases, will fail.

5. (i) Ending inventory:

FIFO: $39 + $43 = $82   LIFO: $35 + $39 = $74

(ii) Gross profit:

FIFO: $65 − $35 = $30   LIFO: $65 − $43 = $22

(iii) Unrealized holding gain is equal to replacement cost minus ending inventory:

FIFO: (2 x $46) − $82 = $10   LIFO: (2 x $46) − $74 = $18

(iv) Comprehensive income = gross profit + unrealized holding gain:

FIFO: $30 + $10 = $40   LIFO: $22 + $18 = $40

The two are identical. As comprehensive income measures total changes in economic well being it is independent of the accounting method and must, by definition, be equal for all methods.

6. A. Adjusting Zenab to FIFO.

Since the LIFO reserve account increased by $1,500, the LIFO effect is $1,500. Under FIFO, COGS would be lower by $1,500 at ($61,300 − $1,500) $59,800. Income before tax would be higher by $1,500 at $6,500.

A comparison of both companies on a FIFO basis is presented below:

	Zenab	Faybech
Sales	$ 92,700	$ 77,000
Cost of goods sold	59,800	52,000
Gross profit	$ 32,900	$ 25,000
Selling and general expense	26,400	21,500
Pretax income	$ 6,500	$ 3,500

B. Adjusting Faybech to LIFO/Current Cost is more complicated. The first step is to calculate an implied inflation rate using Zenab's statements. On a FIFO basis, Zenab's inventories were $24,900 + $3,600 = $28,500 at the beginning of the year. Of that inventory, 70% or (.70 x $28,850) $19,950 were carried on LIFO. The increase in the LIFO reserve implies a specific inflation rate of $1,500/$19,950 = 7.52%. Therefore, Faybech's COGS (pretax income) on an LIFO/current cost basis would increase (decrease) by .0752 x $22,300 = $1,675. This is a decrease in pretax income of close to 50%.

A comparison of both companies on a LIFO basis is presented below:

	Zenab	Faybech
Sales	$ 92,700	$ 77,000
Cost of goods sold	61,300	53,675
Gross profit	$ 31,400	$ 23,325
Selling and general expense	26,400	21,500
Pretax income	$ 5,000	$ 1,825

Note that this solution is incomplete as Faybech is 100% on LIFO while Zenab is only 70% on LIFO. To complete the solution convert the remaining 30% of Zenab's inventories to LIFO using the same inflation rate:

Thirty percent (30%) of Zenab inventory is FIFO (.30 x $28,500) or $8550. Applying the same inflation rate of 7.52% increases COGS (reduces pretax income) by $643. The comparison now becomes:

	Zenab	Faybech
Sales	$ 92,700	$ 77,000
Cost of goods sold	61,943	53,675
Gross profit	$ 30,757	$ 23,325
Selling and general expense	26,400	21,500
Pretax income	$ 4,357	$ 1,825

C. It depends what the purpose of the comparison is. Three possibilities exist:

(1) Comparison of firms' operations.
(2) Comparison of firms' operations and tax policy.
(3) Analysis of firm's "economic" status.

If the purpose is a comparison of a firm's operations with another firm's, then the adjustment should be done on an "as if" basis and a tax adjustment should be made. If the purpose is to compare operations and tax policy, then no tax adjustment should be made. Finally, for evaluation of the economic status no tax adjustment should be made unless liquidation is considered to be imminent.

7. A.

	Year	Zenab (LIFO) 2	1	Faybech (FIFO) 2	1
Current ratio		2.65	2.89	3.68	3.24
Inventory turnover		2.45		1.98	
Gross profit margin		.339		.32	
Pretax income/sales		.054		.045	

B. Faybech's liquidity (as measured by the current ratio) appears to be better. Its inventory turnover is lower, however, implying lower efficiency. Faybech appears to be slightly less profitable as well.

C. (i) Using the FIFO income statements from problem 6, we compute the following ratios:

	Year	Zenab (FIFO) 2	1	Faybech (FIFO) 2	1
Current ratio[1]		3.04	3.20	3.68	3.24
Inventory turnover[2]		2.03		1.98	
Gross profit margin		.355		.32	
Pretax income/sales		.070		.045	

[1]Year 2 = ($33,600 + $5,100)/$12,700
 Year 1 = ($33,500 + $3,600)/$11,600

[2] $$\frac{\$59,800}{(\$25,200 + \$5,100 + \$24,900 + \$3,600)/2}$$

(ii) Using the LIFO income statements from problem 6 (be sure to use the Zenab statement after conversion to 100% LIFO), we compute the following profitability ratios:

Year	Zenab (100% LIFO) 2	Faybech (LIFO) 2
Gross profit margin	.332	.303
Pretax income/sales	.047	.024

Balance sheet adjustments are not possible for Faybech and the 30% of Zenab inventories on FIFO. Thus adjusted current and inventory turnover ratios cannot be computed.

(iii) The hybrid (combination) method of computing the inventory turnover ratio uses the FIFO measure of inventory and the LIFO measure of COGS. The ratios are:

	Zenab	Faybech
LIFO cost of goods sold	$61,943	$53,675
FIFO average inventory	$29,400	$26,300
Inventory turnover ratio	2.11X	2.04X

D. Balance sheet values are most meaningful when the FIFO basis is used. For income statement numbers LIFO numbers should be used. Therefore for the current ratio, we use the FIFO numbers. For the gross profit margin, and pretax/sales we use the 100% LIFO numbers. For the inventory turnover ratio, the combination approach is preferred. However that ratio and the FIFO based ratio are similar in this case:

		Zenab		Faybech	
Year		2	1	2	1
FIFO current ratio		3.04	3.20	3.68	3.24
FIFO inventory turnover		2.03		1.98	
Combination turnover		2.11		2.04	
LIFO gross profit margin		.332		.303	
LIFO pretax income/sales		.047		.024	

Notice that, on the basis of these ratios, Zenab is clearly more profitable than Faybech. The inventory turnover ratios are, however, virtually identical. While Faybech still has a higher current ratio, the difference is smaller than it appears based on the reported balance sheet data.

8.   A.   The LIFO Reserve increased by $4,000. If the company used FIFO, its pretax income would be $4,000 higher. After tax income would be higher by .65 x $4,000 = $2,600.

B. Inventory turnover is COGS/average inventory:

LIFO $3,800,000/[.5($748,000 + $696,800)] = 5.26X
FIFO $3,796,000/[.5($794,000 + $746,800)] = 4.93X

C. Since the firm's ROE is 4.6% and net income is $340,000, then average equity = $340,000/.046 = $7,391,304

If the company used FIFO, equity would be higher by the amount of the LIFO reserve adjusted for taxes. The average LIFO reserve is $48,000. Therefore, average equity should be higher by .65 x $48,000 = $31,200.

FIFO Average Equity = $7,391,304 + $31,200 = $7,422,504
ROE_{FIFO} = $342,600/$7,422,504 = 4.62%

The adjustment of ROE is, in this case, insignificant.

D. There are two reasons to make adjustments to accounting methods. One is to obtain a more accurate measure of the firm's operations and the second is to facilitate comparisons of different firms on the same basis.

For inventory turnover, the adjustment results in a more accurate measure of performance. However, the main purpose of the LIFO to FIFO adjustment is for comparative purposes. It enables the analyst to compare Zeta Corp. to other firms that use FIFO.

E. The combination method (inventory and equity at FIFO, COGS and net income at LIFO) should be used for both inventory turnover and ROE. For inventory turnover, this method better approximates the actual (physical) turnover. The argument for ROE is that FIFO equity better reflects the Company's current value, while LIFO income reflects the current operating profit earned on that equity. For the Zeta Corporation, these adjustments are not significant. In some cases, however, the combination method ratios are quite different.

9. A. (All data in $ thousands)

	1991	1990
FIFO Inventory	$16,141	$11,480
LIFO Inventory	10,491	7,166
LIFO Reserve	$ 5,650	$ 4,314

The LIFO reserve increased by $5,650 - $4,314 = $1,336. On the opening current cost (FIFO) inventory of $11,480, the price level change is $1,336/$11,480 = 11.6%.

B. The price level change implied by the Commodity Price Index is (134.3/126.8) - 1 = 5.9%. Even at its highest point (July) the rate of (136.9/126.8) - 1 = 7.96% is still lower than the inflation rate for Pope & Talbot computed in part A.

C. The calculation in part A assumes that the increase in the LIFO Reserve was all due to the effect of price changes on opening inventory. The company increased its inventory during 1991 and, therefore, part of the increased LIFO reserve is due to the added layer for the current year. As a result, the part A calculation is overstated. However, even if the inventory increase was early in the year (resulting in the largest 1991 LIFO effect) this factor explains less than half of the difference between the rates calculated in parts A and B.

D. The mostly likely explanation for the difference in estimates is that Pope and Talbot's product mix differs from that used to compute the Lumber and Wood Products Index. That index may, for example, include products at a more advanced stage of processing whose prices rose less rapidly than the prices of raw materials. Such products would include costs that change little over time, diluting the effect of increases in lumber prices.

The lesson here is that, when commodity prices are used to estimate the effect of price changes on company inventories, care must be taken to ensure that product mixes between index and inventories are similar.

10. A. January 1, 19X3 inventory = $2,700,000 ($2,000,000 + $700,000).

B. To maintain its inventory balance at $2,700,000, Jofen would have had to increase its purchases by $700,000 + $300,000 = $1,000,000. The $300,000 is the difference between the LIFO and FIFO cost of the inventory. The choice of inventory method does not affect purchases as they reflect actual prices paid.

C. Ignoring taxes and any change in accounts payable, reported cash flow from operations increased by $1,000,000 due to lower purchases.

D. COGS should be increased by $300,000 to exclude the effect of the LIFO liquidation.

E. The LIFO liquidation is not an operating activity. Excluding that income makes net income more useful for evaluating operating performance (net income and cash from operations) and forecasting future performance.

11. A. $COGS_{FIFO} = COGS_{LIFO}$ + Change in Reserve
$4898 = $4894 + $4 (all in $ millions)

B. (i) COGS would have been higher by $128 million.
$4894 + $128 = $5022
(all in $ millions)

(ii) $COGS_{FIFO}$ would have been as calculated in part A, $4898 million. It is not affected by LIFO liquidations.

C.   Purchases = COGS + Change in Inventory
     $4894 - $140 = $4754   (all in $ millions)

     Calculation based on FIFO:
     $4898 - $144 = $4754   (all in $ millions)

D.   To maintain Deere's inventory at the 1990 level of $678 million
     ($140 million higher than the actual 1991 level), purchases would
     have been $268 million higher ($140 million + $128 million LIFO
     reserve). Total purchases would therefore be $4754 million (part C)
     + $268 million = $5022 million. [This is identical to B(i) result.]

E.   Best estimates should ignore distortions caused by price changes and
     effects of LIFO liquidation.

     (i)   Gross profit measures the markup over cost and should use the
            adjusted COGS of $5022 from part B(i).
            ($5848-$5022)/$5848 = 14.12%   (all in $millions)

     (ii)   Turnover ratio should use FIFO inventory and the adjusted COGS
            (all in $ millions):
            $5022/[0.5*($1655+$1799)] = 2.91X

     (iii) Had they not liquidated LIFO reserve would have increased by
            ($128 - $4) = $124 million. Therefore the rate of price level
            change is (all in $millions): $124/(0.8*$1799) = 8.6%.
            Remember that only 80% of Deere's inventory is on LIFO.

F.   Increase assets and equity by $1117 million. Assuming liquidation,
     adjust equity for deferred taxes.

12. ($ millions)

	1991	1990	Change
LIFO Inventory	$40,844	$46,315	$(5,471)
LIFO Reserve	3,619	7,882	(4,263)
FIFO Inventory	$44,463	$54,197	$(9,734)

A.   Since the LIFO reserve dropped by $4,263, COGS$_{FIFO}$ would be higher
     (and pretax income lower) by $4,263 million.

B.   The change would have been $9,734 million rather than the $5,471
     million reported (see above table).

C.   Newsprint and magazine paper prices declined during 1991. However,
     these declines would reduce only the LIFO reserve (the difference
     between inventory at FIFO and inventory at LIFO).

The most likely explanation is that the firm sold a segment or a portion of a segment, eliminating related inventory and LIFO reserves.

13. A. 1. Price decreases may explain part of the drop.

   2. Due to poor demand, the company may have cut back on production. This would not explain why work in process increased.

   3. Excess demand may have depleted inventory levels. This would be consistent with lower finished goods but higher work in process as the company increased production as a result of higher sales.

   B. Any one of these reasons reduces the desirability of LIFO. Declining prices and potential inventory liquidations lessen the tax advantages of LIFO.

   C. For new products, startup expenses are reduced; subsequent cost-of-goods-sold is increased as the capitalized costs are amortized. The net effect depends on the timing of new product introductions.

14. A. For service companies, inventory is an insignificant component of assets and COGS an insignificant cost. The main input of service companies is people. Thus inventory turnover is not a useful measure for such companies.

   B. Capacity utilization is an important measure of operating efficiency for firms with fixed capacity. The fixed cost of such capacity means that utilization is an important determinant of profitability. An airline seat, rental car, or hospital bed that goes unused generates no revenue; the variable cost saved may be very low. This phenomenon explains why airlines sell discount tickets; as long as the marginal revenue exceeds the variable cost, such sales are profitable.

   It is also important to measure costs in relation to either capacity or utilization. As revenues are subject to competitive and regulatory constraints, lower costs are important to profitability. Thus an airline's costs relative to available seat-miles (or to passenger revenue miles) measures the efficiency of its operations.

15. Contracts can provide strong incentives regarding the choice of inventory method. However different contracts may provide incentives for different choices. The following discussion assumes rising prices.

   The management compensation plan provides a mixed incentive. Use of LIFO will reduce income but increase cash from operations. Assuming a tax rate t, and a LIFO effect L, net income will decrease by $(1-t)L$ while cash from operations will increase by tL. The net effect $(2t-1)L$ is positive only at tax rates above 50%. Thus management contracts argue against use of LIFO.

   Bond covenants also argue against LIFO. Working capital is reduced by the LIFO reserve less taxes saved. The annual amount is $(t-1)L$ which is always negative. Retained earnings are also lower under LIFO.

Union employee profit sharing payments will be lower under LIFO, assuming that profits would exceed the minimum level. This would seem to argue for LIFO, to reduce compensation paid.

However, there are also second and third order effects that must be considered. Lower profit sharing payments, for example, will increase net income (and cash from operations), increasing management compensation and easing the effect of bond covenants. These effects require complex calculations and are highly firm-specific.

Some effects are non-quantitative. Lower profit sharing payments may result in higher wage demands from workers. For management, use of FIFO may raise questions about why they failed to obtain tax savings by using LIFO.

Thus, while we can identify many of the factors that motivate the choice of inventory method, the controller's choice will depend on how these factors affect Sechne; there is no simple answer.

Chapter 6 - Solutions

1.   A.   (i)

	Debt ($000)	Rate ($)	Interest ($000)
Development loan	$ 6,000	11.0%	$ 660
Mortgage debt	10,000	9.0	900
Debentures	40,000	10.0%	4,000
Interest Payable			$ 5,560

(ii)

	Debt	Rate	Interest
Development loan[1]	$ 6,000	11.0%	$ 660
Debentures[2]	4,000	10.0%	400
Capitalized interest			$ 1,060

    [1]Development loan assumed to be related to office building.

    [2]As mortgage debt, by its nature, must relate to a specific project and the problem does not state that it stems from the office building, remaining balance is assumed to be financed by the debentures. Management may also prefer to capitalize interest on higher rate debt to report higher income.

(iii) Interest expense = interest payable - amount capitalized
       $4,500,000   =   5,560,000   - $1,060,000

B.   Interest coverage should be based on interest payable, not on interest expense. The capitalization of interest is an accounting decision and does not affect the leverage of the firm. Interest coverage should be computed as:

Pretax income + interest expense
<hr>
Interest payable

C.   The capitalization of interest reduces the comparability of such measures as the interest coverage ratio, cash flow from operations, and profitability. The capitalization of interest improves all of these measures for affected firms. Among the factors that affect the capitalization of interest are:

1. The availability of internal funds limits the firm's ability to capitalize interest; interest can be capitalized *only* on external borrowings. Thus, a firm with excess cash and/or a lower debt/equity ratio will be able to capitalize less interest than a firm that must borrow, even if they are otherwise identical.

2. Firms with lower cost debt capital will be able to capitalize less interest than a firm that must pay a higher interest rate.

3. Capitalized interest becomes part of the carrying amount of the asset and is amortized (depreciated) over time. Different firms may use different methods (accelerated vs. straight line) and lives (longer or shorter) for similar assets. Firms that use accelerated methods and shorter lives will report lower profitability (and interest coverage) in the years following the construction of the asset. Amortization does not, however, affect cash from operations as it is a noncash expense.

    The computation of ratios and other performance measures should, therefore, be based on data that excludes the effect of capitalized interest. Such measures will reflect the actual leverage and cost of capital of the firm and will not be affected by the differences discussed above.

2. A. Brand names are clearly an asset. It is not clear, however, that these assets should be shown on corporate balance sheets.

    One advantage of recognizing brand names on a firm's balance sheet is that it makes the balance sheet more complete; a balance sheet that ignores a major firm asset has limited usefulness for analysis. A second advantage is that the cost of acquiring (or developing) a brand name should be recorded as an investment (asset) in order to properly match revenues and expenses.

    The major disadvantage of brand name recognition is the difficulty of proper measurement. As each brand name is unique, market transactions are not available to value the brand. Thus, the value recognized is subjective; differences from firm to firm may reflect either real differences in the value of brands or different measurement decisions.

    One approach is to capitalize the acquisition cost (for brands acquired) or the advertising and other development costs (for internally developed brands). In the latter case, it is unlikely that the value of the brand will equal the cost of development. A successful brand will be worth much more than the cost of its development; an unsuccessful brand may have no value at all.

    Further, the value of brands does change over time. Despite the quotation from Laing, brands can also become "dilapidated" if they are neglected, if advertising is poor, or if products are defective. The value of a brand will also be affected by changes in market conditions, e.g., pricing decisions and the inroads made by generic brands.

From the point of view of financial analysis, therefore, it is not clear that reporting management's subjective estimate of brand value would be helpful. The "proof of the pudding is in the eating" and a valuable brand should be highly profitable. The evaluation of the profitability might be better left to the analyst.

B. The advantage of amortization is that the income statement should reflect all expenses that help produce income. If profitability is due to a brand name, the amortization of the cost of acquiring that brand name should be an element of expense.

On the other hand, given the subjectivity of brand name valuation, the amortization amount (also affected by the choice of method and life) may be a poor measure of the expired cost. In addition, brand names may not decline in value over time; any such decline is likely to be irregular.

For purposes of analysis, therefore, the amortization of brand name intangible assets should be excluded from income. The evaluation of profitability, however, should consider the role of brand names.

3. A. (i) The deferral of development costs increased pretax income by $4,710,000 in 1991 as these costs would otherwise have been included in operating expense.

(ii) The deferral of development costs increased cash from operations in the amount of $4,710,000. Cash for investment increased by an equal amount. Net cash flow was unchanged.

(iii) The deferred costs will be reported as part of the project investment and will increase the depreciation or amortization cost when the project becomes operational, thus reducing reported income. If the commercial success of a project becomes doubtful, the costs will be written off and will reduce income in the year of the writeoff.

(iv) Future year cash flows will *not* be affected by the cost deferral. If the project is successful, depreciation or amortization will be a noncash expenses; if the project is deemed noncommercial, there will be a noncash writeoff. Thus the decision to capitalize development costs shifts the expenditures from operating to investment cash flows; that shift will never be reversed.

B. (i) The initial effect of cost deferral is an increase in net income and, therefore, equity. The debt-to-equity ratio declines (improves).

That decline will be reversed gradually by amortization of the deferred costs and immediately if they are written off. Thus the debt-to-equity ratio was reduced in 1991 but will trend higher in future years as compared to the ratio based on immediate expensing of the development costs.

(ii) Return on assets increased in 1991 by the cost deferral. Both profits and assets were increased by the same amount; the effect on profits had a greater effect on the ratio.

The cost deferral will tend to reduce the future trend of ROA, however. The higher asset level will reduce the ROA produced by any level of income. In addition, income and assets will both be reduced by future amortization or writeoff of the deferred costs, tending to depress ROA.

The deferral of development costs, therefore, improved both ratios for 1991 at the expense of future ratios.

4. A. Income before extraordinary item and cumulative accounting change = $2770 - $1720 = $1050 (all in $ thousands).

Net income = $3 - $1720 - $ 983 = $(2700) (all in $ thousands).

B. Difference is $(8499) - $(9280) = $781 (all in $ thousands).

Remainder of difference is applicable to prior years.

C. (1) 1991 cash outlay was not expensed, which increases income.

(2) Above is (partially) offset by increased amortization of previous years' capitalized outlays.

D. Whether expensed or capitalized *in this case* CFO is not affected.

E. $4092 - $1739 = $2353 (all in $ thousands).

The $2943 represents outlays made in 1991. The net increase of $2353 consists of the 1991 outlays less amortization of previous years' outlays, that can be deduced as $590 ($2943 - $2353).

F. The increase in 1991 net income was $2,703,500, the *sum* of the 1991 increase of $1,720,500 and the cumulative effect of $983,000. The footnote shows $737,500 ($1,720,500 - $983,000) as it incorrectly *subtracts* the cumulative effect from the 1991 effect.

5. A.

	1984	1985	1986	1987	1988	1989	1990	1991	1992
Amortiza-tion exp.	$ 0	$ 0	$ 0	$ 1	$ 12	$ 27	$ 37	$ 44	$ 64
Unamort-ized cost	0	0	0	34	66	90	110	112	134
Computer software expendi-ture*				$ 35	$ 44	$ 51	$ 57	$ 46	$ 86

*Amortized expense + change in unamortized cost

B. Approximately one year: 1988 amortization = approximately 1/3 of 1987 expenditure. Similarly 1989 amortization = approximately 1/3 of (1987 + 1988) expenditures. For 1992, however, the lag appears to be shorter; amortization expense is higher than expected. This may reflect a shortening of the product development cycle, due to competitive conditions.

C. (i) Research and engineering costs may be difficult to link to specific products while computer software costs can be attributed to specific computers or programs. This distinction may justify the capitalization of the latter but the expensing of the former.

    (ii) The ratio of research and engineering to computer software costs for 1987 was 28.9; for 1992 the ratio was 20.3 ($1754/$86). Assuming that this trend continues, Digital will capitalize and amortize more of its product development costs, increasing its reported profitability and solvency ratios. Both the level and trend will improve as the ratio declines.

D. **As reported (all data in $ millions):**

	1984	1985	1986	1987	1988	1989	1990	1991	1992
Research & eng. costs	$ 631	$ 717	$ 814	$1010	$1306	$1525	$1614	$1649	$1754
Operating income	395	450	829	1612	1635	1336	563	511	(636)
Total assets	5593	6369	7173	8407	10112	10668	11655	11875	11284
Equity	3979	4555	5728	6294	7510	8036	8182	7624	4931
ROA				20.7%	17.7%	12.9%	5.0%	4.3%	(5.5%)
ROE				26.8%	23.7%	17.2%	6.9%	6.5%	(10.1%)

Adjusted to expense computer software costs (all data in $ millions):

	1984	1985	1986	1987	1988	1989	1990	1991	1992
Operating income[1]	$395	$450	$829	$1578	$1603	$1312	$543	$509	$(658)
Total assets[2]	5593	6369	7173	8373	10046	10578	11545	11763	11150
Equity[2]	3979	4555	5728	6260	7444	7946	8072	7512	4797
ROA				20.3%	17.4%	12.7%	4.9%	4.4%	(5.7%)
ROE				26.3%	23.4%	17.1%	6.8%	6.5%	(10.7%)

[1]Decrease reported operating income by change in unamortized cost.
[2]Decrease assets and equity by unamortized cost.

Operating income is lower in all years as software development costs are growing. In all cases adjusted ROA & ROE decline as numerator effect of lower operating income overwhelms denominator effect of lower assets and equity.

E. Adjusted to capitalize and amortize research and engineering costs as well as software development costs (all data in $ millions):

(Years)	1986	1987	1988	1989	1990	1991	1992
Op. income (reported)		$1612	$1635	$1336	$ 563	$ 511	$(636)
Adjustments to op. income:							
Capitalization of research & engineering costs[1]		1009	1294	1498	1577	1605	1690
Amortization of capital. costs[2]		(721)	(847)	(1039)	(1267)	(1456)	(1560)
Net effect of capitalization		$288	$447	$459	$ 310	$ 149	$ 130
Op. income (adjusted)		1900	2082	1795	873	660	(506)
Increase in assets & equity[3]	$1502	$1791	$2238	$2697	$3007	$3156	$3286
Total assets (adjusted)	8675	10164	12284	13275	14552	14919	14436
Equity (adjusted)	7230	8051	9682	10643	11079	10668	8083
ROA		20.2%	18.6%	14.0%	6.3%	4.5%	(3.4%)
ROE		24.9%	23.5%	17.7%	8.0%	6.1%	(5.4%)

[1]Research and engineering costs less amortization of computer software costs.
[2]One-third of sum of capitalized costs over previous three years
[3]Increase equals capitalized costs less amortization. 1992, for example, equals 1992 costs plus 2/3 x 1991 costs plus 1/3 x 1990 costs.

Note that adjusted operating income is higher as growing research costs exceed their amortization. The effect of capitalization on ROA and ROE varies; in some years the numerator effect is more powerful but in others the denominator effect dominates.

F. The capitalization of research or software costs increases cash from operations (and increases cash outflow for investment). In part D, the effect of expensing software costs would be minimal as CFO would be reduced by $57, $46, and $86 million respectively.

The effect of capitalizing engineering costs in part E, however, is highly significant due to their large size. CFO would more than double in 1990 and increase five fold in 1992 as CFO would increase by $1577, $1605, and $1690 million respectively.

6.   A.   Neither the net change in cash nor cash from financing are affected by the accounting method; they remain at $6 and $(30) respectively. Successful efforts (SE) will have lower CFO balanced by lower cash outflows from investing than full costing (FC) as the outflow for dry holes is classified as operations not investment. FC will have higher depreciation/amortization as the cost of dry holes is also amortized.

Effect on income will depend on whether the decrease in (dry hole) expense for FC is offset by increased amortization. In Sonat's case, the decrease in expense of $21 ($382 - $361) is offset by higher amortization of $7 ($200 - $193) resulting in increased income of $14 which is approximately equal to the difference of $16 shown. (All data in millions). [Note that Sonat restated 1990 results for discontinued operations and also reclassified some financial statement data, making an exact reconciliation impossible.]

Therefore, the table should read ($ millions):

	SE	FC
Cash flow from operations	$ 361	$ 382
Cash flow from investing	(325)	(346)
Cash flow from financing	(30)	(30)
Net change in cash	$ 6	$ 6
Net income	94	110
Depreciation, depletion, & amortization	193	200

B.   Sonat's switch to the SE method reduced both reported cash from operations and net income. Despite these adverse effects, the following factors may have justified the change:

(i) For a large mature company, SE is the normal method, and there is little difference between the two methods.

(ii) SE is perceived to be more conservative.

(iii) In a declining oil and gas price environment, the switch to SE may have avoided impairment writedowns of Sonat's oil and gas properties.

(iv) The effect of SE is to reduce both assets and stockholders' equity, possibly increasing return on assets and return on equity ratios.

(v) If Sonat's future exploration is expected to decline, the switch to SE may increase future reported income.

(vi) Sonat may wish to report lower income to avoid "political costs."

7.   A.   The present value of the cash flows, discounted at 10%, is $60 for each asset.

B. **Asset A**

Year	Net Asset	Cash Flow	Depreci- ation	Income	ROA
1	$ 60	$ 36	$ 30	$ 6	10%
2	30	23	20	3	10%
3	10	11	10	1	10%

Asset B

Year	Net Asset	Cash Flow	Depreci- ation	Income	ROA
1	$ 60	$ 26	$ 20	$ 6	10%
2	40	24	20	4	10%
3	20	22	20	2	10%

C. The pattern for Asset A is the sum-of-the-years' digits method. The pattern for Asset B is the straight line method.

8. (i) The choice of method has no effect on reported cash flows as depreciation is a noncash expense.

(ii) Accelerated depreciation methods report lower net income (higher depreciation expense) and lower equity (higher accumulated depreciation) than the straight line method. The net effect on ROA is usually negative as the lower numerator dominates the calculation.

(iii) Accelerated methods result in higher depreciation expense initially, but a declining trend thereafter. The effect on total depreciation expense depends on the growth rate of capital spending (whether the effect of higher depreciation expense on new assets offsets the impact of declining depreciation expense on old ones).

9. **Depreciation expense   19X3   19X4**

(i) Sum-of-years' digits: base is $8000 ($9000 - $1000), SYD = 15

5/15ths = $2666.67   4/15ths = $2133.33

(ii) Double declining balance: base is $9,000, rate is 40% (2 x 20%)

.40 x $9000 = $3600   .40 x $5400* = $2160

(iii) Straight line: base is $8000 ($9000 - $1000), rate is 20%

.20 x $8000 = $1600   (same) $1600

(iv) MACRS (150% declining balance): base is $9000, rate is 30%

  .30 x $9000 = $2700   .30 x $6300* = $1890

*$9000 less previous year's depreciation

10. (i)   ($9000 - $1800)/8 = $ 900

   (ii)   ($9000 - $1800)/9 = $ 800

   (iii) ($9000 - $1080)/8 = $ 990

   (iv)   ($9000 - $1080)/9 = $ 880

11. A. $(66) - $19 = $(93) [Cumulative effect would disappear and 1991 earnings increase would not have occurred.]

   B. We can infer that the level of production in all three years was lower than the "normal" level at which the accounting change would make no difference. At higher levels of production, pro forma net income would be lower as depreciation expense would be higher under the units-of-production method.

   C. The change in deprecation method had no effect on cash flow in 1991 as depreciation is a noncash expense.

   D. The change in method should tend to stabilize Cummins' net income in future years as depreciation expense has become a variable cost rather than a fixed cost.

12. A. The accounting change applied only to newly acquired property so no restatement of prior year depreciation was required.

   B. The trend of depreciation expense will be lower because depreciation expense on older property (accelerated methods) will be declining while depreciation expense on new property (straight line method) will be lower. The net effect will be to increase reported net income.

   C. Increase in pretax income equals interest capitalized less amortization of capitalized costs ($ millions):

1987	1988	1989
$11 - $5 = $6	$16 - $7 = $9	$20 - $8 = $12

   Increase in net income equals pretax effect x (1 - tax rate).

D. Increase in CFO (decrease in CFI) is equal to the amount of interest capitalized. Amortization has no impact on cash flow components.

Increase in CFO:	$11	$16	$20
Decrease in CFI	$11	$16	$20

E. Times interest earned = EBIT/interest expense

As reported = ($251 + $39)/$39 = 7.36X
Adjusted   = ($239 + $59)/$59 = 5.05X

13. A. 1992: Book value of property retired = $6381 - $4423 = $1958 million
            Proceeds of sale   1203
            Loss on retirement $(755)

1991: Book value of property retired = $4306 - $3822 = $ 484 million
            Proceeds of sale   133
            Loss on retirement $(351)

B. The facility was probably part of the acquisition of another company; additions at cost reflects capital expenditures only.

C. See Exhibit 6S-1 for calculations of average depreciable life and average age of property by category.

These data can be used to compare Daniel with other companies, although classification differences may make comparisons difficult. They can also be examined for levels and trends that convey information about the age of Daniel's property and future capital spending requirements.

Exhibit 6S-1A shows that the average depreciable life of Daniel's fixed assets is slightly more than 16 years, ranging from less than eight years for automotive and transport to more than 38 years for buildings. These averages can be compared with averages for similar categories of other companies to judge whether Daniel uses lives that are more or less conservative than those used by other companies. If Daniel uses shorter lives, its earnings should either be adjusted upwards or accorded a higher multiple (see discussion of quality of earnings in Chapter 14). If its lives are too long, the reverse would be true.

Levels and trends within categories should also be examined. The average life for computers, for example, appears quite long considering the rate of technological change. The average life of Daniel's automotive equipment also looks too long, but has been declining.

Exhibit 6S-1B shows the extent to which Daniel's fixed assets have been depreciated. Except for buildings and other transportation equipment, the company's property assets are more than halfway through their depreciable lives. Inadequate earnings and cash flows may have reduced capital expenditures from the level necessary to maintain the most modern facilities. While competitors may be in the same position (and comparisons should be made), the data suggest that Daniel may have heavy capital expenditure requirements ahead.

A. Average depreciable life (years) = average carrying amount/depreciation expense:

($ millions)	1990	1991	1992
Buildings	25166/577 = 43.6	26301/734 = 35.8	29250/761 = 38.4
Machinery	40731/2596 = 15.7	41763/2671 = 15.6	45383/2759 = 16.4
Computers	8140/1061 = 7.7	6830/945 = 7.2	7815/907 = 8.6
Office	5200/400 = 13.0	4759/434 = 11.0	5355/471 = 11.4
Automotive	1795/154 = 11.7	1862/209 = 8.9	2095/273 = 7.7
Transport	4485/186 = 24.1	8663/292 = 29.7	4183/545 = 7.7
Other	7244/477 = 15.2	7454/520 = 14.3	7671/535 = 14.3
Totals*	92761/5451 = 17.0	97632/5805 = 16.8	101752/6251 = 16.3

B. Average age (%) = accumulated depreciation/ending gross investment ($ millions):

At Year End	1990	1991	1992
Buildings	5788/25166 = 23.0	6309/26301 = 24.0	7034/29250 = 24.0
Machinery	25935/40731 = 63.7	26150/41763 = 62.6	28201/45383 = 62.1
Computers	4877/8140 = 59.9	3851/6830 = 56.4	4470/7815 = 57.2
Office	2997/5200 = 57.6	2794/4759 = 58.7	3081/5355 = 57.5
Automotive	1194/1795 = 66.5	1207/1862 = 64.8	1328/2095 = 63.4
Transport	2707/4485 = 60.4	2968/8663 = 34.3	500/4183 = 12.0
Other	4258/7244 = 58.8	4604/7454 = 21.2	4914/7671 = 64.1
Totals*	47756/92761 = 51.5	47883/97632 = 49.0	49528/101752 = 48.7

C. Average age (years) = accumulated depreciation/depreciation expense ($ millions):

At Year End	1990	1991	1992
Buildings	5788/577 = 10.0	6309/734 = 8.6	7034/761 = 9.2
Machinery	15935/2596 = 10.0	26150/2671 = 9.8	28201/2759 = 10.2
Computers	5877/1061 = 4.6	3851/945 = 4.1	4470/907 = 4.9
Office	2997/400 = 7.5	2794/433 = 6.4	3081/471 = 6.5
Automotive	1194/154 = 7.8	1207/209 = 5.8	1328/273 = 4.9
Transport	2707/186 = 14.6	2968/292 = 10.2	500/545 = 0.9
Other	4258/477 = 8.9	4604/520 = 8.9	4914/535 = 9.2
Totals*	47756/5451 = 8.8	47883/5805 = 8.2	49528/6251 = 7.9

*Excludes land and construction in progress.

It should also be noted that machinery, the largest category, is also among the oldest. There has been major modernization of the "other transportation" segment (see the large expenditures in 1991 and retirements in 1992) that has made this segment the "youngest" of the company.

Exhibit 6S-1C shows the average age in years. While the average age has declined over the 1990 - 1992 period, 7.9 years does not suggest the most modern fixed assets. Here again, note that the key machinery category is, on average, ten years old. An average age of nearly five years for computers is surprising. However notice the effect of 1991 capital expenditures on the other transportation segment.

14. A. Restructuring reserves include prior, present year, and future expenditures. The reserve at year end shows the amount of future expenditures. In 1991 and 1992, cash outflows partly reflect prior year charges and partly current year charges. The 1990 increase in the restructuring reserve indicates that less than one-fifth of that year's charge resulted in a cash outflow in that year.

Over the three year period, Digital's charges totalled $3.15 billion; fully half of that amount remained to be spent at June 27, 1992.

B. The "big bath" theory states that firms attempt to report all of the "bad news" at once. Yet Digital has taken restructuring charges in each year, and the amounts have been increasing. This behavior is the opposite of what one would expect from the "big bath" theory.

C. The restructuring charges taken in 1990 - 1992 will tend to increase reported earnings in future years. Asset writedowns reduce future depreciation and amortization expense. The accrual of lease rentals, severance costs, and other operating items means that these expenses will not burden future operating results. As indicated in the answer to part A, these charges have negative implications for future cash flows from operations as the accruals are liquidated.

15. A. Most of the restructuring provision had no impact on cash flows as it represents past expenditures for property and acquired goodwill. It appears that only $11.8 million represents 1990 and future year cash outflows. The portion not expended in 1990 will affect cash flows in subsequent years.

B. Although the cash consequences of the provision were minor, the effect on future turnover ratios and reported income may be significant.

(i) The property writedown and absence of depreciation charges increases Comsat's return on assets (EBIT/average assets) in years after 1990.

(ii) The asset turnover ratio (sales/average assets) will also increase as average assets are lower following the 1990 writedowns.

(iii) Post-1990 net income should benefit from the absence of depreciation and amortization of the written down assets and from the absence of operating costs also included in the restructuring charge for 1990. Any gain from the operating changes will also increase future reported earnings.

16. A. (i) The revaluation has no impact on either cash flow or reported income (except for any "decrements" that are charged to earnings). Return on equity is, however, reduced when assets are revalued and the increment is included in equity.

(ii) There is no effect on cash flow or reported income in following years, excluding any revisions in the revalued amounts. As these assets are not depreciated, the revaluation has no impact on reported income. ROE, however, remains depressed by higher reported equity.

(iii) When assets are sold, gain or loss should be measured against the revalued amounts, rather than original cost. As a result, gains on the sale of these assets will be smaller (or losses will be reported). Cash flow from operations is not affected by asset sales.

B. The argument for revaluation is the disclosure of the true value of the firm's assets. This disclosure allows the financial statement user to measure operating results against the real investment in these assets rather than an obsolete cost. This permits the user to evaluate the "opportunity cost" of using the assets in operations rather than selling them.

On the other hand, revaluations are subjective by their nature. Management can manipulate revaluations and provide a misleading (either too high or too low) indication of the value of the firm.

C. For some assets, broadcast licenses and newspaper titles for example, amortization is not appropriate. The value of such properties does not change with the passage of time, but reflects economic trends and management performance.

For films, television programs, and books, however, the case against amortization is weaker. While some assets of this type may not diminish in value over time (the value of a classic film may increase over time), other titles may have little value following the period of initial distribution.

The footnote data in exhibit 6P-6 is insufficient to answer the question of whether amortization is appropriate, as it depends on the specific assets included in the balance sheet categories.

D. (i)   If these assets were amortized, then net income would be reduced by revaluation as amortization would be based on the (higher) revalued amount.

   ·(ii)   Cash from operations would not, however, be affected as amortization is a noncash expense.

Chapter 7 - Solutions

1. Deferred taxes can be found in all of the categories listed. Examples are:

   (i) Deferred tax credits expected to reverse within one year.

   (ii) Deferred income tax resulting from use of accelerated depreciation for tax purposes and straight line for financial reporting.

   (iii) Deferred tax offset to valuation allowance for marketable equity securities or to currency translation adjustment.

   (iv) Deferred tax asset (debit) due to accrual for compensation or other expenses to be paid in next year.

   (v) Deferred tax assets (debits) recognized that will not be recovered within the next year, such as for postretirement benefit costs that will not be funded within one year.

2. (i) Correct: Under SFAS 109, changes in tax law must be reflected in the deferred tax liability in the period of enactment.

   (ii) Correct: Answer to (i) also applies to deferred tax assets.

   (iii) Correct: The tax consequences of events that have not been reflected in the financial statements (such as future earnings or losses) are not recognized.

   (iv) Incorrect: This statement was true of APB 11 but is false under both SFAS 96 and SFAS 109.

3. Permanent differences are items of income or expense that affect *either tax return income or financial income, but not both.* Examples include:

   ○ Tax-exempt interest income (not reported on tax return)

   ○ Interest expense on amounts borrowed to purchase tax-exempt securities (not deductible on tax return)

   ○ Amortization of acquisition goodwill (not reported on tax return)

   ○ Tax or other nondeductible government penalties (not reported on tax return)

   ○ Statutory mineral depletion in excess of cost basis depletion (not reported in financial statements)

   ○ Premiums on key-person life insurance policies (not deductible on tax return)

◇ Proceeds from key-person life insurance policies (not reported on tax return)

      Permanent differences, depending on their nature, either increase or decrease the firm's effective tax rate from the statutory rate.

4.   A.   The higher tax expense relative to taxes payable understates net income and therefore equity. If the deferred tax liability is not expected to reverse, there is no expectation of a cash outflow and no liability should be recognized.

       B.   Deferred tax liabilities represent payments that may eventually have to be made. Changes in tax law and other unforseen events may result in cash flow consequences. Conservatism suggests that liability recognition is appropriate.

       C.   Because the deferred taxes will be payable (if at all) only in future years when timing differences reverse, the liability should be stated at the present value of those future tax payments. The remaining portion (difference between carrying amount and present value) should be considered equity. In addition, analysis of income tax footnote disclosures may suggest that a portion of the deferred tax liability will never require cash, further increasing equity.

5.   Before answering the specific questions in this problem, we must determine the cost of each asset. We can use the information about asset L to do this:

      Year 2 depreciation under the sum-of-the-years' digits method with a five year life is 4/15ths. Therefore the depreciation base (cost − salvage value) must be $12,000/(4/15) = $45,000 and cost must be $48,000 ($45,000 + $3,000).

      This information can be used to prepare a depreciation schedule under each of the three methods:

Depreciation Expense

Year	Asset K Straight Line[1]	Asset L SYD[2]	Asset M DDB[3]
1	$ 9,000	$ 15,000	$ 19,200
2	9,000	12,000	11,520
3	9,000	9,000	6,912
4	9,000	6,000	4,147
5	9,000	3,000	3,221
Total	$ 45,000	$ 45,000	$ 45,000

[1]Base = $45,000 (cost − salvage value); expense = $45,000/5
[2]Base = $45,000; expense based on 5/15ths, 4/15ths, 3/15ths, etc.
[3]Base = $48,000 (salvage value ignored); rate = 40%
      First year expense = .40 x $48,000 = $19,200, leaving $28,800
      Second year expense = .40 x $28,800 = $11,520, leaving $17,280
      Third year expense = .40 x $17,280 = $ 6,912, leaving $10,368
      Fourth year expense = .40 x $10,368 = $ 4,147, leaving $ 6,221
      Fifth year expense = $3,221 to leave salvage value of $ 3,000

A.   Double declining balance method is used on the tax return for all three assets; year two depreciation expense under that method is $11,520.

B.   Financial statement depreciation expense in year two is:
Asset K (straight line) $ 9,000
Asset M (double declining balance)   11,520

C.   (i)   At the end of year two, accumulated depreciation is
Asset K (straight line) $ 18,000
Asset L (SYD)   27,000
Asset M (DDB)   30,720
Tax Return (DDB)   30,720

Therefore the deferred tax liability is:

Asset K: .34 ($30,720 - $18,000) = $4,324.80
Asset L: .34 ($30,720 - $27,000) = 1,264.80
Asset M: no deferred tax as method is the same

(ii)   At the end of year five, accumulated depreciation is the same under all methods and there will be no deferred tax asset or liability.

6.   A.   Assuming that Mother Prewitt continues to buy machines in the future, the depreciation timing difference will never reverse and there will be no expected cash consequences. In this case the deferred tax liability can be treated as equity.

Assuming that the installment sale is not expected to recur, the tax on the sale will be paid in 1993 and will require cash. For that reason, the $27,200 of deferred taxes should be considered a liability when calculating liquidity, solvency and leverage ratios.

On the other hand, for many companies installment sales recur. When the installment method is permitted for tax purposes, such sales are no different from the depreciation example. The cash consequences of deferred tax items depends on their probability of reversal, not on their nature.

B.   (i)   Under APB 11, no adjustment would be made; only when the timing differences reverse would the new rates be reflected in the financial statements (tax expense would include the difference between the balance sheet liability and the amount paid). (See discussion of gross change method on page 517.)

(ii)   Under SFAS 96, enacted changes in tax rates are reflected and the deferred tax liabilities would be restated to their amounts based on the 40% tax rate. The incremental liability would be recorded as part of income tax expense regardless of when (or if) paid.

(iii)   Same as SFAS 96.

C. A valuation allowance would be required if it were deemed "more likely than not" that some or all of the deferred tax asset would not be realized.

7. A. Total (deferred + current) income taxes payable at December 31 (in $ millions):

1988	1989	Increase
$13,844	$13,999	$155

As income 1989 tax expense (from exhibit) was $2,028 million, we estimate income taxes paid at $1,873 million (income tax expense less the increase in deferred income taxes).

This estimate differs from actual 1989 income taxes paid of $2,881 million by approximately one billion dollars. Exxon must have additional income tax asset or liability balances that have been included in other balance sheet categories. If we had those balances we would be able to reconcile income tax expense to income taxes paid.

Portions of Exxon's footnotes that were not included in Exhibit 7P-1 reveal that a 1989 acquisition increased Exxon's deferred tax liability by close to $2 billion. In addition, the adoption of SFAS 96 in that year decreased the deferred tax liability by about $500 million. Even with these items, however, a large discrepancy remains, probably due to undisclosed balances.

B. Taxable income (per income tax returns) can be estimated as pretax income + (deferred tax expense/statutory rate):

$$\$4953 + (\$157/.34) = \$5415 \text{ million}$$

This result exceeds pretax earnings, as expected given the negative deferred tax expense for 1989.

C. (i) Income tax expense/pretax income

$$\$1978/\$4953 = 39.9\%$$

(ii) Taxes payable/taxable income

$$\$2130/\$5415 = 39.4\%$$

(iii) Cash taxes paid/pretax income

$$\$2881/\$4953 = 58.2\%$$

Both taxes payable and cash taxes paid were high relative to tax expense in 1989 due to the Valdez provision. Exxon created a reserve but did not obtain a tax deduction for expenditures that were not made prior to year end. 1990 income taxes payable (and cash taxes paid) will be lower than normal as Exxon receives the tax benefits. Absent the Valdez provision, Exxon appears to have positive deferred income tax expense due (primarily) to its higher depreciation expense for tax purposes.

Therefore, to use 1989 effective tax rates as predictors of future rates, adjustment for the Valdez provision is required. Note that this provision will distort (ii) and (iii) in the opposite direction in the year(s) when cash payments are made and tax deductions are realized. Income tax expense/pretax income is not affected by the timing of the Valdez payments and is the most useful (as a predictor) of the effective tax rates for that reason.

8. A. Cost-of-goods-sold was higher for financial reporting purposes than for tax purposes. As the deferred tax effect of the difference was negative, Exxon must have had lower tax deductions than financial reporting deductions.

    B. One possibility is that Exxon wrote down inventory (under the lower of cost or market rule) for financial reporting purposes but was unable to do so for tax purposes. Secondly, Exxon used LIFO for financial reporting outside the United States but did not (or could not) use it for tax purposes.

9. A. Exxon shows a timing difference for interest of $134 million, indicating that interest expense for tax reporting was higher than that for financial reporting. This suggests that Exxon reported interest paid rather than interest expense.

    Using Exxon's effective tax rate of about 40% (from problem 7A), the timing difference for interest can be estimated as:

    $134/.40 = $335 million

    and interest reported for tax purposes as:

    $1265 + $335 = $1600 million.

    Alternatively, using the statutory tax rate of 34%, the timing difference for interest can be estimated as:

    $134/.34 = $394 million

    and interest reported for tax purposes as:

    $1265 + $394 = $1659 million approximately equal to the $1700 million actually paid.

    B. 1. Interest accrued on discount or zero coupon bonds.

        2. Interest accrued between coupon payment dates.

        3. Difference in amounts of interest capitalized on the tax return versus the financial statements.

10. A. Catalina was using SFAS 96 so that deferred taxes were already adjusted to current tax rates and any restatement of acquisitions had taken place prior to the adoption of SFAS 109.

    Even under SFAS 109, Catalina could not recognize all of its deferred tax assets, suggesting that the new standard had no effect on the recognition of deferred tax assets.

B. (i) The net accrued tax asset (liability) as of March 31 was:

1991	1992	Change
$(455)	$1,303	$1,758

When combined with income tax expense, this produces an estimate of taxes paid of $3669 ($1911 + $1758) (all data in $ millions).

(ii) Deferred tax assets reconcile exactly:

Balance at March 31, 1991 $ 363 million
F 1992 deferred tax expense   2,836
Balance at March 31, 1992 $3,199 million

Taxes payable, however, do not reconcile:

Balance at March 31, 1991 $ 818 million
F 1992 current tax expense   4,747
Subtotal $5,565
Balance at March 31, 1992   1,896
Estimate of taxes paid $3,669

This estimate is the same as that obtained in part (i). Actual tax paid is $415 million lower [$3669 - $3254]. There must be an undisclosed prepaid income tax account of $415 million at March 31, 1991.

C. (i) Income tax expense/pretax income:

$1911/($4760+$1911) = 28.65%

Alternate calculation: (income tax expense/expected tax at statutory rate) x statutory rate:

($1911/$2264) x 34% = 28.65%

(ii) Taxable income = pretax income + (deferred tax expense/statutory rate) = $6671 + $2540/.34 = $14,141 million

current tax expense/taxable income

$4,747/$14,141 = 33.57%

(iii) Cash taxes paid/pretax income

$3,254/($4760 + $1911) = 48.78%

Catalina's low 1992 effective tax rate resulted from the recognition of the benefit of operating losses. In view of the valuation allowance, there may be some doubt as to whether these benefits will be realized.

The third ratio was affected by the apparent prepayment [part B (ii)] at the beginning of the year.

As neither the first nor third ratio appear to be useful predictors, we are left with the second. This ratio is close to the statutory rate, reflecting the absence of permanent differences. This ratio appears to be most useful for predictive purposes.

D. $ 811/.34 = $2385 million
$1101/.34 = $3238 million

In both cases, the accumulated tax expense is lower than the accumulated book expense by the amount shown. This must be true if the timing differences create deferred tax assets as taxable income must have exceeded pretax income as a result of lower expenses.

Deferred tax assets from depreciation are rare. Catalina may have accelerated depreciation on some assets (due to obsolescence) but could not change tax depreciation.

The deferred revenue difference is more straightforward. Catalina must have received payments that had to be recognized for taxes but the revenues were deferred for financial reporting purposes.

E. (i) The existence of the valuation allowance tells us that management is uncertain that future profitability will be sufficient to receive the benefit of all deferred tax assets. This suggests that future effective tax rates may be low if the company receives the benefits of the postponed tax deductions.

Reported effective tax rates will also be affected by any changes in the valuation allowance. If profitability improves, the valuation allowance can be reduced, further increasing reported income. On the other hand, disappointing profits may require an increase in the valuation allowance, reducing net income further.

(ii) Deferred revenue and the provision for doubtful accounts both largely originated in 1992 and should reverse in 1993. If the company is not generating taxable income, the benefit of these tax deductions may be lost. This possibility would justify the valuation allowance. The depreciation differences will reverse over a longer time period, allowing more time for taxable income to develop.

11. A. The deferred tax effect of postretirement health benefits was $13,636 as disclosed in the listing of deferred tax assets and liabilities at June 30, 1992. The effect of the new standard on reported income can be estimated as (in $ thousands):

	Cumulative	F1992	Total
Pretax	$ 30,893	$ 4,720	$ 35,613
Income tax	11,832	1,808	13,640
Net	$ 19,061	$ 2,912	$ 21,973

The net amount and tax impact of the cumulative effect are included in the description of the accounting change, as is the net amount of the F1992 effect. The tax rate used to compute the cumulative effect can be computed ($11,832/$30,893) as 38.3%. Applying that rate to the F1992 effect completes the table. The total income tax effect of $13,640 approximates the deferred taxes attributable to postretirement health benefits ($13,676), with an error of less than 1%. This congruence is expected as Clorox changed only its accounting method for financial reporting, not its method for tax reporting. Thus the entire effect of the accounting change generates deferred taxes.

B. (i) Restructuring charges normally consist of a mixture of past, present, and future cash flows. The amount representing future cash flows generates deferred tax effects as tax deductions are available only when the outflow takes place. The deferred tax assets at year end 1991 and 1992 result from timing differences of approximately $110 million and $81 million respectively (both computed at the F1991 effective tax rate of 38.8%).

(ii) The results of (i) tell us that only $15 million ($125 – $110) of the 1991 restructuring charge consisted of 1991 and prior year cash flows. The $29 million decline ($110 – $81) during 1992 should approximate the cash outflow for that year.

(iii) The remaining deferred tax asset at June 30, 1992 reveals that approximately $81 of cash outflows remain and can be expected to occur in F1993 and future years.

C. (i) Income tax expense/pretax income

$93,107/($117,765+$93,107) = 44.15%

(ii) Taxable income = pretax income + (deferred tax expense/statutory rate) = $210,872 – ($10,261/.34) = $180,693

Taxes payable/taxable income
$79,777/$180,693 = 44.15%

(iii) Cash taxes paid/pretax income
$73,709/($117,765+$93,107) = 34.95%

D. The cumulative effect of adopting SFAS 106 does not affect the tax rates computed in part C. The income tax component of the cumulative effect is not included in income tax expense but is netted against the cumulative effect itself. This can be seen by reconciling the net deferred tax liability. That liability rose by approximately $2 million in the year ended June 30, 1992 despite $13 million of deferred tax expense for that year. The $11 million deferred tax asset resulting from the cumulative effect is "missing" and is needed to reconcile.

The deferred tax effect of the restructuring charge resulted in taxes payable and taxes paid for 1992 that were below income tax expense; tax deductions were received in 1992 for expenses that were recognized for financial reporting purposes in 1991.

E.   The deferred tax liability probably should not be considered a liability for Clorox. Looking at its components, the effects of leases and restructuring expenses, the two that will clearly reverse over time, nearly offset. Assuming that capital expenditures do not decline and that foreign earnings are not remitted, those two components will not reverse. Thus, in total, it seems unlikely that the deferred tax liability will result in a cash outflow for Clorox for the near future.

"Safe harbor" leases, it should be noted, were the result of investments that took advantage of tax law provisions that were subsequently repealed. Thus, in contrast to normal leases, they are not recurring in nature and will reverse over time.

12. A.   Assuming that Deere's ongoing operations do not change, and that tax laws remain unchanged, these deferred tax liabilities should not be treated as real liabilities for purposes of analysis. While timing differences connected with past installment sales and depreciable assets will reverse in the future, those reversals will be offset by new timing differences from future installment sales and depreciable assets. Thus we can expect that these liabilities will not diminish and, therefore, will not require cash outflows.

B.   The deferred tax liability relating to depreciation was $88 million at October 31, 1991 as compared with $81 million at October 31, 1990. The increased liability means that Deere's tax depreciation exceeded the financial reporting amount by $21 million ($7 million/.34).

13. A.   *Postretirement benefits*: under SFAS 109 Dresser accrues the present value of future benefits.

Warranty reserves: Dresser accrues estimated future costs.

Restructuring costs: Dresser has accrued future payments.

Bad debt reserves: Dresser accrued an estimate of uncollectible receivables.

Pensions: Dresser's pension funding (tax deduction) must be below pension cost.

Deferred compensation: accrued but payable in future years

NOL carryforwards: Dresser has prior years' losses that are carried forward; they will generate cash inflows when they can be used to offset current year taxable income.

7-9

These items will generate cash inflows when they can be used to offset future taxable income (thus making current year tax payments unnecessary). The factors involved are:

1.   When timing differences reverse: some of them are short term in nature (deferred compensation, bad debts) while other are longer term (postretirement benefits).

2.   The effect of new timing differences: if Dresser's warranty reserves, for example, increase each year, then the deferred tax asset will increase each year.

3.   The trend of taxable income: higher taxable income will enable Dresser to take full advantage of NOL carryforwards and reversing timing differences.

4.   The pattern of future taxable income: taxes are determined on a jurisdiction-by-jurisdiction basis. Taxable income must match (by tax jurisdiction) NOLs and reversing timing differences for Dresser to obtain all future tax benefits.

B.   The valuation allowance indicates that Dresser believes that there is significant doubt that it will realize the entire tax benefit from its deferred tax assets. This may be due to either timing issues or jurisdiction issues (see part C).

C.   The NOL carryforwards are the most likely candidate; some or all may be in tax jurisdictions where future profitability cannot be forecast with confidence, or where the carryforward period is likely to expire before profitability returns.

Restructuring costs are another possibility. Tax deductions may not offset taxable income for the same reasons as for NOLs.

D.   Dresser has taken advantage of the "indefinite reversal" provisions of GAAP and has not provided deferred taxes on the undistributed earnings of its foreign affiliates. Should conditions change, and Dresser receives that income (as dividends or by selling subsidiaries), the company will have to recognize additional income tax expense.

14.   A.

	1991 Tax Rate	1992 Tax Rate
Q1	25.5%	20.7%
Q2	24.0	25.1
Q3	26.1	(594.9)

B.   Using a tax rate of 17% for 1992 Q3 alone, tax expense would have been $16,660. The actual tax expense for Q3 was $583,000 (income) for a difference of $600,000

C.   On a pretax basis, 1992 Q3 declined by 97% from 1991 Q3 ($98 vs. $3244). Net income, however, declined by only 72% ($681 vs. $2396) because 1992 Q3 included the tax benefit of revising the tax rate on earnings that has already been reported for the first two quarters of 1992.

D.   (i)   One possibility is to make comparisons only on a pretax basis, thus avoiding any distortion from changes in the estimated tax rate.

    (ii)   A second method would be to exclude the effect of revisions of previously reported earnings. Thus, net income for 1992 Q3 would be computed as $61,000 ($98,000 – $17,000) where $17,000 is the tax expense for Q3 after excluding the $600,000 effect of the change in estimate.

E.   1992 Q1: Tax expense = $191,000 (.17 x $ 1,123,000), making net income $932,000, 5% higher than reported Q1 net income

    1992 Q2: Tax expense = $633,000 (.17 x $ 3,723,000), making net income $3,090,000 or 11% higher than reported Q2 net income.

    These adjusted net income amounts also improve the comparisons with 1991 quarterly data due to the use of the lower tax rate.

Chapter 8 - Solutions

1. A.

	American Airlines		Eastern Airlines	
	1987	**1988**	**1987**	**1988**
Current assets	$2,146.3	$2,615.0	$1,022.4	$ 999.9
Current liabilities	2,071.0	2,795.6	1,192.7	1,153.8
Net working capital	$ 75.3	$ (180.6)	$ (170.3)	$ (153.9)
Current ratio	1.03X	0.94X	0.86X	0.87X
Quick ratio	0.84	0.76	0.67	0.69
Cash ratio	0.49	0.46	0.28	0.35

B.   Unlike other payables, the air traffic liability will not require cash outlays (other than incidental costs); instead this obligation is satisfied as customers use their tickets on flights. The air traffic liability should therefore be excluded from computations of short-term liabilities.

C.   **Adjusted Computations:**

Current liabilities	$2,071.0	$2,795.6	$1,192.7	$1,153.8
Air traffic liability	(577.0)	(800.0)	(390.5)	(302.4)
Current liabilities	$1,494.0	$1,995.6	$ 802.2	$ 851.4
Net working capital	652.3	619.4	220.2	148.5
Current ratio	1.44X	1.31X	1.27X	1.17X
Quick ratio	1.17	1.06	0.99	0.94
Cash ratio	0.68	0.64	0.41	0.47

As expected, all of American Airlines' liquidity measures improve when the air traffic liability is removed from current liabilities.

D.   Eastern's short-term liquidity position is weaker than that of American over the two-year period shown. Eastern's ratios appear to improve slightly in 1988. However, the improvement in the current and quick ratios evaporates when the air traffic liability is eliminated. This liability declined from $390.5 million to $302.4 million due to reduced advance purchases by customers. Other liability categories increased proportionately and current assets (except cash) declined. The higher cash balance may have been required to meet potential reductions in credit availability.

E. The decline in air traffic liability indicates that fewer customers were willing to purchase tickets in advance, presumably due to the deterioration in Eastern's financial position. In contrast, American's air traffic liability increased, although the growth should be compared to past fluctuations and to growth for the rest of the industry.

2. (i) Interest expense = Interest paid + change in bond discount
$8562 = $7200 + $1362

(ii) Interest expense = Market rate x [face value − discount]
$8562 = .12 x [face value − $8652]

Therefore, face value = ($8562/.12) + $8652 = $80,000

(iii) Coupon rate = interest paid/face value = $7200/$80,000 = 9%

3. The table below presents *approximate* market values using the following approach. The bonds and notes (other than the variable interest notes) were arranged in chronological order. Then, using the given yields to maturity (YTM), the other YTMs were estimated by interpolation. The estimated YTMs were then used to calculate the present value of interest and principal payments. This analysis assumes (for simplicity) that coupon payments occur on June 30 and December 31 and semiannual compounding.

Coupon	Description	Maturity	Book Value	Market Value	YTM	Explanation
Sonat Variable	Revolving Credit	1994	$240	$240	5.32%	Var. rate/No adjustment
9.000%	Loan	1993	8	9	5.00%	
9.875%	Notes	1996	200	220	7.16%	Given
8.650%	Notes	1997	56	59	7.30%	
9.410%	Notes	1997	35	38	7.30%	
9.500%	Notes	1999	100	111	7.55%	
9.000%	Notes	2001	100	108	7.81%	Given
7.250%	Zero Coupon	2005	250	229	8.00%	
Southern Natl. Gas						
9.625%	Notes	1994	100	107	6.49%	Given
10.000%	Notes	1995	100	111	6.65%	
9.850%	Loan	1997	4	5	6.95%	
6.750%	Notes	1999	40	39	7.25%	
8.875%	Notes	2001	100	109	7.57%	Given
Other			2	2		
Totals			$1,335	$1,387		

4.　A.　Proceeds are $56,742 = \$100,000/(1.12)^5$

B.

	1991	1992	1993	1994	1995
Earnings before interest & taxes	$50,000	$50,000	$50,000	$50,000	$50,000
Cash flow from operations before interest & taxes	60,000	60,000	60,000	60,000	60,000
Interest expense	6,809	7,626	8,541	9,566	10,714
Cash flow from operations	60,000	60,000	60,000	60,000	60,000
Times interest earned	7.34	6.56	5.85	5.23	4.67
Times interest earned (cash basis)	[Infinite, since no interest is paid. In 1995, the bond will be retired and the payment reported as a financing cash outflow.]				

C. $56,742 x .12 = $6809 annual interest expense paid in cash.

	1991	1992	1993	1994	1995
Earnings before interest & taxes	$50,000	$50,000	$50,000	$50,000	$50,000
Cash flow from operations before interest & taxes	60,000	60,000	60,000	60,000	60,000
Interest expense	6,809	6,809	6,809	6,809	6,809
Cash flow from operations	53,191	53,191	53,191	53,191	53,191
Times interest earned	7.34	7.34	7.34	7.34	7.34
Times interest earned (cash basis)	8.81	8.81	8.81	8.81	8.81

D.   Cash flow from operations is higher when zero coupon bonds are issued because interest is never reported as an operating cash outflow. [Note the infinite cash basis coverage ratio.] Interest coverage, however, is lower after the first year, and declines as interest expense increases over time, reflecting the steadily increasing principal amount. Conventional bonds (if sold at par) result in a constant cash outflow from operations and constant interest expense. Given the Null Company's "steady state," the interest coverage ratio is constant on both accrual and cash flow bases.

E.   Given the tax deductibility of accrued but unpaid interest on zero coupon bonds, cash flow from operations will be higher for both cases. The reported cash flow differences will remain unchanged. For the zero coupon case, cash flow from operations is even more misleading as the firm must generate sufficient cash from operations to repay the debt at maturity. The obligation must be repaid, regardless of its cash flow classification.

5. A. Adding principal and interest payments:

PV of $20,000,000, to be paid in 10 years[1]   = $ 9,127,800
+ PV of 20 payments of $1,000,000 each[2]   =   13,590,330
   Financing cash inflow = proceeds   = $22,718,130

[1] PV factor (n=20, r=.04) = .45639 x $20,000,000 = $9,127,800
[2] PV factor (n=20; r=.04) = 13.59033 x $1,000,000 = $13,590,330

January 1, 1994: Cash and debt liability each increased by
$22,718,130.

Balance sheet at December 31	1994	1995
Long-term debt	$22,626,855	$22,433,206
Accrued interest	905,074	897,328
Total liability	$23,531,929	$23,330,534
Interest expense	$ 1,813,799	$ 1,798,605
Cash from operations	$(1,000,000)	$(2,000,000)

Calculations:

Interest expense (income tax ignored)
Year ended December 31, 1994:
July 1: $22,718,130 x .04 = $908,725
Interest payment of $1,000,000 (no impact on expense)
Reduction of bond premium = $1,000,000 - $908,725 = $91,275
Liability balance on July 1 = $22,718,130 - $91,275 = $22,626,855

December 31: $22,626,855 x .04 = $905,074 interest expense, shown as
accrued interest on December 31, 1994 balance sheet

January 1, 1995:
Interest payment of $1,000,000 (no impact on expense)
Interest payment of $1,000,000 (no impact on expense)
Reduction of bond premium = $1,000,000 - $905,074 = $94,926
Liability balance on January 1 = $22,626,855 - $94,926 =$22,531,929

Year ended December 31, 1995:
July 1: $22,531,929 x .04 = $901,277 interest expense
Interest payment of $1,000,000 (no impact on expense)
Reduction of bond premium = $1,000,000 - $901,277 = $98,723
Liability balance on July 1 = $22,531,929 - $98,723 = $22,433,206

December 31: $22,433,206 x .04 = $897,328 interest expense, shown as
accrued interest on December 31, 1995 balance sheet.

January 1, 1996:
Interest payment of $1,000,000 (no impact on expense)
Reduction of bond premium = $1,000,000 - $897,328 = $102,672
Liability balance on January 1 = $22,433,206 - $102,672 = $22,330,534

Operating cash outflow
1994: One interest payment on July 1, 1994, $1,000,000

1995: Two interest payments of $1,000,000 each, on January 1 and July 1, $2,000,000

Balance sheet impacts

1994: effect of bond issuance
    reduction of bond premium at July 1
    interest payable at December 31
    interest expense reduces equity

1995: reduction of interest payable and bond premium at January 1
    reduction of bond premium at July 1
    interest payable at December 31
    interest expense reduces equity

B.   The purchase price must be equal to the face amount since the market interest rate is equal to the coupon rate.[3]

The carrying amount of the bonds on July 1, 1997 will be $21,997,050.[4] The gain from repurchase is the difference between the purchase price and carrying amount: $20,000,000 - $21,997,050 = $1,997,050. It is a gain because a liability has been extinguished for a lesser amount of assets. Because of the change in interest rates since the bonds were issued, Derek has captured the remaining bond premium. The journal entry would be:

Bonds payable	20,000,000	
Premium on bonds payable	1,997,050	
Cash		20,000,000
Gain on extinguishment		1,997,050

[3]This can be shown, as well, by using present values: purchase price = present value of $20,000,000, to be repaid in 6.5 years: PV factor (n=13, r=.05) = .53032 x $20 million = $10,606,400 plus PV of 13 payments of $1,000,000 each: PV factor (n=13, r=.05) = 9.39357 x $1,000,000 = $9,393,570; total is $20,000,000.
[4]Present value of $20,000,000, to be repaid in 6.5 years: PV factor (n=13, r=.04) = .60057 x $20 million = $12,011,400 plus PV of 13 payments of $1,000,000 each: PV factor (n=13, r=.04) = 9.98565 x $1,000,000 = $9,985,650; total = $21,997,050. The carrying amount could also be determined by extending the analysis in part A (reducing the bond premium at the time of each interest payment) to July 1, 1997.

C.   The gain is not a component of continuing, operating income but should be considered nonrecurring. It is a consequence of the change in interest rates rather than the firm's operating activities, and cannot be expected to recur.

D.   1.   The gain provides a one-time increase in reported net income.

       2.   The decrease in leverage (as a lower amount of higher coupon debt is issued to replace the lower coupon debt) may help the firm avert or delay technical default on bond covenants. The repurchase may also allow the firm to eliminate limiting

covenants on this specific debt issue. Thus even if new debt must be issued to raise the funds needed for repurchase, the firm may wish to retire the bond issue.

6. A. 1992 interest expense = $18,095,550 [.0725 x $249,580,000]

    B. Liability on December 31, 1992 = $267,775,550

        As no cash interest is paid, interest expense of $18,095,550 is added to the prior liability balance of $249,580,000.

    C. Zero coupon notes have no effect on CFO at any time; interest expense on conventional bonds affects CFO every year. When income taxes are considered, the zero-coupon notes will generate an annual tax benefit despite the absence of any interest payment. Thus CFO is always higher when zero coupon notes are issued rather than full coupon notes. The 1992 effect is $18,095,550; the effect over the life of the notes is the difference between the face amount and the proceeds at the time of issuance.

    D. For both conventional notes and zero coupon notes, cash from financing includes the proceeds from issuance and the amount paid for redemption. For conventional notes, the amounts are approximately the same (the difference being any premium or discount and the cost of issuance). The net amount over the life of the issue is approximately zero.

        For zero coupon notes, however, the redemption amount includes *all* accrued interest from the time of issuance. As a result the net effect over the life of the note issue is to increase the cash outflow from financing activities. This effect occurs when the notes are issued and when they are repaid. Thus there would be no impact on cash from financing for 1992.

7. A. (i) $\dfrac{\text{Debt}}{\text{Equity}}$ $\dfrac{\$4,000,000}{\$28,000,000}$ = 0.14

        When the preferred shares are nonredeemable, they should be considered stockholders' equity.

        (ii) $\dfrac{\text{Debt}}{\text{Equity}}$ $\dfrac{\$21,500,000^1}{\$10,500,000^2}$ = 2.05

            [1]$4,000,000 + $16,000,000 [redemption value of preferred stock] + $1,500,000 [preferred dividends in arrears (2 x 100,000 x $7.50)].
            [2]$28,000,000 - $16,000,000 [redemption value of preferred stock] - $1,500,000 [dividends in arrears]

        When the preferred shares are redeemable at the option of shareholders, they should be treated as debt, and stated at their redemption value. The dividend payments in arrears should also be included as they must be paid before common shareholders can receive any distributions.

B. Book value per common share:

(i)   ($28,000,000 - $15,000,000)/200,000 = $65 per share

(ii) $12,000,000/200,000 = $60 per share

C. Redeemable preferred shares should be considered as debt in computing solvency ratios since they constitute a fixed preference in liquidation and the dividend payments are fixed and often cumulative. Many redeemable preferred issues have the equivalent of "sinking-fund" provisions that also suggest their treatment as debt. Note that the SEC requires that redeemable preferred shares be reported separately from stockholders' equity.

8. First year effects, capital versus operating lease method:

(i)   Current ratio will be lower when the lease is capitalized as current liabilities now include the current portion of the capitalized lease obligation.

(ii)   The debt-to-equity ratio will be higher because the present value of the minimum lease payments must be reported as debt.

(iii) Operating income will be higher under capitalization. It is decreased only by depreciation. Under the operating lease method it is decreased by the full amount of the lease payment. [Depreciation is almost always lower, even when an accelerated depreciation method is used.] The interest component of lease expense (capital lease method) is a non-operating expense.

(iv)   Net income in the first year is lower under the capital lease method as total lease expense (the sum of depreciation and interest expense) exceeds the annual rental (lease expense under the operating lease method).

(v)   Cash flow from operations is higher when leases are capitalized as only a portion (interest component) of the annual rental payment is reported as an operating cash outflow; the remainder is considered a financing cash outflow.

9. **Effect of choice of interest rate on lessee:**

		9% versus 10%	
		First Year	Lease Term
i	Interest expense [Lower interest rate reduces interest expense.]	Lower	Lower
ii	Amortization expense [Lower interest rate increases present value of minimum lease payments, creating higher asset amount to be amortized over lease term.]	Higher	Higher
iii	Total lease expense [The net effect for the first year depends on the lease amounts; over the lease term, however, total expense equals total lease payments regardless of the choice of interest rate.]	Indeter-minate	Equal
iv	Cash from operations [Lower interest rate shifts expense from interest to amortization (see i and ii); as cash from operations is decreased only by interest expense, a decrease in interest expense increases CFO, both in the first year and over the least term.]	Higher	Higher
v	Average assets [Lower interest rate increases present value (see ii) resulting in higher average assets, both in first year and over lease term.]	Higher	Higher
vi	Average liabilities [Lower interest rate increases present value recognized as liability, both in first year and over lease term.]	Higher	Higher

10. A. DQE: Capitalization Table

Reported long-term debt	$1,420,726
Redeemable preferred	45,437
Capital leases	87,861
Current portion of debt	119,428
Sinking fund debt	28,665
Total debt	$1,702,117
Nonredeemable preferred	$ 121,906
Common equity	1,111,121
Total equity	$1,233,027

Reported total debt/total equity ratio: 1.38X
    [$1,702,117/$1,233,027]

B.   **Computation of coverage ratios:**

Reported interest coverage:
Earnings before interest and tax	$ 281,644
Reported interest expense	$ 131,397
Reported times interest earned ratio: [$281,664/$131,397]	2.14X

Fixed charge coverage:
Reported interest expense	$ 131,397
Operating lease payments (Note E)	65,414
Reported fixed charges	$ 196,811

EBIT prior to fixed charges [EBIT + operating leases]	$ 347,058

Fixed charge coverage ratio: [$347,078/$196,811]	1.76X

Alternate computation of fixed charge coverage:

Reported interest expense	$ 131,397
Other fixed charges (see discussion)	104,737
Reported fixed charges	$ 236,134

EBIT prior to fixed charges [EBIT + operating leases]	$ 347,058

Fixed charge coverage ratio: [$347,078/$236,134]	1.47X

DISCUSSION: The fixed charge coverage ratio is intended to include the firm's fixed obligations, regardless of whether they are shown on the balance sheet. Part D (Note E) of Exhibit 8P-3 shows the lease payments of DQE for 1991. Interest on capital leases is already included in interest expense. The first fixed charge calculation includes operating lease payments, fixed charges that are reported as operating expenses. Thus both EBIT and fixed charges must be increased by $65,414.

The second fixed charge calculation includes the amortization of capital leases as well as operating lease payments. While capital lease amortization is the payment of principal (rather than interest), it is a fixed charge. Thus $104,737 (operating leases plus amortization of capital leases) has been added back to fixed charges. As amortization is not an operating expense, there is no effect on EBIT.

Preferred dividends have been ignored. When included in fixed charges, they must be measured on a pretax basis [preferred dividends/(1 - tax rate)], as they are paid out of after tax earnings. Calculations thus require income tax data not provided in this problem. Their inclusion would reduce fixed charge coverage.

Further adjustments to fixed charges could be made for other required debt payments (such as sinking fund payments); the data for these adjustments was not included in Exhibit 8P-3. These ratios could also be calculated on a cash flow basis (using cash paid for interest rather than interest expense, and cash from operations rather than net income).

11. A.   (All amounts in $ thousands)

   (i)   Present value of capital lease obligations $132,729
          Long-term portion shown on balance sheet   (87,861)
          Short-term portion $ 44,868

          Minimum 1992 payment is $52,998 (Note E). Therefore
   interest portion must be $52,998 - $44,868 = $8,130.

          Interest rate = $8130/$132,729 = 6.125%

   (ii)   Based on the pattern of lease payments the interest rate is
          approximately 10%

   B.   The dissimilar interest rates are a function of the imprecision of
   the disclosures and different assumptions regarding the time value
   of money implicit in the two estimation methods. Different
   estimation methods will produce similar results when the initial
   payment or the first few payments are not a significant portion of
   the total liability, true when the lease term is relatively long.

          In the case of DQE, the 1992 payment of $53 million is more
   than 25 percent of the total payments of $178 million and the first
   three years' payments of $119 million are nearly 67% of the total.
   As a result, variations in the *timing of lease payments within the
   year* distort the estimation of the implicit interest rate.

   C.   **Future minimum lease payments (Exhibit 8P-3D, $ thousands):**

	Capital Leases	Operating Leases
1992	$ 52,998	$ 66,507
1993	35,134	65,187
1994	31,000	62,468
1995	14,589	61,236
1996	8,395	61,221
Thereafter	36,000	1,302,161
Total	$ 178,116	$ 1,618,780

          Nearly 80% ($142,116/$178,116) of the capital lease payments
   will be made over the next five years and the annual payments
   decline by more than 84% over that period (from $52,998 to $8,396).
   Finally, the payment schedule suggests that only 4 or 5 years remain
   after 1996. In contrast, for the operating leases only 20% of the
   payments are due over the next five years ($316,619/$1,618,780), the
   decline in annual payments is less than 8% over the 5 year period,
   and the schedule suggests another 22 annual payments
   ($1,302,161/$61,221) after 1996. The disclosures reveal "operating
   lease" payments that are long-term and fairly constant over time;
   these leases should be capitalized.

   D.   Computation of the present value of operating leases:

          Assuming that future (after 1996) payments will equal the 1996
   amount of $61,221 implies that 21.26 payments remain
   ($1,302,161/$61,221). Using this payment schedule and an interest
   rate of 10%, the present value of the operating leases would be

$571,132. An interest rate of 6.125% would result in a present value of $799,803.

E.   Impact on statement of cash flows:

Interest expense = .10 x $571,132 = $57,113 (alternately: .06125 x $799,803 = $48,988).

Amortization of capital lease liability = total lease payment less interest expense = $66,507 - $57,113 = $ 9,394 (alternately: $66,507 - $48,988 = $17,519). The amortization component of the lease payment would be reclassified from operating cash flow to financing cash flow, increasing the former and decreasing (increasing the outflow) the latter.

F.   Effect of capitalization of operating lease on leverage and interest coverage ratios:

	At 10%	At 6.25%
Reported long-term debt	$ 1,420,726	$ 1,420,726
Redeemable preferred	45,437	45,437
Capital leases	87,861	87,861
Short-term portion of debt	119,428	119,428
Sinking fund requirements	28,665	28,665
Reported debt	$ 1,702,117	$ 1,702,117
PV of operating leases	571,132	799,803
Adjusted debt	$ 2,273,249	$ 2,501,920
Total equity	$ 1,233,027	$ 1,233,027
Reported debt/equity ratio	1.38	1.38
Adjusted debt/equity ratio	1.84	2.03
Reported interest expense	$ 131,397	$ 131,397
Add: interest on leases	57,113	48,988
Adjusted interest expense	$ 188,510	$ 180,385
EBIT	$ 338,757	$ 330,632
Reported coverage ratio	2.14	2.14
Adjusted coverage ratio	1.80	1.83

DISCUSSION: Capitalization of the operating leases worsens both the leverage and interest coverage ratios significantly. As seen in the above table, use of a 10% interest rate increases the debt/equity ratio from 1.38X to 1.84X; use of the lower interest rate of 6.125% (higher present value) results in an even higher debt/equity ratio of 2.03X.

The interest coverage ratio is also adversely affected by capitalization of the operating leases. This ratio declines from 2.14X to 1.80X (10% rate) or 1.83X (6.125% rate).

Note that the higher interest rate results in a lower (better) debt/equity ratio but a lower (worse) interest coverage ratio. Thus management's choice between a higher or lower rate may depend on which ratio is more important (perhaps because of debt covenants).

The adjustments to EBIT require additional comment. When a capital lease replaces an operating lease, EBIT is increased by the lease payment but decreased by depreciation expense (interest expense is excluded from EBIT). The net effect depends on the interest rate used to capitalize the lease; a high interest rate shifts more of the lease payment to interest and reduces depreciation (as the present value is lower).

As total lease expense (interest plus depreciation) equals total lease payments over the life of the lease, they will also be equal *on average* for each year. As these are existing (rather than new) leases, we can make the simplifying assumption in the above computations that interest expense = (lease payment - depreciation expense).

12. A. The following states the effects of Tolrem using the capital lease method as compared with the operating lease method.

(i)   Cash from operations is higher as only the interest portion of lease expense is deducted; total lease expense is deducted for operating leases.

(ii)   Financing cash flow is lower for capital lease, as part of lease rental is treated as amortization of liability and classified as financing cash outflow.

(iii) Investing cash flow is not affected by the lease treatment. However, the firm will report capital leases in the statement of cash flows (or a footnote) as noncash investment activities.

(iv)   Net cash flow is the actual rental payment and is unaffected by the lease treatment.

(v)   Debt/equity ratio is higher for capital lease, as it records the present value of minimum lease payments as debt *and* reduces net income (and therefore equity) in first year.

(vi)   Interest coverage ratio is usually (not always) lower for capital lease method, which reports interest expense but also higher EBIT, see (vii). For coverage ratios well above 1.0, the ratio will decline. If the increase in interest expense exceeds the increase in EBIT, the ratio will decline even for firms with very low coverage ratios.

(vii) Operating income is lower for operating lease; for capital lease, interest portion of lease expense is nonoperating.

(viii) Net income is higher for operating lease; total lease expense (interest plus depreciation) is higher for capital lease.

(ix)   Deferred tax assets are higher for capital lease; as lease treatment for tax purposes is unaffected by accounting choice, capital lease will result in deferred tax asset as taxable income (operating lease) exceeds pretax income (capital lease).

(x)   Taxes paid are unaffected by choice of method (see ix).

(xi) Pretax return on assets is higher for operating lease as pretax income is higher and assets are lower; capital lease reduces income and reports lease assets.

   Post-tax return on assets is higher for same reasons.

(xii) Pretax return on equity: both pretax income and equity are higher for operating lease than for capital lease. The higher pretax income should increase the ratio in all but exceptional cases. Post-tax return on equity should be higher for same reason. However as increase in post-tax income equals (for first year) increase in equity, there may be more exceptional cases.

B. Net income (viii) will be lower for the operating lease after the "crossover" point. As total net income over the life of the lease is unaffected by the accounting choice, higher net income (operating lease) in the early years must be offset by lower net income in later years.

C. Consistent use of the operating lease method in place of capitalization will not change the direction of the effects shown in part A, but will increase their magnitude. New leases will keep Tolrem from reaching the crossover point for net income, keeping net income and return ratios higher than if the leases were capitalized.

13. A. Present value of 10 annual payments of $2,400 plus the present value of a single payment of $4,000 due 10 years hence, both discounted at 9% is:

   ($2,400 x 6.4177) + ($4,000 x .4224) = $17,092

B.
Interest expense (.09 x $17,092)	= $1,538
+ Depreciation expense ($17,092-$4,000)/10	= 1,309
Total lease expense	= $2,847

C. Total lease expense will decline over the lease term. Interest expense will fall as a fixed interest rate is applied to a declining liability. Depreciation expense remains constant as Dale uses the straight-line method. Total lease expense would decline faster if the firm used an accelerated depreciation method.

14. A. Convertible securities should be treated as equity when the stock price is significantly higher than the conversion price and it is expected that the debt will be converted rather than repaid. These securities should be included in debt when the stock price is significantly below the conversion price. Option pricing models may be used to estimate the value of the equity component when the stock price is close to the exercise price and conversion is uncertain. In this case the analyst should also evaluate the impact on ratios of both repayment and conversion. For the example shown, the differences are significant.

	1990	1991
Short-term debt & capital leases	$ 3,087	$ 2,569
Long-term debt	40,186	32,563
Capital lease obligations	23,691	20,696
Total debt	$ 66,964	$ 55,828
Stockholders' equity	$ 102,622	$ 110,715
Reported debt/equity ratio	.65	.50
Adjusted debt (less convertible debt)	$ 28,447	$ 37,434
Adjusted equity (add convertible debt)	$ 141,139	$129,109
Adjusted debt/equity ratio	.20	.29
Interest expense	$ 9,633	$ 8,560
Earnings before interest & taxes	23,560	16,526
Reported times interest earned ratio	2.45	1.93
Adjusted interest [Reported interest less 1990 (1991) adjustment of $38,517 x .135 ($18,394 x .135)]	$ 4,433	$ 6,083
Adjusted times interest earned ratio	5.31	2.72

B. Bondholders whose bonds were not called would not exercise the conversion right even when the stock price exceeded the conversion price. Given the high interest rate on the bonds, there is no reason to convert the bonds to shares unless the dividend yield is higher (not the case for Vicorp, which had no common stock dividend). In addition, they retain the superior safety and lower downside risk of the bondholder. As for bondholders whose bonds were called, the stock price was probably below the conversion price at the time of the call.

15. A.
1992 minimum lease payment =	$ 5,154	
Principal due in 1992	(2,445)	
Interest portion	$ 2,709	
Interest rate ($2,709/$23,141)		11.7%

The footnote shows the total present value of $23,141 and the current maturity of $2,445; the difference between the minimum lease payment and the interest portion must be the interest component. Note that the alternate method of estimating the interest rate (using the actual lease payments and their present value) yields a similar rate of 11.9%.

B. The capital lease payment of $5,154,000 includes $2,445,000 of current maturities (reported as financing cash flow); the remaining $2,709,000 is interest (reported as operating cash flow). The entire

$17,936,000 of operating lease rentals will be reported as operating cash flow.

C.   The operating leases should be capitalized.

Nearly 52% ($20,876 of $40,012) of the capital lease payments are due within the next five years; the annual payments decline by more than 28% over that period (from $5,154 to $3,695). Finally, the payment schedule suggests that little more than five years of payments remain, making the total life of the capital leases approximately ten years.

The operating lease disclosures show 46% of the payments due within the next five years ($81,497 of $ 175,717), the decline in annual payments is 21% over the five year period, and the schedule suggests nearly seven additional years, making the total life nearly 12 years.

The disclosures reveal "operating lease" payments that are long term, fairly constant over time, and not significantly different from those considered capital leases; these leases should therefore be capitalized.

D.   Present value of operating leases can be computed from the minimum lease payments shown in Exhibit 8P-4:

1992	$ 17,936
1993	17,195
1994	16,695
1995	15,498
1996	14,173
Thereafter	94,220
Total	$ 175,717

Assuming that post-1996 annual payments will remain at $14,173 implies that 6.65 payments remain ($94,220/$14,173). We use this payment schedule, number of payments, and the interest rate of 11.70% (derived in part A) to compute a present value of $96,129.

E.   Reported ($ thousands):   **1991**

Short-term debt and capital leases	$ 2,569
Long-term debt	32,563
Capital lease obligations	20,696
Total reported debt	$ 55,828
PV of operating leases	96,129
Adjusted debt	$151,957
Stockholders' equity	$110,715
Reported debt/equity ratio	0.504
Adjusted debt/equity ratio	1.373

Earnings before interest and tax	$ 16,526
Interest expense	$ 8,027
Capitalized interest	533
Interest expense before capitalization	$ 8,560
Interest on capitalized operating leases	11,247*
Adjusted interest expense	$ 19,807
Adjusted earnings before interest and tax	$ 27,773**
Reported coverage ratio	1.93
Adjusted coverage ratio	1.40

*11.7% x $96,129.

**As interest expense is nonoperating, EBIT must be increased by $11,247. A more sophisticated calculation would increase EBIT by the difference between the lease payment and estimated depreciation expense.

F.   (i)   Current value of Vicorp's operating lease obligations at 7% would be $119,595 (all other data unchanged). The capital lease obligation would increase by $5,281.

(ii) and (iii)   Total adjusted debt would be $180,704 (reported debt of $55,826 + $5,281 + $119,595). [Equity would be reduced as well, but we have ignored this effect for simplicity.]

The adjusted debt/equity ratio would now be 1.632.

Adjusted interest expense at 7% would be $16,215 ($19,807 - $3,592[1]), EBIT would be $24,181 ($27,773 - $3,592) and the times interest earned ratio would be 1.49 ($24,181/$16,215).

This difference must also be subtracted from EBIT. At the lower interest rate, the present values are higher, increasing depreciation expense. As before, we make the simplifying assumption that net income is the same under both methods so that lease rentals = interest + depreciation.

---

[1]Interest on existing capital lease liability:

($23,141 x .117)	$ 2,707	
Interest recomputed ($28,422 x .07)	(1,990)	
Difference		$ 717
Interest on operating leases at 11.7% (part E)	$11,247	
Interest recomputed ($119,595 x .07)	(8,372)	
Difference		2,875
Total reduction in interest expense from leases		$ 3,592

16.   A. and B.

	Caramino	Aglianico	Difference
Operating income	$ 20,000	$ 20,000	$
Depreciation expense[1]	(8,624)		(8,624)
Lease rental		(10,000)	10,000
EBIT	$ 11,376	$ 10,000	$ 1,376
Interest expense[2]	(2,650)		(2,650)
Earnings before tax	$ 8,726	$ 10,000	$ (1,274)
Income tax expense	(3,490)	(4,000)	510
Net income	$ 5,236	$ 6,000	$ (764)

[1]The present value of the minimum lease payments is $43,121 ($10,000 + 4 payment annuity of $10,000 per year at 8%). Assuming zero residual value, depreciation = $43,121/5 = $8,624.
[2] Interest expense = 8% x ($43,121-$10,000) = $2,650

Caramino's EBIT is higher by $1,376; Aglianico reports rental expense but no depreciation expense since it does not record any asset. Because total lease expense (depreciation plus interest) is higher than the lease rental, Caramino's EBT is lower by $1,274. After a deferred income tax offset of $510, Caramino's net income is $764 lower.

Caramino's deferred tax debit (asset) results from the difference between financial reporting (capital lease) and tax reporting (operating lease). The $1,274 timing difference results in a deferred tax debit of $1,274 x .40 = $510

C. and D.   Caramino reports higher cash from operations by $10,000. Since the tax rate is 40%, Aglianico (operating lease firm) reports aftertax operating cash *outflow* of $6,000. Caramino (capital lease firm) pays no interest but, since it uses the operating lease method for taxes, receives a tax deduction of $4,000 for the annual payment of $10,000. Caramino's aftertax operating cash *inflow* is $4,000.

The difference ($6,000 + $4,000 = $10,000) is recorded by Caramino as a *financing* cash outflow; this is the amount of the lease payment considered a reduction of the capitalized lease liability for 1993. [Note that the lease payment is made at the beginning of the year and, therefore, has no interest component; there is no accrued interest as the lease has just begun.]

E.   There is no impact on investing cash flow for either firm. Caramino would report the present value of the capital lease as a noncash investment activity.

F.

	Caramino	Aglianico
Cash from operations	$ 4,000	$ (6,000)
Cash for financing	(10,000)	0
Cash for investing	0	0
Net cash flow	$ (6,000)	$ (6,000)

The net cash outflow for each firm is the lease payment of $10,000 less the tax deduction of $4,000 (40% tax rate). However the classification of cash flow components depends on the lease method used.

G. By using the capital lease method, Caramino reports higher debt and lower income. However the firm also reports higher cash from operations. The choice of method may reflect the effect of different debt covenants or simply a preference among financial characteristics.

17. A. The fair market value of the asset is $125,000. The present value of the MLPs is $128,392 (at 8%, the lower of the lessee and lessor rates); the asset must be capitalized at the (lower) fair market value.

B. The existence of the bargain purchase option requires depreciation over the estimated economic life of the asset rather than the (shorter) lease term.

C. The option creates the presumption that the asset will be held past the expiration date of the lease. Otherwise it must be assumed that use of the asset will revert to the lessor at expiration, requiring the lessee to depreciate the leased asset over the (shorter) lease term.

18.

		1st Year	9th Year
(i)	Assets	Higher	Higher
(ii)	Revenues	Higher	Lower
(iii)	Expenses	Higher	Lower
(iv)	Asset turnover ratio	Higher	Lower
(v)	Interest income	Higher	Higher
(vi)	Cost of goods sold	Higher	No effect
(vii)	Net income	Higher	Lower
(viii)	Retained earnings	Higher	Higher
(ix)	Taxes paid	No effect	No effect
(x)	Post-tax ROA	Higher	Lower
(xi)	Cash from operations	Higher	Lower
(xii)	Investment cash flow	Lower	Higher

Assets are higher because inventory is replaced with (higher) receivables because of the recognition of manufacturing profit. Assets remain higher throughout the lease term.

Revenues are higher in Year 1 as the sales-type lease recognizes a sale whereas the operating lease method does not. In later years, interest revenue from the sales-type lease should be lower than lease revenue for the operating lease. This effect is more pronounced over time; in year 9 interest income is low given the small remaining receivable. The revenue effect increases the asset turnover ratio in the first year. Both the revenue and asset effects reduce turnover in the ninth year.

Expenses are higher in year 1 due to the recognition of cost of goods sold. In later years, there is no expense for the sales-type lease; the operating lease method reports depreciation expense in every year, however.

Initial period income and income-related ratios are higher for the sales-type lease because the sale (and income) is recognized at the inception of the lease. In later years, however, income is higher for the operating lease.

Income taxes paid are the same since the lease cannot be considered a completed sale for tax purposes.

Cash from operations is higher for the first year due to recognition of the sale (the investment in the lease is classified as an investing cash outflow). In later years the operating lease method shows higher cash from operations as rental income exceeds the interest income recorded for the sales-type lease (income taxes paid are the same).

[See Exhibit 8-15 (pages 607-610) and the accompanying text for further explanation of these effects.]

19. A. The present value of the minimum lease payments receivable of $170,271 (at 10%, the lower of lessee and lessor rates) is more than 90% of the fair market value of $185,250. Therefore the lease should be capitalized by the lessee, Baldes. It would be useful to know whether the lessee has guaranteed the residual value of the leased asset.

B.

Leased assets	$ 170,271
Long-term lease obligation	$ 167,298
Current portion of lease obligation	2,973
Total lease obligation	$ 170,271

Note that there are no income or cash flow statement effects at the inception of the lease.

C. (i) **Balance sheet effects of capital lease:**

	12/31/95	12/31/94	01/01/94
Leased assets	$170,271	$170,271	$170,271
Accumulated depr.	17,028	8,514	0
Leased assets (net)	$153,243	$161,757	$170,271
Current portion of lease obligation	$ 3,597	$ 3,270	$ 2,973
Long-term portion of lease obligation	160,431	164,028	167,298
Total lease obligation	$164,028	$167,298	$170,271

No impact on balance sheet if operating lease method applied.

[Deferred tax assets reflecting the difference between total expense under the two methods would also be reported.]

(ii) **Income statement effects of capital lease:**

Years ended December 31,	1995	1994
Interest expense[1]	$ 16,730	$ 17,027
Depreciation expense[2]	8,514	8,514
Total expense	$ 25,244	$ 25,541

[1]Interest expense for: 1994 = .10 x $170,271
1995 = .10 x $167,298
[2]Deprecation expense = $170,271/20 for each year

The income statement would show lease expense of $20,000 each year under the operating lease method.

(iii) **Statement of cash flow effects of capital lease:**

Years ended December 31,	1995	1994
Cash from operations	$(16,730)	$(17,027)
Financing cash flow	(3,270)	(2,973)

The operating lease method reports $20,000 cash outflow from operations for each year.

D. As in part A, the PV of the MLPs is more than 90% of the fair market value, permitting capitalization. However, for the lessor to capitalize the lease, revenue recognition criteria must be satisfied as well. These conditions are:

(i) Collectibility of MLPs is reasonably assured, and

(ii) There are no significant uncertainties regarding the amount of costs yet to be incurred by the lessor or other obligations under the provisions of the lease agreement.

To evaluate these issues, information would be needed regarding the financial condition of Baldes and any remaining obligations of Malbec.

E. The operating lease method has no effect on Malbec's balance sheet at the inception of the lease since the lessor has merely entered into a rental arrangement - an executory contract.

F. **Sales-type lease reporting by lessor:**

Malbec's gross investment in the lease:

MLPs ($20,000 x 20)	$ 400,000
Unguaranteed residual value	5,500
Gross investment	$ 405,500

Net investment:

Present value of 20 payments at 10%	$ 170,271
PV of $5,500, 20 periods hence at 10%	818
Net investment	$ 171,089

Unearned income: $405,500 - 171,089 = $ 234,411

Journal entry at inception (1/1/94):

Gross investment	$ 405,500	
Cost of goods sold	149,182	
Sales revenue		$170,271
Inventory		150,000
Unearned income		234,411

Balance Sheet Effects, January 1, 1994:

Inventory (reduction due to sale)	$(150,000)

Gross investment in sales-type lease	$ 405,500
Less: unearned interest income	(234,411)
Net investment	$ 171,089

Income Statement Effects, Year Ended December 31, 1994:

Sales revenue	$ 170,271
Cost of goods sold	(149,182)
Income effect	$ 21,089

G. **Balance Sheet Effects:**

	12/31/95	12/31/94
Sales-type lease:		
Net investment in lease, current portion	$ 3,498	$ 3,180
Net investment in lease, long-term	156,020	159,518
Operating lease:		
Assets under lease	$ 150,000	$ 150,000
Accumulated depreciation	(14,450)	(7,225)
Net assets	$ 135,550	$ 142,775

Income Statement Effects:

	12/31/95	12/31/94
Sales-type lease:		
Sales revenue	$ ---	$ 170,271
Cost of goods sold	---	(149,182)
Sales profit	---	$ 21,089
Interest income	$ 16,820	17,109
Pretax income	$ 16,820	$ 38,198
Operating lease:		
Rental income	$ 20,000	$ 20,000
Depreciation expense	(7,225)	(7,225)
Pretax income	$ 12,775	$ 12,775

Statement of Cash Flows:

	12/31/95	12/31/94
Sales-type lease:		
Cash from operations:		
Sales profit	$ ---	$ 21,089
Inventory reduction	---	150,000
Interest income	$ 16,820	17,109
Cash from operations	$ 16,820	$ 188,198
Investment cash flow:		
Net investment in lease	$ ---	$(171,089)
Reduction in net investment	3,180	2,891
Investment cash flow	$ 3,180	$(168,198)
Operating lease:		
Rental income	$ 20,000	$ 20,000
Cash from operations	$ 20,000	$ 20,000

NOTE: There is no effect on investment cash flow when the operating lease method is used.

Cash from operations--indirect method:

	12/31/95	12/31/94
Sales-type lease:		
Pretax income	$ 16,820	$ 38,198
Inventory reduction	---	150,000
Cash from operations	$ 16,820	$ 188,198
Operating lease:		
Pretax income	$ 12,775	$ 12,775
Depreciation expense	7,225	7,225
Cash from operations	$ 20,000	$ 20,000

20.   A.   The first step must be to estimate the interest rate used by Knogo to capitalize its existing sales-type leases. Part C of Exhibit 8P-5 can be used to derive the following, ignoring the allowance for uncollectibles, executory costs, and residual value for simplicity:

Minimum lease payments ($ thousands):

Year	Amount
1993	$ 7,705
1994	6,943
1995	5,207
1996	3,021
1997	1,107
Total	$ 23,983
Unearned income	(5,298)
Present value	$ 18,685

The resulting interest rate is 11.9541%.

Next we use this interest rate to determine the present value of Knogo's operating leases:

Minimum lease payments ($ thousands):

Year	Amount
1993	$ 10,166
1994	8,097
1995	6,177
1996	3,921
1997	2,283
Total	$ 30,644
Unearned income	(6,905)
Present value	$ 23,739

We now assume that Knogo can convert these operating leases to sales-type leases. The firm would recognize sales equal to the present value of the MLPs and recognize COGS equal to the carrying value of the leased equipment. As we do not have this amount, we will assume that Knogo has the same gross margin percentage as on its sales-type leases:

Gross profit percentage = $50,084/$80,695 = 62.07%

Gross profit on present value of operating leases = $23,739 x .6207 = $14,734. COGS = $23,739 - $14,734 = $9,005, which is our estimate of the carrying value of the assets on lease.

The balance sheet effects of the conversion of the operating leases to sales-type leases would be:

1.   Assets rise by $14,734 as leased equipment replaced by present value of MLPs.

2.   Liabilities increase reflecting deferred taxes on the "sale" (we assume that tax treatment of leases is unchanged so that taxes paid do not change). [The deferred tax liability would be $14,734 x marginal tax rate.]

3.   Equity increases by the recognized gross profit of $14,734 less the deferred income tax liability.

B. Use of the sales-type lease method results in higher reported profits initially due to recognition of the manufacturing profit immediately rather than over time.

Assets, liabilities, and stockholders' equity are all increased as the (higher) present value of MLPs replaces the original inventory cost of the leased assets.

Cash from operations increases initially as the manufacturing profit is recognized. Cash for investment is negative as the firm reports an outflow for its "investment" in the MLPs.

Financial ratios are improved by the sales-type lease treatment due to higher income and CFO.

21. A. The data needed to calculate the ratios for each of the five options follows ($ thousands):

Financing Method Number		1 Pref. Stk.	2 Conv. Bond	3 Zero Bond	4 Cap. Lease	5 Oper. Lease
CFO before interest & rent	Given	$ 390	$ 390	$ 390	$ 390	$ 390
Rental payments[1]	New	0	0	0	0	163
CFO before interest		$ 390	$ 390	$ 390	$ 390	$ 227
Interest paid[2]	Given	$ 200	$ 200	$ 200	$ 200	$ 200
	New	0	100	0	100	0
Total		$ 200	$ 300	$ 200	$ 300	$ 200
Preferred dividends	Given	$ 0	$ 0	$ 0	$ 0	$ 0
	New	100	0	0	0	0
Total		$ 100	$ 0	$ 0	$ 0	$ 0
Long-term debt + capital lease liability[3]	Given	$2,000	$2,000	$2,000	$2,000	$2,000
	New	0	1,000	1,100	937	0
Total		$2,000	$3,000	$3,100	$2,937	$2,000
Tangible fixed assets	Given	$5,000	$5,000	$5,000	$5,000	$5,000
	New	1,000	1,000	1,000	1,000	0
Total		$6,000	$6,000	$6,000	$6,000	$5,000

[1]Lease payments for a $1,000,000 lease (10 years at 10%) would be $163,000/year. These are recorded as *rental payments* for the operating lease but not for the capital lease. Therefore, for the operating lease only are they deducted from CFO.

[2]Note that no interest is paid on the zero coupon bond (see note 3).

[3]Unpaid interest on the zero coupon bond increases the liability. For the capital lease, the excess of the lease payment over the interest factor ($163,000 − $100,000) reduces the liability.

Times interest earned (cash basis):   **1.30**   **1.30**   1.95   **1.30**   1.13

$$\frac{\text{CFO Before interest}}{\text{Interest paid + preferred dividends}}$$

Fixed charge coverage (cash basis):   **1.30**   **1.30**   1.95   **1.30**   1.07

$$\frac{\text{CFO Before interest and rent payments}}{\text{Interest paid + rent payments + preferred dividends}}$$

Debt to gross tangible assets: 0.33   0.50   **0.52**   0.49   0.40

$$\frac{\text{Long-term debt + capital lease liability}}{\text{Gross tangible fixed assets}}$$

The resultant ratios for each of the five options are listed above. Those ratios that violate the applicable covenant are in boldface. Note that each of the five financing options violates at least one of the covenants. Each option violates two different covenants, except for the zero coupon bond, which violates only the debt/tangible assets covenant.

The zero coupon would seem to be the "best" as its coverage ratios are high (no cash interest payment) and the debt to assets limit is barely violated. It violates this covenant because debt increases to reflect the unpaid interest.

B.   The best approach is to combine the zero coupon bond, which violates only the debt/assets covenant, with another financing method that brings down that ratio without lowering either of the other ratios excessively. Preferred stock dominates all other choices as it has the lowest debt/assets ratio yet no other choice has higher coverage ratios. Thus the optimal choice is a combination of preferred stock and zero coupon bonds. Because neither choice creates rent payments, the first two ratios are identical. Therefore, we must consider only the first and third constraints:

CFO/(interest + preferred dividends) must exceed 1.80.

Long-term debt/gross assets must be less than 0.50.

If P dollars are raised via preferred shares and Z dollars via zero coupon bonds, then P + Z = $1,000,000. For the zero coupon bonds, the amount of debt at year end is 1.1Z because of the accrual of unpaid interest. These constraints reduce to the following equations ($ thousands):

I: $390/($200 + $100p) > 1.80   where p = P/$1,000,000

II: $\frac{\$2,000 + \$1,100\ (1-p)}{\$6,000} < 0.50$

These reduce to the following constraints:

I: .167 > p   II: p > .091

Thus, .167 > p > .091

One possibility would be to issue 85% zero coupon bonds and 15% preferred (p = .15):

CFO = $390 (neither issue reduces CFO)

Interest paid = $200 (neither issue creates interest payments)

Preferred dividends = $15 ($150 x 10%)

Long-term debt = $2935 [$2,000 + ($1100 x .85)]

Tangible fixed assets = $6000 (same effect for both choices)

Times interest earned and fixed charge coverage ($390/$215) = 1.81
Debt to tangible fixed assets (2935/6000) = .489

Another possibility would be 90% zero coupon bonds and 10% preferred (p = .10):

CFO = $390

Interest paid = $200

Preferred dividends = $10 ($100 x 10%)

Long-term debt = $2990 [$2,000 + ($1100 x .90)]

Tangible fixed assets = $6000 (same effect for both choices)

Times interest earned and fixed charge coverage ($390/$210) = 1.86
Debt to tangible fixed assets (2990/6000) = .498

Thus the decision is a tradeoff between the two ratios. As p increases, Sleepman reduces its debt ratio but also its coverage ratio. At the extremes (p = .167 and p = .091), the firm will be right on the edge of violating one covenant. The decision would be based on management's view of which ratio has the lower risk of being violated (or which ratio the lender considers more significant). Note, however, the zero coupon bond increases in amount as interest accrues and (all other things being equal) puts increasing pressure on the debt-to-fixed-assets ratio over time.

CHAPTER 9 - SOLUTIONS

1. A.   The lower discount rate used to compute the projected benefit obligation for 1990 and 1989 increased service cost but reduced interest cost for those two years. However, as the impact on service cost is greater the net effect was an increase in total pension cost.

    B.   (i)   Pension cost would decline because the assumed return on assets component (assumed rate times value of plan assets) would rise.

    (ii)-(iii)   The return on assets assumption has no effect on the actual difference between the PBO and plan assets. However, as the difference between the expected return and actual return is deferred, the changed assumption will change the amount deferred (equal to the decline in pension cost). Assuming no change in funding, the pension liability reported on the balance sheet will decline by this same amount.

2. Generally such shifts in status occur when the increase in plan assets during the year is smaller than the increase in the ABO.

    For Alcoa, plan assets actually decreased in 1990 from $2,891.3 to $2,795.4. Benefits paid out were larger than the sum of contributions and actual ROA, as the reconciliation below shows:

Plan Assets ($ millions)

Opening balance	$2,891.3 million
Actual return on assets	53.0
Contribution[1]	40.0
Benefits paid (Balancing figure)	(188.9)
Closing balance	$2,795.4

[1]Reconciliation of accrued (prepaid) pension cost:

Opening balance [(48.6) + 18.5]	$ (30.1)
Pension cost	85.9
Contribution (balancing figure)	(40.0)
Closing balance [(48.8) + 64.6]	$ 15.8

    The total ABO for all plans at December 31, 1990 is equal to $2,836 ($1239.7 + $114.3 + $1363.5 + $118.5) as compared with $2,744 ($2517.1 + $196.5 + $27.4 + $3.0) at December 31, 1989.

    Footnote N indicates that the actual return on assets was $183.7 below the expected return. Had the expected return been achieved, plan assets would have been $2,979.1, greater than the total ABO. (However the ABO may still have exceeded assets for some plans.)

Thus it is reasonable to assume that the largest factor contributing to the shift in plans to underfunded status was the low realized ROA. This trend should not be expected to continue in the future if the expected ROA is an appropriate estimate of long term trends. Under this assumption, years of underperformance will be offset by years of overperformance. (In fact, such overperformance occurred in 1991, shifting almost all plans back into the overfunded category.)

3.   A.   SFAS 87 requires that, for pension plans whose assets are below the accumulated benefit obligation (ABO), the difference must be immediately recognized on the balance sheet. However, the excess of the ABO over the plan assets must be adjusted for the (prepaid) accrued pension (asset) liability. This asset/liability excludes unamortized actuarial gains/losses, prior service costs, and the transition asset/liability related to these plans, because of their delayed recognition. In Note N, the "underfunded" plans are disclosed separately from those with assets exceeding accumulated benefits. The degree of underfunding is computed below:

Status of Underfunded Plans ($ millions)

	1990	1989
ABO (vested and nonvested)	$(1,482.0)	$(30.4)
Plan assets	1,353.8	0.5
ABO in excess of plan assets	(128.2)	(29.9)
Accrued pension cost[1]	64.6	18.5
Minimum liability	$ (63.6)	$(11.4)

[1]Given in note but can be checked as follows:

	1990	1989
PBO	$(1,621.1)	$(38.9)
Plan Assets	1,353.8	0.5
PBO in excess of plan assets	$ (267.3)	$(38.4)
Adjustments:		
Unamortized transition (asset) liability	$ 78.8	$ 12.9
Unamortized prior service cost	103.8	(1.5)
Unamortized actuarial losses	20.1	$ 8.5
Accrued pension cost	$ (64.6)	$(18.5)

B.   The minimum liability increases the liability shown on the balance sheet. By combining the overfunded and underfunded plans, the total accrued liability recognized on Alcoa's balance sheet at December 31, 1990 and 1989 can be computed as:

	1990	1989
Net prepaid (accrued) pension cost	$ (15.8)	$ 30.1
Minimum liability recognized	(63.6)	(11.4)
Net prepaid (accrued) pension cost recognized on the balance sheet	$ (79.4)	$ (18.7)

C.   The minimum liability has not been included in pension cost or net income. A "deferred charge" has been created to offset the additional liability of $63.6 and $11.4 at December 31, 1990 and 1989, respectively. In the short run, therefore, the minimum liability is a "cosmetic" accounting entry with no cash flow or income consequences. The "deferred charge" or "pension intangible" is really just a means of deferring recognition of a charge to equity, and should be recognized as such in the analysis of Alcoa's financial statements.

However, this treatment does not ensure that the liability will never affect reported income. Future amortization of the unamortized items, especially prior service cost, will quickly affect pension cost and net income in the following years. Ultimately, cash flow will be affected as well, as the shortfall of plan assets compared to the benefit obligation must be funded.

D.   (1)   PBO - Plan Assets = $3039.6 - $2795.4 = $244.2 million
     (2)   ABO - Plan Assets = $2836.0 - $2795.4 = $40.6 million
     (3)   PBO alone = $3039.6 million
     (4)   ABO alone = $2836.0 million

Using the PBO is more appropriate for a going concern analysis. The ABO should be used when the liquidation of the company or the pension plan is being considered and analysis must be based on the present status.

If the focus is solely on the liability of the pension plan itself, then the gross liability (before deducting plan assets) should be used. From the point of view of the employer (plan sponsor), however, the net liability is the appropriate measure of exposure.

4.   A.   **Projected benefit obligation ($ millions)**

Opening balance	$ (2,912.7)
Service cost	(76.2)
Interest cost	(229.6)
Prior service cost and actuarial gains and losses (balancing figure)	(10.0)
Benefits paid	$ 188.9
Closing balance	$ (3,039.6)

B.

Service cost	$ 76.2 million
Interest cost	229.6
Recurring cost	**305.8**
Prior service cost and actuarial gains and losses	10.0
Gross cost	**315.8**
Actual return on assets	(53.0)
Nonsmoothed cost	**262.8**
Reported cost	**$ 85.9**

Each of the three alternative measures of cost is three to four times as large as the amount reported by Alcoa.

C. **Forecast of Pension Cost ($ millions)**

	1991E	1990A
Service Cost[1]	$ 88	$ 76
Interest cost [1991: .08 x $3,040]	243	230
Recurring and gross cost	**331**	**306**
Expected return on assets [1991: .09 x $2,795]	(252)	(237)
Nonsmoothed cost	**79**	**69**
Net amortization[2]	37	17
Net pension cost	$ 116	$ 86

E = Estimated   A = Actual

[1]Alcoa has changed neither the discount rate nor the rate of compensation increase; the PBO gain of about 3% due to other factors is too small to affect service cost. Thus we must guess based on trends in payroll. Assuming the same percentage increase as in 1990 results in an estimate of $88.

[2]Amortization of transition asset (same as 1990)	$ 3 M
Amortization of prior service cost based on application of 1990 rate ($61.6/14) to 1990 year end level of $149.1	34
Assume no amortization of actuarial loss because of corridor method. [10% of PBO is 304.]	
Total amortization	$ 37 M

Note: The actual 1991 pension cost of Alcoa was ($ millions):

	1991E	1991A
Service cost	$ 88	$ 83
Interest cost	243	241
Recurring and gross cost	**331**	**324**
Expected return on assets	(252)	(249)
Nonsmoothed cost	**79**	**75**
Net amortization	37	21
Net pension cost	$ 116	$ 96

E = Estimated   A = Actual

The most significant error in our estimate was in the forecast of net amortization. Alcoa apparently used a longer amortization period than assumed, lowering the amortization component of pension cost. (The amortization period used is not explicitly disclosed.) As a result, our forecast overestimated the increase in 1991 pension cost.

D.   To deduce prior service cost and actuarial gains and losses, first analyze the net amortization, making some assumptions:

Analysis of net amortization ($ millions):

Amortization of transition liability[1]	$ 2.8
Amortization of unamortized prior service cost[2]	14.0
Net amortization	$ 16.8

[1]$19.6 − $16.8 = $2.8

[2]Balancing figure assuming no amortization of unrecognized actuarial losses as corridor method prevails.

Analysis of net actuarial (gains) losses ($ millions):

Opening balance	$ (29.7)
Deferred losses on plan assets[1]	183.7
Actuarial gains and losses[2]	(91.5)
Closing balance	$ 62.5

[1]See footnote to pension cost (Exhibit 9P-1).
[2]Balancing figure.

Unamortized prior service cost ($ millions):

Opening balance	$ 61.6
Amortization[1]	(14.0)
Prior service cost[2]	101.5
Closing balance	$ 149.1

[1]Brought forward from analysis of net amortization.
[2]Balancing figure.

This leaves us with an increase in prior service cost of $101.5 and an actuarial gain of $91.5.

E.   The prior service cost arises from amendments to the pension plan. Such adjustments can be expected as labor union contracts are renegotiated periodically. It should be noted that the PBO is not much higher than the ABO, suggesting that some of the company's plans are flat benefit or career average plans. Flat benefit plans are often a bargaining issue in labor negotiations and, therefore, are adjusted periodically for inflation.

Actuarial gains/losses can be manipulated by management through changes in assumptions. In this case an actuarial gain may have been desirable to offset the increased prior service cost. However, as Alcoa did not change its compensation growth rate or its discount rate, the gain must result from changes in undisclosed factors such as estimates of retirement age, quit rates, and mortality rates. Thus, one cannot tell whether the actuarial gain represents a deliberate offset or reflects objective actuarial factors alone.

5.   A.   The expected return can be estimated as plan assets times expected rate of return on assets: $2,131 x .097 = $207 million. The amount deferred equals actual return – expected return: $622 – $207 = $415 million.

B.   The contribution can be calculated from the change in the firm's pension liability after backing out the minimum liability:

	Overfunded	Underfunded	Total
Closing balance (10/31/91) less minimum liability	$ 225	$ 388 (359)	$ 613 (359)
	$ 225	$ 29	$ 254
Opening balance (10/31/90) less minimum liability	$ 118	$ 327 (277)	$ 445 (277)
	$ 118	$ 50	$ 168
Change			$86

This change of $86 million must be current period pension cost less contributions. Since pension cost is $73, the company must have received a "refund" of $13 (possibly from a plan termination):

Opening balance	$ 168
Pension cost	73
(Contribution) refund[1]	13
Closing balance	$ 254

[1]Balancing figure.

C.   **Plan assets ($ millions):**

Opening balance	$ 2,131
Return on assets	622
Contribution (refund) [from (B)]	(13)
(Benefits paid)[1]	(60)
Closing balance	$ 2,680

[1]Balancing figure.

6.   A.   Reported pension cost was $73 million.

B.   Recurring cost equals the sum of the service and interest cost components: $64 + $231 = $295 million.

Gross pension cost includes recurring costs, actuarial gains and losses, and additions to prior service cost. It is readily obtainable as the change in PBO before benefits paid. Therefore, gross pension cost is:

Closing PBO	$3,309 million
plus benefits paid	60
less opening PBO	(2,617)
Gross pension cost	$ 752 million

Nonsmoothed pension cost equals gross pension cost less the actual return on plan assets: $752 - $622 = $130 million. Each measure is significantly above reported pension cost for Deere's U.S. plans.

C.   The actuarial loss results from recalculation of the PBO at 10-31-91 based on current assumptions. Deere decreased its discount rate to 8.3% at 10-31-91. This decrease resulted in a higher present value of future pension benefits (higher PBO). It is also possible that revised assumptions regarding retirement ages, quit rates, and other undisclosed assumptions contributed to the actuarial loss.

Prior service costs represent the increase in the PBO due to plan amendments adopted in 1991 that increased pension benefits.

Prior service costs and actuarial losses can be computed by subtracting recurring cost from gross pension cost: $752 - $295 = $457.

D.   **Projected benefit obligation ($ millions):**

Opening balance	$ 2,617
Service cost	64
Interest cost	231
Prior service cost and actuarial gains/losses	457
Benefits paid	(60)
Closing balance	$ 3,309

MORE DETAILED ANSWER TO PARTS "C" AND "D":

The total of prior service costs and actuarial gains and losses can be broken down further as follows:

Assuming no amortization, new prior service cost must at least equal the change in unamortized prior service cost: $225 - $141 = $84 million (increase in PBO).

Similarly the change in net unamortized loss is $345 - $273 = $72 million (gain). Since from 5A, the actual return deferred is $415 (gain), then actuarial losses must be at least: $415 - $72 = $343 million (increase in PBO, or loss).

The (minimum) new prior service costs and actuarial losses are, therefore: $84 + $343 = $427 million (increase in PBO).

The difference between this sum and the actual change of $457 - $427 = $30 million must be due to amortization. We need to break out that amortization between prior service cost and net gains and losses. One method of doing this is shown below, along with a reconciliation of the net amortization and deferral ($millions):

Net amortization and deferral:

Amortization of transition asset[1]	$ (45)
Deferred gain on plan assets[2]	415
Amortization of unrecognized net loss[3]	5
Amortization of unrecognized prior service cost[4]	25
Net amortization and deferral	$ 400

[1]$168 - $123 = $45.
[2]Answer 5A.
[3]Assumes amortization over fifteen years of unrecognized net gains greater than 10% of the higher of plan assets at fair value or the projected benefit obligation: ($345 - $261.7)/15 = $5.6
[4]Balancing figure.

This assumption yields new prior service cost of $109 and an actuarial loss of $109 - $457 = $348 as shown below:

Unrecognized net actuarial (gains) losses ($ millions):

Opening balance	$ 345
Amortization of deferred loss[2]	(5)
Deferred gain on plan assets[1]	(415)
Actuarial loss[3]	**348**
Closing balance	$ 273

[1]Answer 5A.
[2]Footnote 3 from net amortization and deferral.
[3]Balancing figure.

Unamortized prior service cost ($ millions):

Opening balance	$ 141
Amortization[1]	(25)
New prior service cost[2]	**109**
Closing balance	$ 225

[1]Footnote 4 from net amortization and deferral.
[2]Balancing figure.

E.   Gross pension cost and Nonsmoothed pension cost can be calculated on an ABO basis as follows ($ millions):

Closing ABO	$ 2,931
Plus: benefits paid	60
Less: opening ABO	(2,244)
Gross pension cost	$ 747

Nonsmoothed pension cost (on an ABO basis) is equal to gross pension cost less the actual return on plan assets: $747 - $622 = $125.

Recurring cost on an ABO basis has two components: service cost and interest cost. The latter can be estimated as (discount rate x beginning ABO). Service cost on an ABO basis is not disclosed but can be approximated by applying the ABO/PBO ratio to total service cost. Thus, recurring cost would be:

$$
\begin{array}{lr}
(\$2244/\$2617) \times \$64 = & \$\ \ 55\ \text{million} \\
.09 \times \$2244 = & \underline{\ \ 202} \\
\text{Total} & \underline{\$\ 257}\ \text{million}
\end{array}
$$

7.   A.   In the footnote, the "underfunded" plans (ABO less than plan assets) are disclosed separately from those with assets exceeding accumulated benefits. The degree of underfunding is computed below ($ millions):

Pension Status (Underfunded Plans)	1991	1990
ABO	$ (1,573)	$ (1,238)
Plan assets	1,185	911
ABO in excess of plan assets	(388)	(327)
Accrued Pension Cost[1]	29	50
Minimum liability	$ (359)	$ (277)

	1991	1990
[1]PBO	$(1,600)	$(1,266)
Plan assets	1,185	911
PBO in excess of plan assets	(415)	(355)
Adjustments:		
Unrecognized transition asset	(20)	(27)
Unrecognized prior service cost	224	140
Unrecognized net loss	182	192
Accrued pension cost	$ (29)	$ (50)

B.   Recognition of the minimum liability makes the balance sheet liability equal to the amount by which these plans are underfunded (using the ABO as a measure of the pension liability).

C.   Deere recognized the deferred tax effect of the minimum liability because it expects to receive a tax deduction for the contributions it makes in future years.

D.   One possibility would be to record the difference between the PBO and plan assets as a liability in place of the actual balance sheet liability:

$$
\begin{array}{lll}
\text{PBO} & \$1709 + \$1600 = & \$3,309\ \text{million} \\
\text{Plan assets} & \$1495 + \$1185 = & \underline{\$2,680} \\
\text{Liability} & & \underline{\$\ \ 629}
\end{array}
$$

At present Deere shows $225 + $388 = $613 million as a balance sheet liability. Thus the adjustment to the liability is relatively small. However, at present, most of the recognized liability is offset by an intangible asset of $249 million that should be eliminated.

Therefore, debt should be increased by $629 - $613 = $16 million and equity should be reduced by $16 + $249 = $265 million to reflect the increased liability and the elimination of the intangible asset.

8.   A.   **Combined Status of U.S. Plans ($ millions)**

	October 31, 1991	October 31, 1987
Accumulated benefit obligation (ABO)	$ (2,931)	$ (1,789)
Excess of PBO over ABO	(378)	(272)
Projected benefit obligation (PBO)	(3,309)	(2,061)
Plan assets	2,680	2,043
Excess of PBO over plan assets	(629)	(18)
Unrecognized (gain)/loss	273	(48)
Unrecognized prior service cost	225	115
Unrecognized transition asset	(123)	(213)
Minimum liability recognized	(359)	---
Pension liability (balance sheet)	$ (613)	$ (164)

B.   The funded status of the plan has deteriorated over the four year period to a deficit of $629 million. The PBO has increased by 60%, nearly twice the 31% increase in plan assets.

C.   (i)   The underfunded status is almost entirely recognized on Deere's balance sheet, mainly because of the minimum liability provision.

          (ii)   The underfunded status is not recognized in equity. First, most of the minimum liability is offset by an intangible asset (see pension footnote). Second, Deere has deferred recognition of the actuarial losses and increase in prior service cost.

          (iii) The underfunded status has been recognized in pension cost only to a limited extent. 1991 pension cost is twice 1987 pension cost. About half of the increase is due to higher service cost (some of that increase is due to the lower discount rate). The remainder results from the fact that interest cost has risen faster than expected return on assets, reflecting the increasing excess of PBO over plan assets.

               The calculations in 5B show that no contribution was made to the U.S. plans in 1991. Thus the deterioration of plan status appears not to have affected Deere's funding decisions.

D.   The points made in parts A-C suggest that both pension cost and contributions will rise in future years. The increased cost will reflect amortization of the deferred losses and prior service cost as well as the increasing gap between PBO and plan assets (interest

cost should continue to rise faster than expected return on assets).
This gap should necessitate increased contributions as well.

9. **Forecast of Pension Cost ($ millions)**

	1992E	1991A
Service cost[1]	$ 75	$ 65
Interest cost [1992: .083 x $3,309]	275	231
Recurring and gross cost	350	295
Return on assets[2] [1992: .097 x $2,680]	(260)	(207)
Nonsmoothed cost	90	88
Amortization of transition asset[3]	(14)	(45)
Amortization of unrecognized losses[4]	---	5
Amortization of prior service cost[5]	40	25
Net (reported) pension cost	$ 116	$ 73

E = Estimate   A = Actual

[1]Service cost should increase because the discount rate for 1992 will
be 8.3% (the discount rate used at 10-31-91) rather than the 9% used for
1991. It should also increase because of increases in employee payroll.
Note that service cost was flat in 1991 versus 1990, despite the fact that
the discount rate was increased. Seventy-five million dollars ($75
million) is an estimate based on the above factors.
[2]We assume that Deere continues to use a ROA assumption of 9.7%. Note
that the 1991 component is the net of the actual ROA (622) and the
deferral (415) as computed in Question 5(A).
[3]Computed by dividing the unrecognized amount ($123) by 9 years. As
Deere adopted SFAS 87 at 10/31/85, there should be 9 years of amortization
remaining. The computation for 1991 may have been distorted by Deere's
acquisition in that year.
[4]As 10% of the PBO (greater than plan assets) exceeds the
unrecognized loss, no amortization is required, assuming that Deere uses
the corridor method.
[5]The amortization for 1991 implies an amortization period of 5.64
years ($25 divided into opening balance of $141). Applying the same period
to the year end 1991 balance of $225 results in amortization of $40
($225/5.64).

[NOTE: Deere reported fiscal 1992 pension cost of $96 million; lower
service cost and interest cost accounted for the error in the forecast
shown above.]

10.   A.   Actuarial assumptions should reflect the economic characteristics of
the plan jurisdiction. Such factors as interest rates, inflation,
and expected market returns will vary by country, requiring a
different set of actuarial assumptions for each.

       B.   The employees in these plans are, apparently, fully vested; no
further employee service is required to receive benefits.

       C.   These plans are unfunded; there are no pension assets. Note that the
balance sheet liability is equal to the ABO as a result of the
minimum liability provision of SFAS 87.

11. A. **Net amortization ($ millions)**

Amortization of transition asset[1]	$ (204)
Amortization of unrecognized net gain[2]	(174)
Amortization of unrecognized prior service cost[3]	125
Net amortization	$ (253)

[1]$2951 - $2747 = $204.
[2]Amortization over fifteen years of unrecognized net gains greater than 10% of the higher of the plan assets at fair value or the PBO ($4,902 - $2,287)/15 = $174 [corridor method].
[3]Balancing figure.

While the IBM footnote provides no information about its amortization of unrecognized gains and losses, some must be present (otherwise amortization of prior service cost would be negative, which is impossible). It is possible, however, that IBM amortizes the _entire_ gain, rather than using the corridor method.

We cannot be certain that our estimate of the second and third components is correct, although the total is known. The offset would be the new actuarial losses and prior service cost in parts b and c. As these are both the result of "reestimating" the PBO, a small error can be tolerated.

B. **Unrecognized net (gain) loss ($ millions)**

Opening balance (12-31-89)	$(4,902)
Deferred losses on plan assets	1,859
Amortization of unrecognized net gain[1]	174
1990 actuarial loss[2]	204
Closing balance (12-31-90)	$(2,665)

[1]Brought forward from 11A.
[2]Balancing figure.

C. **Unrecognized prior service cost ($ millions)**

Opening balance (12-31-89)	$ 1,092
Amortization[1]	(125)
New prior service cost[2]	356
Closing balance (12-31-90)	$ 1,323

[1]Brought forward from 11A.
[2]Balancing figure.

12. A. **Prepaid (accrued) pension cost ($ millions)**

Opening balance (12-31-89)	$ 655
Pension income for 1990	390
1990 contribution[1]	0
Closing balance (12-31-90)	$ 1,045

[1]Balancing figure.

B. **Plan assets ($ millions)**

Opening balance (12-31-89)	$ 22,867
1990 return on assets	160
1990 contribution[1]	0
1990 benefits paid[2]	(802)
Closing balance (12-31-90)	$ 22,225

[1]From 12A.
[2]Balancing figure.

C. **Projected benefit obligation ($ millions)**

Opening balance (12-31-89)	$ (15,451)
Service cost	(573)
Interest cost	(1,309)
Actuarial loss[1]	(204)
New prior service cost[2]	(356)
Benefits paid	802
Closing balance (12-31-90)	$ (17,091)

[1]From 11B.
[2]From 11C.

13. A. Prepaid pension cost results from the net effect of pension cost (income) and contributions. As IBM recognized pension income, its prepaid pension (asset) account rose.

The 1990 decline in the excess of plan assets over PBO was due primarily to the low return on assets. Due to the smoothing provisions of SFAS 87, that low return had no immediate impact on pension income. The impact of the 1990 decline in pension assets may, however, be seen in future years.

B. IBM's pension cost (income) has been driven by two factors. One is the excess of plan assets over the PBO; the second is the use of a higher ROA assumption (9%) than discount rate (8 1/2%). As a result of these two factors, the return on assets component of pension cost has been rising faster than the interest cost component. Rising amortization of deferred investment gains (due to high returns in 1988 and 1989) and flat service cost (due to employee reductions) have been additional factors in the growth of IBM's pension income.

14. A. Income taxes are the primary motivating factor. Contributions to pension plans are tax deductible and earnings generated by plan assets are not taxed. Both of these tax advantages are unavailable for nonpension plans, except in limited circumstances.

B. The answer to this question is not clear, as IBM could use the money to fund its own operations. However, it is a point well worth considering in evaluating IBM. Some possible reasons are listed below:

1. IBM may not have alternative investment opportunities providing a sufficient return.

2. The money may be invested to build up "financial slack."

3.   Tax deductions are available for limited funding.

4.   Given the volatility and the uncertainty associated with health costs, IBM may be attempting to hedge some of the risk by investing money in a "more stable" environment.

5.   IBM has historically eschewed debt. Thus, as part of the corporate culture it may have wanted to minimize the debt associated with these benefits.

C.   Pay-as-you-go expense is equal to the actual payments for health benefits. Under SFAS 106, IBM must accrue for benefits earned by employee service, even though benefit payments may be far in the future. Nonpension plans are, therefore, accounted for like pension plans.

D.   IBM previously accrued postretirement liabilities for employees only when they retired. SFAS 106 accrues such liabilities for employees during their working years. Additionally, it is not clear whether (or how) IBM used present value to measure accrued benefits.

The cumulative difference between the two methods is the transition liability of $2,613 million (the cumulative effect of $2,263 + $350 tax benefit) taken by IBM upon adoption of SFAS 106.

E.   IBM adopted the new standard by recognizing the transition liability of $2613 million as a charge against 1991 earnings. As the liability has been fully recognized, there is no deferred transition amount.

15.   A.   1991 expected ROA is actual return minus deferred return or $325 − $198 = $127 million. Given the assumed rate of 9%, this implies assets at 1-1-91 of $1,411 million ($127/.09).

B.   The accrued liability can be calculated as $776 million by completing the following schedule:

Plan Status, January 1, 1991 ($ millions)

Accumulated postretirement benefit obligation	$ (4,800)
Plan assets	1,411
Excess of APBO Over plan assets	(3,389)
Accrued liability prior to adoption of SFAS 106	776
Transition liability	$ (2,613)

C.   The loss represents the effect of recalculating the APBO based on updated information less the deferral of return of assets above the expected level. Since the deferral was $198 million (gain), the deferred actuarial loss must be $315 million. (Unrecognized loss less deferred gain = $117 − $(198) = $315.)

D.   (i)   **Accrued liability**

1-1-91 balance	$ 776
Transition liability	2,613
Benefit cost	394
12-31-91 balance	(3,700)
Contribution	$ 83

(ii) **APBO**

1-1-91 balance	$ 4,800
Service cost	132
Interest cost	389
Actuarial loss	315
12-31-91 balance	(5,449)
Benefits paid	$ 187

Benefits paid can also be computed by reconciling plan assets:

1-1-91 balance	$ 1,411	million
1991 return on assets	325	
1991 contribution	83	
12-31-91 balance	(1,632)	
Benefits paid	$ 187	million

E. $207 million, the excess of benefit cost of $394 million over benefits paid of $187 million.

16.   Required assumptions are listed below the table:

Postretirement Benefit Cost ($ millions)

			1992E	1991A
Service cost[1]			$ 145	$ 132
Interest cost	[1992: .085 x $5,449]		463	389
Return on assets	[1992: .09 x $1,632]		(147)	(127)
Amortization[2]			0	0
Net benefit cost			$ 461	$ 394

E = Estimate   A = Actual

[1]Estimate a 10% increase given higher payroll costs and health care inflation.
[2]Assuming that IBM uses the corridor method, none is required. 10% of the APBO = $545 million, well in excess of the deferred net loss.

[NOTE: IBM reported net benefit cost of $447 million for 1992.]

17.   Because Fibreboard recognized the entire transition obligation when it adopted SFAS 106, there is no unrecognized obligation.

18.   As the plan is unfunded, there are no assets on which a return can be earned or assumed.

19. **APBO ($ thousands)**

Balance 1-1-91 [transition liability]	$ 3,102
1991 service cost	68
1991 interest cost	178
Actuarial loss	3
Subtotal	$ 3,351
Less: balance 12-31-91	3,153
Benefits paid	$ 198

20. Benefit cost was $246 million, benefits paid were $198 million. The adoption of SFAS 106 increased cost by $48 million as compared to the pay-as-you-go method.

21. **Nonpension Benefit Cost ($ thousands)**

	1992E	1991A
Service Cost[1]	$ 75	$ 68
Interest cost[2] [1992: .08 x $3,153]	252	178
Amortization	0	0
Net benefit cost	$ 327	$ 246

   E = Estimate   A = Actual

   [1]Assume 10% increase reflecting higher payrolls and effect of health care inflation.
   [2]The interest cost for 1991 looks odd. Assuming an 8% discount rate, it should have been .08 x $3,102 = $248 thousand. We have no explanation for this discrepancy. Given the absence of significant actuarial gains or losses, it is unlikely that the discount rate changed.

22. (i)   Fibreboard could have increased the discount rate, reducing the APBO. Reducing the assumed health care cost trend rate would also have reduced the reported obligation.

    (ii) Neither of these changes would affect benefit cost for 1992 if they were implemented at year-end; they would reduce 1993 benefit cost by reducing the service cost component.

23. A.   The deferred tax impact of $(1175) thousand implies a timing difference of $3456 thousand ($1175 divided by .34, the statutory tax rate).

         The pension plan footnote shows net pension cost of $608 thousand. As net accrued pension expense has increased $210 thousand (from $11,554 in 1990 to $11,764 in 1991) there must have been a contribution of $398 ($608 - $210) thousand in 1991.

         FBD reported net periodic postretirement benefit cost of $3348 thousand for 1991 and a year end accrued benefit cost of $3153 thousand; the difference of $195 thousand reflects the benefits paid during the year (and the amount deductible that year).

We can now compare the amounts deducted on FBD's tax return with the amounts recognized in the financial statements ($ thousands):

	Tax Return	Financial Statements
Pension benefits	$ 398	$ 608
Other benefits	195	3,348
Totals	$ 593	$ 3,956

The difference of $3956 − $596 = $3363 thousand should be the timing difference for 1991. The small discrepancy between this result and the actual timing difference of $3456 thousand determined above may be due to:

- An effective tax rate other than the 34% .

- Some benefit payments may be deductible in a year other than the year of payment.

- Undisclosed supplemental plans or defined contribution plans may have generated timing differences.

This exercise shows how the analysis of deferred taxes can be used to generate quite accurate forecasts of tax deductible amounts that differ from those used in the financial statements.

B.   There is no difference.

C.   Presumably, FBD was still using APB 11 which did not limit the amount of deferred tax assets that could be recorded.

24. A.   The computation of net pension cost is shown in the table below. As shown in the table, net pension cost is actually a benefit of $12.2 million.   Note that in 1987 an investment return based on the expected long-term rate of return of 9.0% is still credited against pension cost, despite the negative return in that year. The excess of plan assets over the projected benefit obligation ($215.1 million) represents the cumulative effect of changing to SFAS 87 and is amortized over 15 years at the rate of $14.3 million per year. The closing balance of unrecognized investment and actuarial losses as of December 31, 1986 represents the net gain or loss from investment and actuarial experience up to that date. As it is being amortized over 10 years, only $3.1 million ($31.4/10) is included in 1987 pension cost.

Anheuser-Busch
Computation of 1987 Pension Cost ($ millions)

Service cost		$ 23.0
Interest on PBO [9% x $398.7]		35.9
Actual ROA [5% x $666.1]	$ 33.3	
Less: deferred ROA [$(59.9) - $33.3]	(93.2)	
Expected ROA [9% x $666.1]		(59.9)
Subtotal		(1.0)
Amortization of transition amount (gain) [$215.1 million/15 years]		(14.3)
Amortization of deferred loss [$31.4 million /10 years]		3.1
Net pension cost (benefit)		$ (12.2)

B.   The adverse investment and actuarial experience in 1987 had no effect on 1987 pension expense. The 1987 expense was based upon December 31, 1986 data. Future (1988 and beyond) pension expense will increase because of:

1.   amortization of deferred losses (due to the market crash),

2.   possible reduction of the ROA assumption, and

3.   a decline in the calculated expected ROA due to the decline in the market value of plan assets.

In 1987, the plan status deteriorated. The ratio of plan assets to the projected benefit obligation, a measure of the plan's health, declined because plan assets fell and the PBO grew. Nevertheless, the plan remains overfunded at year end. The plan's future status will be affected by the sponsor's choice of assumptions for the discount rate, return on assets, and compensation increases as compared to actual changes in the benefit obligation, actual return on plan assets, and company contributions.

Chapter 10 - Solutions

1.   A.   Debt should be increased by:

             $ 20 million   (present value of operating lease)
                 5   (guarantee)
                 7   (present value of take-or-pay agreement)
             $ 32 million

There is no effect on equity as each obligation is offset by a corresponding asset:

             Leased assets for operating lease
             Receivable for Crockett's obligation to repay debt
             Supply agreement

The recomputed debt-to-equity ratio is:

             ($12 + $32)/$20 = 2.2X as compared with .6X before adjustment

       B.   The additional interest expense is:

             Lease (effective interest
               rate is about 18%)   .18 x $20 = $ 3.6
             Bond guarantee   .10 x   5 =   0.5
               Total $ 4.1

Before adjustment, the interest expense is $1.0 million and the times interest earned ratio is 5.0, implying EBIT of $5.0 million.

             After adjustment, the ratio is:

                 ($5.0 + $4.1)/($1.0 + $4.1) = 1.78 X

No adjustment has been made for the take-or-pay contract as it does not affect 1993 interest expense. Adjustments in future years will be based on the implicit interest rate of 21%.

       C.   Reasons for entering into off-balance-sheet obligations:

             1.   Avoidance of or mitigation of the risk of violating debt covenant restrictions.

             2.   Leased assets revert to lessor after eight years, limiting risk of obsolescence.

             3.   Guarantee of Crockett debt may lower interest rate, increasing profitability of investment.

             4.   Contract with PEPE secures source of supply and possibly advantageous pricing.

D. Additional information needed for full evaluation:

1. (Lease) Useful life of leased assets; conditions under which lease can be canceled; nature of leased assets.

2. (Guarantee) Financial condition of Crockett; bond covenants.

3. (Take-or-pay) Alternate sources of supply; quantity to be purchased relative to total needs; price provisions of contract.

2. A. **Capitalization,** December 31

($ millions)	1991	1990
Current portion of debt	$ 1,331	$ 1,516
Long-term debt	4,861	4,122
Capital leases	312	363
Total debt	$ 6,504	$ 6,001
Stockholders' equity	9,828	9,385
Total capital	$16,332	$15,386

	1991	1990
Total Debt/Equity	$6504/$9828 = **0.66**	$6001/$9385 = **0.64**

	1991	1990
Total assets	$26,182	$25,975
Average total assets		$26,078	

	1991	1990
Pretax income	$ 1,420	$ 2,175
Interest expense	558	568
EBIT	$ 1,978	$ 2,743

	1991	1990
Interest coverage ratio	**3.54**	**4.83**

	1991	1990
Return on assets (ROA)	**7.58%**	**10.56%**
[EBIT/Average total assets]		[On ending assets]

Alternate calculation:

	1991	1990
Earnings before interest and tax	$ 1,978	$ 2,743
Plus: minority interest	16	12
Less: reinvested equity earnings	(120)	(119)
Alternate EBIT	$ 1,874	$ 2,636

	1991	1990
Alternate interest coverage ratio	**3.36**	**4.64**

	1991	1990
ROA [Alternate EBIT/Ave. TA]	**7.19%**	**10.15%**

The alternate calculation removes that portion of equity method earnings not received as dividends and thus not available for debt service. Similarly it adds back minority interest, a deduction from earnings not requiring cash.

B & C. Adjustments need to be made to debt (to adjust capitalization table), total assets (for return on assets ratio), and to interest expense (to adjust EBIT for interest coverage and ROA ratios).

The adjustments follow:

(i) (Caltex) In lieu of pro rata consolidation, add 50% of Caltex debt (short and long term) and 50% of interest expense. Total assets must be adjusted by Texaco's share of Caltex assets (see Note 3).

(ii) (Star Enterprise) Assume that non-current liabilities (NCL) are debt; Texaco has 50% interest in Star. Therefore, add 50% of NCL to Texaco debt. Total assets must also be increased by Texaco's share of Star assets less Texaco's share of equity in Star which has been reported as a component of investments and other assets. As no data on Star's interest expense is provided, we estimate 9% on assumed debt.

(iii) (Other equity affiliates) Note 3 provides Texaco's share of assets for equity affiliates as a group. For debt assume that non-current liabilities are debt; Texaco's percentage ownership (based on equity) is 26.7% (1991) and 26.5% (1990). Estimated interest adjustment is again 9% on assumed debt.

NOTE: When equity method affiliates are proportionately consolidated, adjusted EBIT will include the parent's pro rata share of the affiliate's EBIT and adjusted interest expense. In some cases, interest coverage will improve after adjustment.
When the balance sheet is proportionately consolidated, the parent's (net) investment in the affiliate must be deducted to avoid double counting.

(iv) (Note 10) Operating leases are clearly long-term and should be capitalized. Present value at 13% discount rate = **$571** [1991]. 13% is approximate rate on capital leases. Operating leases can be approximated as a stream of $88 per year for 12 years.

Due to lack of data use same number for prior year **$571** [1990].

Interest adjustment is $74 (13% x $571).

(v) (Note 14) Environmental reserves are already recognized; no adjustment required unless there is belief that they are inadequate.

(vi) (Sale of receivables) Assume that proceeds were used to reduce debt. We must use *ending balance* of receivables outstanding = **$0** [1991] and **$300** [1990, assuming that full facility was used. This is important enough to check for accuracy.] The amount outstanding should be added to assets as well as debt. Interest expense is again imputed at 9%.

(vii) (Note 15) The commitments appear to be "throughput" agreements. It is not clear whether the "gross" or "net" exposure should be used. Using the "net" exposure requires adding **$328** (1991) and **$341** (1990) to Texaco's assets and debt. Interest adjustment at assumed 9% rate is **$30** for 1991 (**$30** for 1990).

(viii) (Forward exchange contracts and interest rate swaps). These are of interest for what they tell us about Texaco's operations. The risk is a small percentage of the principal amount and can be ignored for this analysis.

Exhibit 10S-1 is the revised capitalization table. Exhibit 10S-2 shows the adjustments to total assets and Exhibit 10S-3 shows adjustments to interest expense. The adjusted ratios are:

	1991	1990
Interest coverage	$2665/$807 = **3.30**	$3472/$843 = **4.12**
Total debt/ equity	$8970/$9828 = **0.91**	$8615/$9385 = **0.92**
Return on assets	$2665/$30609 = **8.71%**	$3472/$30648 = **11.33%**

Exhibit 10S-1
Adjusted Capitalization
($ millions)

	1991	1990
Current debt	$ 1,331	$ 1,516
Long-term debt	4,861	4,122
Capital leases	312	363
Total debt--as reported	$ 6,504	$ 6,001
Adjustments:		
Caltex: 50% short-term debt	461	492
50% long-term debt	214	157
Star: 50% noncurrent liabilities	381	304
Other: 26.7% (26.5%) NCL	511	459
Operating leases	571	571
Receivables sold	---	300
Throughput agreements	328	341
Adjusted total debt	$ 8,970	$ 8,625
Stockholders' equity	9,828	9,385
Total capital--adjusted	$18,798	$18,010

Exhibit 10S-2
Adjustments to Total Assets
($ millions)

	1991	1990
Total assets as reported	$ 26,182	$ 25,975
Texaco share of affiliates	6,818	6,471
Less: net equity*	(3,329)	(3,010)
Operating leases	571	571
Receivables sold	---	300
Throughput agreements	328	341
Adjusted total assets	$ 30,570	$ 30,648
Average: $ 30,609		

*Must subtract to avoid double counting, as share of total assets now included.

Exhibit 10S-3
($ millions)

	1991	1990
Interest Expense:		
As reported:	$ 558	$ 568
Adjustments:		
Caltex: 1/2 interest expense	65	75
Star: assume 9% x debt	34	27
Other: assume 9% x debt	46	41
Operating leases @ 13%	74	74
Receivables sold: 9% x debt	--	27
Throughput agreements @ 9%	30	31
Adjusted interest expense	$ 807	$ 843
Earnings Before Interest & Tax:		
Reported pretax income	$ 1,420	$ 2,175
Reported interest expense	558	568
Adjustments:		
Caltex: 1/2 EBIT	829	708
Star: 1/2 EBIT	167	215
Other: proportionate EBIT	196	183
Operating leases @ 13%	74	74
Receivables sold: 9% x debt	--	27
Throughput agreements @ 9%	30	31
Less: equity in NI of affils.	(609)	(509)
Adjusted EBIT	$ 2,665	$ 3,472

D. Adjusting for Texaco's off-balance-sheet financing results in higher reported leverage, lower interest coverage, but higher return on assets. The higher ROA derives from the proportionate consolidation of affiliates.

3. A. Caltex itself uses off balance sheet financing that needs to be taken into account when assessing the leverage of Caltex (and therefore Texaco). We must look at:

      (i)   50% owned affiliates
      (ii)   Operating leases
      (iii) Contingent liabilities
      (iv) Financial instruments

   B. Unfortunately, the Caltex footnote data are not very informative. Some rough adjustments are, however, possible:

      (i)   (Equity affiliates) We can replace Caltex's equity with its share of assets and liabilities:

($ millions)

	1991	1990
Caltex share of total assets	$ 4,506	$ 4,416
Less: Caltex equity	(1,293)	(1,093)
Increase in assets	$ 3,213	$ 3,323

The effect on debt can be estimated by assuming that all noncurrent liabilities are debt:

	1991	1990
Addition to Caltex debt	$ 903	$ 542

Using the interest rate on Caltex debt of 9.7% [$131/$1349], the estimated interest expense is:

	1991	1990
	$ 88	$ 53

The adjustment to EBIT requires an addition of the Caltex share of the operating income of its affiliates plus interest expense less the reported equity in net income of affiliates:

	1991	1990
	$312	$ 88

(ii)   (Operating leases) The present value is $146 million when capitalized at 9.7% (rate on Caltex debt). This amount should be added to assets and debt. Additional interest expense is $14 ($146 x 9.7%).

(iii) (Contingent liabilities) The total of debt guarantees ($15 million) and letters of credit outstanding ($54 million) at December 31, 1991 is $69 million. There may be some liability from litigation and tax claims.

(iv)   (Financial instruments) These disclosures are, like those for Texaco, informative about operating and financing activities rather than useful for adjustment purposes.

Using these data, we can further adjust Texaco's ratios (remember that only one-half of each Caltex adjustment is applicable to Texaco):

$ millions	1991	1990
Adjusted debt (Exhibit 10S-1)	$ 8,970	$ 8,615
Additional adjustments	559	378
Second adjusted debt	$ 9,529	$ 8,993
Debt/equity	.97	.96
Adjusted total assets (Exhibit 10S-2)	$ 30,570	$ 30,648
Additional adjustments	1,714	1,769
Second adjusted total assets	$ 32,284	$ 32,417
Average: **$ 32,350**		
Adj. interest expense (Exhibit 10S-3)	$ 807	$ 843
Additional adjustments	51	33
Second adjusted interest expense	$ 858	$ 876
Additional EBIT adjustments	$ 166	$ 44
Adjusted EBIT (Exhibit 10S-3)	2,665	3,472
Second adjusted EBIT	$ 2,831	$ 3,516
Second adjusted interest coverage	3.30	4.01
Second adjusted return on assets	9.25%	11.47%

C.   It would be useful to know whether Caltex's affiliates, in turn, have their own off-balance-sheet liabilities. It would also be helpful to know more about transactions with Texaco (and with the other 50% stockholder, Chevron) to obtain a better idea of the role that Caltex plays. Caltex appears to be more than an investment; how much more we can't tell from the data provided.

    This case illustrates the importance of obtaining information on affiliates in order to assess the impact of the accounting and financing methods they employ and how they affect the risk of the parent company.

4.   A.   Cell 1: no sale has taken place as seller retains both risks and benefits.

    Cell 2: while benefits have been transferred, risks have not; unless they are minor, no sale has taken place.

    Cell 3: while risks have been transferred, benefits have not; sale is incomplete.

    Cell 4: Sale is complete as both benefits and risks have been transferred to the buyer.

    B.   Cell 2: SFAS 77 states that transfers of receivables with recourse can be recognized as sales even though seller retains the effective credit risk.

    C.   The sale of receivables with recourse improves reported liquidity, turnover, and leverage ratios as the receivables and debt (repaid from proceeds of sale) are reduced. The effect on profitability depends on the relationship of sales price to carrying amount and on the effective interest rates.

D. The sale of receivables results in an immediate improvement in cash flow from operations. The effect on future cash flow from operations depends on whether sales continue in the future. If no further sales are made, future cash flows are reduced due to the absence of receivable collections from the receivables sold in the current period.

5. A. Receivables have been reduced at December 31, 1991 by $66,796,000, the amount of sold receivables that remain outstanding. Assuming that there was no gain or loss on the sale and that proceeds were used to repay debt, the above amount should be added to both accounts receivable (current assets) and short-term debt (current liabilities):

Current ratio:

As reported = $642,641/$374,272 = 1.72X

Adjusted = $\dfrac{(\$642,641 + \$66,796)}{(\$374,272 + \$66,796)}$ = 1.61X

Receivable turnover ratio:

As reported = $\dfrac{\$1,979,986}{(\$129,823+\$182,283)/2}$ = 12.69X

Adjusted) = $\dfrac{\$1,979,986}{(\$129,823+\$66,796+\$182,283)/2}$ = 10.45X

As reported # of days receivables = 365/12.69 = 29 days

Adjusted # of days receivables = 365/10.45 = 35 days

The cash cycle equals days of receivables plus days of inventories less days of payables. Neither inventories nor payables are affected by the sale of receivables. Therefore, the increase in days of receivables of six days increases the cash cycle by the same number of days. Thus, the sale of receivables improved the reported cash cycle by six days. [Using data not provided, the cash cycle is 19 days as reported, but 25 days after adjustment.] We assume that the amount of receivables sold remained outstanding throughout the year.

B. **Debt-to-equity ratio:**

As reported: ($88 + $193,484)/$385,725 = .50X

Adjusted: ($88+$193,484+$66,796)/$385,725 = .68X

Times interest earned:

As reported = \$73,932/\$16,020   = 4.61X

$$\text{Adjusted} = \frac{\$73,932 + \$5,524^*}{\$16,020 + \$5,524^*} \qquad = 3.69X$$

> *8.27% x \$66,796 where 8.27% is the interest rate obtained by relating 1991 interest expense to total debt at December 31, 1991.

Return on assets:

As reported = \$73,932/\$953,481[@]   = 7.75%

> [@]Current liabilities + long-term debt + stockholders' equity

Adjusted (\$73,932+\$5,524)/(\$953,481+\$66,796)   = 7.79%

C.   The sale of receivables in 1991 increased cash flow from operations for that year by \$66,796. Without that effect, 1991 cash from operations would have decreased from \$72,272 (1990) to \$32,153 (1991 after adjustment). [All data in \$thousands]

The effect on the 1991-1992 comparison depends on receivable sales in 1992. The 1991 sales "borrowed" cash flow from 1992. If 1992 sales of receivables equal the 1991 level, 1992 CFO will be "normal" but the 1991-1992 comparison will be distorted because the 1991 CFO was overstated. If 1992 receivable sales are higher or lower than the 1991 level, 1992 CFO and the 1991-1992 comparison will both be distorted.

6.   A.   The discount appears to be interest expense, the difference between the face amount of the receivables sold and the (discounted) proceeds of sale. This would equal the amount of interest expense if Honeywell had kept the receivables but borrowed \$100 million. Thus, it should be reclassified from selling expense to interest expense.

B.   The receivables sale reduced current assets by \$ 100 million and current liabilities by \$97.2 million (assuming the proceeds were used to reduce short-term debt). Adding these amounts back to current assets and current liabilities respectively decreases the current ratio from 1.19 (reported) to 1.14 (adjusted).

Average receivables were reduced by \$50 million for 1990. Adding that amount to average reported receivables of \$1169.4 million reduces the turnover ratio from 5.40 (reported) to 5.17 (adjusted).

The receivables sale improves both ratios and, therefore, the comparison with 1989. The current ratio for 1989, for example, was 0.94; while the 1990 ratio is still higher, the adjustment reduces the improvement.

C.   By adding the assumed debt reduction to total (short and long-term) debt, the 1990 debt-to-equity ratio becomes .52 rather than the reported .46.

To adjust the interest coverage ratio (times interest earned), $2.8 million must be added to *both* EBIT and interest expense, reflecting the reclassification of the discount. The adjustment reduces the interest coverage ratio from 5.87X to 5.74X.

Return on assets (EBIT/average total assets) is affected by both the adjustment to EBIT and the addition of $50 million ($100/2) to the denominator. These adjustments reduce ROA from 13.35% to 13.27%.

D.   The 1990 receivables sale increased reported cash from operations by $97.2 million. Adjustment for this nonoperating factor reduces the 1990 amount to $624.1 million and the increase from the 1989 CFO is now 28% (rather than 48% as reported).

The comparison with 1991 CFO depends on receivables sales in that year. Even if 1991 receivable sales equal those of 1990 (making 1991 CFO "normal"), 1991 CFO will appear low relative to the inflated 1990 CFO. *[NOTE: this is what actually happened; Honeywell's sold receivables outstanding at December 31, 1991 were $65 million, and reported CFO declined in that year.]*

7.   A.   Assuming use of the proceeds of sale to reduce debt, the receivables sale has reduced both current assets and current liabilities by $281 million. Adding this amount to both sides of the balance sheet *increases* the current ratio from .64 to .70; because the current ratio is less than one, the receivables sale reduced it.

The receivables turnover ratio, however, was sharply improved by the receivables sale. Adding back one-half of the sold receivables reduces the turnover ratio from 14.9X to 8.0X. (If an equal amount of receivables sold were outstanding one year earlier, we would add back the entire $281 million to average receivables, reducing the ratio to 5.5X.)

B.   **Reported Capitalization**, December 31, 1991 ($ millions)

Short-term debt	$ 224.7
Long-term debt	2,267.1
Total debt	$ 2,491.8
Stockholders' equity	1,333.1
Total debt/equity	$2491.8/$1333.1 = **1.87**
Average total assets	$ 6,315.4
Interest expense	$ 331.3
EBIT	504.9
Interest coverage ratio	**1.52**
Return on assets	**7.99%**
[EBIT/average total assets]	

Adjustments for off-balance sheet techniques:

The footnotes disclose operating lease and other commitments that must be added to the balance sheet to compute adjusted leverage, coverage, and return ratios. Reported interest expense and total debt indicate an interest rate of 13.3%, used in the adjustments that follow.

The adjustments for operating leases and the Trunkline transportation agreement are straightforward and their total present value at 13.3% is $102.3 million; the Petrolane disclosure gives only the total lease payments of $118.6 million; we have chosen to allocate that total equally over the remaining 15 year term, for a present value of $50.3 million. As Panhandle discloses only the range of payments on the PEPL contract, we have allocated the average amount over the ten-year life of the contract for a present value of $116.9 million.

The redeemable preferred stock has a redemption value of $16.8 million which is added to total debt along with the $281 million of receivables sold during the year. Each of these commitments has been used to adjust interest expense and EBIT and to compute adjusted ratios.

Adjusted Capitalization, December 31, 1991 ($ millions)

Short-term debt	$ 224.7	
Long-term debt	2,267.1	
Total debt as reported		$ 2,491.8
Adjustments:		
Receivables sold	281.0	
Operating leases	102.3	
Petrolane	50.3	
PEPL	116.9	
Redeemable preferred	16.8	
Subtotal		567.3
Total debt after adjustments		$ 3,059.1
Stockholders' equity		$ 1,333.1

Adjusted debt/equity $3059.1/$1333.1 = **2.29**

Adjusted average
   total assets $6315.4+$550.5[*]= $6865.9

   [*]Increased by total adjustments except for redeemable preferred (already on balance sheet) to reflect assets corresponding to off-balance-sheet liabilities recognized. We assume that same amount was outstanding one year earlier so that the total amount increases average assets.

Interest expense	$ 331.3
Adjustments:	
Redeemable preferred	1.8[*]
Leases	13.6
Petrolane	6.7
PEPL	15.5
Receivables sold	37.4
Adjusted interest expense	$ 406.3

[*]Must be grossed up to pretax amount required to pay preferred dividends from after tax income.

```
Adjusted EBIT ($504.9+$75.0)          $ 579.9

Adjusted interest coverage ratio         1.43

Adjusted return on assets               8.45%
```

    C.   The effect of receivables sales on cash from operations depends on the year-to-year change in the amount outstanding. Increases improve CFO for that year while declines reduce it. Thus we need to know the year-end balances to accurately adjust CFO.

        The operating leases and throughput agreements, however, decrease CFO as compared with asset ownership. All payments are considered operating outflows. However if leases or other obligations were capitalized, a portion of those payments would be an investment outflow and CFO would be higher.

    D.   The adjustments in part B suggest that Panhandle's leverage is somewhat greater than the reported data would suggest. The company's use of off-balance-sheet financing keeps these obligations hidden from data base users and others who do not go beyond the reported balance sheet.

8.   A.   If the bonds were converted, Alleghany would record a gain of $31,418,000, the difference between the face amount of the bonds and the carrying amount of the shares. [Note that conversion of the bonds would require Allegheny to surrender virtually all of its American Express shares; 59,600 x 22.8833 = 1,363,844 shares.]

    B.   Dividend income is 1,366,000 shares @$.94 = $1,284,000 or $1,197,000 after the effective tax rate of 7.2% [.20 x 36%] on dividend income. Interest expense is $59,600,000 x .065 = $3,874,000 or $2,479,000 after 36% tax. The net cost is therefore, $1,282,000 per year or 2.15% of the face amount of bonds.

    C.   By selling the exchangeable bonds rather than selling the American Express shares, Allegheny avoided the payment of capital gains taxes. When the bonds are exchanged, Allegheny will receive a higher price than if it had sold the shares (exchangeable bonds are sold with an exchange price above current market). In the meanwhile Allegheny enjoys the use of the funds at a low net cost.

9.   A.   [The calculations are shown in the table below.]

        Morrison Knudsen (MK) received proceeds of $166,235 after deducting underwriting expenses of $5570. The latter, however, are accounted for separately (straight line amortization) and must be added back to obtain the beginning balance of the bond obligation.

        Interest then must be computed using the 7.25% yield at issue. But this yield is based on semiannual compounding.

        For 1990, interest is computed for the two months ended June 30 and then for the six months ended December 31; for each period a semiannual rate of 3.625 % (7.25%/2) is used. For 1991, the annual accrual is computed by compounding the semiannual rate:

$$(1.03625)^2 = 1.0738$$

Net proceeds of sale	$166,235	thousands
Underwriting expenses	5,570	
Carrying amount at issue	$171,805	
Interest to 6-30-90	2,076	[$171,805 x 1/3 x .03625]
Balance at 6-30-90	$173,881	
Interest to 12-31-90	6,303	[$173,880 x .03625]
Balance at 12-31-90	$180,184	
Interest to 12-31-91	13,300	[$180,184 x .07381]
Balance at 12-31-91	$193,484	

B. Conversion would transfer debt to equity of $180,184 at December 31, 1990 ($193,484 at December 31, 1991). The resultant debt-to-equity ratios would be:

At December 31, 1990:   .04   [.70 before conversion]
      December 31, 1991:   .00   [.50 before conversion]

To adjust the times interest earned ratio, deduct interest expense on the zero coupon bonds (from part A) from total interest expense. The resulting ratios are:

For 1990: $\dfrac{\$72,935}{(\$11,172 - \$8,379)} = 26.1X$ [6.5X before conversion]

For 1991: $\dfrac{\$73,932}{(\$16,020 - \$13,300)} = 27.2X$ [4.6X before conversion]

To compute primary earnings per share, first compute the average number of shares outstanding for each year by dividing net income by earnings per share:

1990: $36,481,000/2.93 = 12,450,853
1991: $35,145,000/2.60 = 13,517,308

The additional number of shares outstanding from conversion of the LYONs would be 3,122,500 (500,000 x 6.245). Earnings per share on conversion would be (assuming a 34% tax rate):

1990: $\dfrac{\$36,481,000 + \$5,530,000}{12,450,853 + \ \ 2,081,667^*} = \$2.89$

1991: $\dfrac{\$35,135,000 + \$8,778,000}{13,517,000 + \ \ 3,122,500} = \$2.64$

*For 1990, the shares are assumed outstanding only following issuance of the bonds.

C. (i)   The advantage of LYONs versus nonconvertible zero coupon bonds is the lower interest rate that LYONs buyers will accept because of the convertibility.

    (ii) The advantage of LYONs versus full coupon bonds is twofold. First, there is no cash interest expense, although the company receives a tax deduction each year. Second, the company is, in effect, selling equity at a price that is higher each year. *[NOTE: The number of shares remains constant but the debt converted increases each year.]* For a full coupon convertible bond, the conversion price remains fixed. Thus LYONs should be less dilutive in the long run.

10. A. Syntex has issued, and is obligated to repay, bonds with a face value of 20 billion yen. If the counterparty to the swap is unable to perform by servicing the debt it has assumed, Syntex is liable for the full amount of the debt.

B. Syntex would recognize a loss if the counterparty were unable or unwilling (and could not be forced to) perform. The loss would equal the difference between the current dollar value of these bonds ($157.1 million at December 31, 1992) and the recognized liability (based on the exchange rate on the swap date) of $100 million.

C. Because of intermarket differences in exchange rates, firms like Syntex can sometimes obtain a lower net cost of debt by borrowing in one currency (based on interest rates in that currency) and swapping the obligation for an obligation in another currency. We can assume that Syntex wished to borrow dollars at a floating rate and was able to obtain a lower interest rate by engaging in the swap transaction.

D. We would have to compare the interest rate (and other terms) on this debt with the rate and terms available if Syntex has issued floating rate U.S. dollar bonds with the same maturity directly.

E. If Syntex had simply maintained the yen debt, its debt would have risen (as the yen appreciated against the dollar) and its debt-to-equity ratio would be higher. In addition, Syntex would have had higher interest expense, decreasing the interest coverage ratio, because:

1. The higher value of the yen would increase interest expense when translated into U.S. dollars.

2. Syntex would have continued to pay interest expense based on yen interest rates; the swap enabled the company to pay interest at (lower) variable U.S. dollar rates.

11. A. The analyst should consider recognizing the following obligations:

1. Debt guarantees of $177 million.

2. The present value of the throughput contracts (the $166 million of affiliated company debt would be a good proxy for those obligations).

3. The present value ($37 million) of Amoco's take-or-pay contracts.

4. The present value of Amoco's future environmental obligations.

Only the fourth obligation would reduce Amoco's equity; the remaining obligations would be offset by assets.

B.   The arguments for recognizing these obligations are:

1.   Amoco's credit rating is the basis for the borrowings for items 1-3 and therefore these obligations affect Amoco's debt capacity.

2.   Amoco has either a primary or secondary (guarantees) obligation to make payments to service these obligations.

The arguments against recognizing these obligations are:

1.   Amoco's future liability is uncertain in timing and amount (items 1 and 4 especially).

2.   These items represent contracts only and not debt obligations of the firm.

C.   To fully evaluate these obligations, we would need further information about them. For example:

1.   What is the credit standing of the primary obligators? This affects the likelihood that Amoco will have to make payments.

2.   What are the pricing conditions of the throughput and take-or-pay contracts. Minimum prices (that may exceed future market prices) would strengthen the argument that these are debt obligations rather than simply contracts.

3.   What is the range of possible environmental costs? How much insurance does Amoco have? Are there other parties that might share the cost?

12.   Aluminum producers that have take-or-pay contracts for energy and/or bauxite have converted significant variable costs into fixed costs. Therefore, their marginal costs are much lower than if these contracts had not been entered into. Under these conditions, aluminum producers will continue production as long as revenue exceeds *marginal costs*, even though they lose money based on *total costs*.

Chapter 11 - Solutions

1. A. 1990: Cost method, unless Burry can argue that it has "significant influence" over Bowman.

    1991: Equity method, unless Burry does not have "significant influence." If the equity method is appropriate, a retroactive restatement of the Investment in Bowman account and retained earnings is required.

    B. 1990: Income and Cash from Operations would be equal to the dividends received during the year: $152,000 (.19 x $800,000).

    There would be no effect on the carrying amount of Burry's investment in Bowman which would remain at the acquisition cost of $10 million.

    1991: The equity method must be applied retroactively to 1990:

Acquisition cost:	$10,000,000
Less: Share of 1990 loss (.19 x $600,000)	(114,000)
: Dividends received (.19 x $800,000)	$ (152,000)
Restated carrying amount, January 1, 1991	$ 9,734,000

    NOTE: The reduction of $266,000 is charged to retained earnings.

    Because Burry acquired an additional 1% for a total share of 20%, a retroactive restatement of the investment account and retained earnings is required. Burry must reduce the carrying amount of $10,000,000 by its share of the net loss and dividends received, for an adjusted carrying amount of $9,734,000 ($10,000,000 - $114,000 - $152,000).

    1991 transactions and entries:

Restated carrying amount, January 1, 1991	$ 9,734,000
Plus: Additional acquisition cost	500,000
: Share of 1991 income	
(.20 x $2,000,000)	400,000
Less: dividends received	(200,000)
(.20 x $1,000,000)	
Carrying amount, December 31, 1991	$10,434,000

    Income would be equal to Burry's proportionate interest in the earnings of Bowman: $400,000 (.2 x $2,000,000).

    Cash from operations would equal the amount of dividends received from Bowman: $200,000 (.2 x $1,000,000).

    The difference between earnings recognized and cash received (equity in undistributed earnings = .2 x ($2,000,000 - $1,000,000)) would be added to the carrying amount of Burry's investment in Bowman: $200,000, making that amount $10,434,000 ($9,734,000 + $500,0000 + $200,000).

C. 1990: same as B

Income of $152,000 (.19 x $800,000)

No effect on investment

1991: income equal to cash flow from dividend payments of $200,000 (.2 x 1,000,000).

The investment account would be $10,500,000 (10,000,000 + 500,000) at the end of 1991.

D. 1990: Burry would recognize its proportionate share of Bowman's loss: ($114,000) = [.19 x $(600,000)]

Investment account would be $9,734,000 a decrease of $266,000 ($152,000 + $114,000) reflecting the share of loss and the dividends received.

[Alternate calculation: share of undistributed loss for 1990 = .19 x [($600,000) - $800,000] = .19 x ($1,400,000) = $(266,000)]

1991: Income equal to $400,000 (.2 x $2,000,000)

Cash from operations equal to $200,000 (.2 x $1,000,000)

Investment account equals $10,434,000, an increase of $700,000 including the $200,000 difference between income and cash flow and the additional investment of $500,000.

E. The answer depends on the relationship between Burry and Bowman. It is unlikely that the purchase of an additional 1% interest changed that relationship. Thus B, which uses different methods for the two years, does not provide useful information. The choice is between the cost method (C) and the equity method (D).

The advantage of the cost method is that Burry's income statement records only the cash flow (dividends) received. If Burry is a passive investor in Bowman, the cost method provides the best information. This is especially true of Bowman shares are marketable; the stock price is the best measure of its value to Burry.

The equity method is more appropriate when Burry is actively involved in managing Bowman and thus earning its share of the profits of Bowman. The payment of dividends may be discretionary (especially if Bowman is privately held) on the part of the major shareholders.

2. A. Purchase price was $3,100 ($4,000 - $900).

The balance of and the change in the valuation allowance are irrelevant.

B.   Mark to market return =
      realized gain/loss + change in market valuation allowance (MVA)

      (i) $900 + $(700) = $200

             The removal of Nachum shares from the portfolio increased the valuation allowance; we can deduce that Nachum shares must have been $700 above cost one year earlier. As the gain was $900, 1991 appreciation must be $200.

      (ii) $900 + $700 = $1600

             The opposite case, in that removal of Nachum shares reduced the valuation allowance. By the same reasoning, the 1991 gain must be $1600.

3.   The investments are accounted for as follows:

      W and Y using the equity method, as ownership exceeds 20%

      X (noncurrent) at lower of cost or market

      Z (current) at lower of cost or market

A.   (i)   Realized gains/losses = 0 as there were no sales

      (ii)   Unrealized gains/losses:

             X: $300,000 (3 x $100,000) recovery of previously recorded unrealized loss; included in stockholders' equity

             Z: None as cost below market

             W and Y: market value changes not recognized under equity method.

      (iii) Dividend income:

             X: $10,000   (100,000 x $.10)
             Z: 0
             Total $10,000   (dividends are not recorded as income for W and Y, instead they are reported as reductions in the carrying amount of the investment)

      (iv)   Equity in income of affiliates:

             W: .25 x $200,000   = $ 50,000
             Y: .40 x   900,000   =   360,000
             Total $ 410,000

B.   As the market value of X shares was below cost, valuation allowances were required:

      12/31/91:   100,000 x $4.00 ($50 - $46) = $400,000
      12/31/90:   100,000 x $1.00 ($50 - $49) = $100,000

C. Mark to market returns for 1991:

Firm	Dividends	+ Market Value Change	=	Total Return
W	$ 17,000	$ (600,000)		$ (583,000)
X	10,000	300,000		310,000
Y	72,000	1,600,000		1,672,000
Z	0	450,000		450,000
Total	$ 99,000	$ 1,750,000		$ 1,849,000

Note that only for firm X is the total return reported in the financial statements, and in that case the return is reported primarily as an adjustment to stockholders' equity.

4. A. Cost method is used for 19X6:

No effect on sales.

Income recognized = dividends received of $10 (.01 x $1000)

Cash from operations = dividends received	$ 10
Cash for investment = cost of shares	(100)
Net cash flow	$ (90)

Equity method is used for 19X7:

No effect on sales

Income recognized = proportionate share of earnings
= $660   (.30 x $2200).

Cash from operations = dividends received	$ 360
Cash for investment = cost of shares	(3,190)
Net cash flow	$(2,830)

B. 19X6

December 31, 19X6 (cost method) $ 100

19X7
The equity method must be applied retroactively to 19X6:

Initial acquisition cost	$ 100
Plus share of 19X6 earnings (1% of $2,000)	20
Less dividends received	(10)
Adjusted carrying amount, January 1, 19X7	$ 110
January 1, 19X7 shares purchased	$ 3,190
Equity in 19X7 earnings	660
Less: 19X7 dividends received	(360)
Carrying amount, December 31, 19X7	$ 3,600

C. The additional share purchases would require that Potter use the purchase method of accounting to reflect its ownership of San Francisco. Potter cannot use the pooling method because:

(i)   It owned 30% (more than the maximum allowed of 10%) of San Francisco prior to the acquisition of the controlling interest,

(ii) The combination was completed over a little more than two years, whereas pooling can be used only if the transaction is completed within one year, and

(iii) Potter used cash for its purchases not stock.

The assets and liabilities of San Francisco must be consolidated with those of Potter using fair market values at January 1, 19X8 (San Francisco only). Some off-balance-sheet items (contingencies and postemployment benefits) may also be recognized. Information on fair values and off-balance-sheet items, as well as full financial statements for San Francisco, would be needed to evaluate the effect of the acquisition on Potter's 19X8 financial statements.

5.   A.   There would be no change in HP's reported income as the market value of the portfolio exceeds its cost.

     B.   No. While these investments apparently cannot be considered cash equivalents under SFAS 95, there is probably little difference between cost and market value due to their short maturities.

     C.   [NOTE: The $1,000,000 profit on the sale of Baruch-Foster in 1991 was recognized as part of income from investments but has been transferred to income from affiliates. We use tax rates of 35% for 1991 and 36% for 1992.]

($ thousands)	1991	1992
Operating income[1]	$11,920 x .65 = $ 7,748	$15,505 x .64 =$ 9,923
Marketable securities[2]	$22,141 x .65 = $14,392	$ 8,570 x .64 =$ 5,485
Affiliates	$(1,540)+$650 = (890)	(4,585)
Total	$21,250	$10,823

[1]Sales and other operating revenues less operating costs.

[2]Income from investments less interest expense, as debt is assumed to finance the investment portfolio.

D. **First, disaggregate HP's assets:**

($ thousands)	1990	1991	1992
Operating	$ 437,907	$ 450,170	$ 484,596
Short-term and marketable securities	114,978	100,321	81,188
Affiliates	30,042	24,677	19,720
Total assets	$ 582,927	$ 575,168	$ 585,504

ROA:			
Operations		1.7%	2.1%
Investments & marketable securities		13.4%	6.0%
Affiliates		(3.3%)	(20.7%)
Total		3.7%	1.9%

E. First, notice that operating income rose in 1992 but net income declined because of the sharp decline in reported income from marketable securities and affiliates. While the ROA of operating activities remained very low, it increased significantly in 1992.

Income from marketable securities fell sharply, both in absolute and ROA terms. But, as these data reflect only *realized* gains, they are not very meaningful (see later parts of problem).

The one remaining equity affiliate, Atwood Oceanics, also performed worse in 1992 on both absolute and ROA terms. As Atwood accounts for barely 3% of total assets, however, it is a small factor in HP's total operations.

This disaggregation produces useful data, therefore, only for HP's operating activities.

F.

($ thousands)	1991	1992
Pretax reported income	$ 22,521	$ 9,202
Less: realized gains (ii)	11,341	1,920
Equals: dividends and interest (i)	$ 11,180	$ 7,282
(iii) None recognized (see part A)		

NOTE: The $1 million pretax gain on the sale of Baruch-Foster has been reclassified (per Note at C on page 11-5).

G. Mark to market returns

MVA (market value - cost):

1990:	$154,004 - $81,180	=	$72,824
1991:	135,034 - 71,794	=	63,240
1992:	128,063 - 68,060	=	60,003

Mark to market return = reported return + change in MVA:

1991:	$22,521 + $(9,584)	=	$12,937
1992:	9,202 + (3,237)	=	5,965

Return on assets = mark to market return/opening market value:

```
1991:          $12,937/($154,004 + $33,798)   =      6.9%
After tax:     $12,937 x .65 = $8,409                5.0%

1992:          $5,965/($135,034 + $28,527)    =      3.6%
After tax:     $5,965 x .66 = $3,937                 2.4%
```

H.

($ thousands)	1991	1992
Atwood (change in market value)	$ (15,400)	$ 800
Baruch-Foster (gain on sale)	1,000	0
Total	$ (14,400)	$ 800

```
1991 ROA = $(14,400)/$34,777           =      (41.4%)
1992 ROA = $800/$14,400                =       5.6%
```

I.   **Pretax returns**

	1991		1992	
	$ thousands	ROA	$ thousands	ROA
LOCM investments:				
Reported return (part C)	$ 14,392	13.4%	$ 5,485	6.0%
Mark to market (part G)	12,937	6.9%	5,965	3.6%
Equity method affiliates:				
Reported return (part C)	(890)	(3.3%)	(4,585)	(20.7%)
Mark to market (part H)	(14,400)	(41.4%)	(800)	5.6%

For the LOCM investments, 1992 returns were lower than 1991 returns under both methods. However the decline is much less severe under mark to market than reported. For both years, the mark to market returns are quite low; earnings on risk free cash equivalents would have been at least as high.

For the equity affiliates, the mark to market returns are quite different from those reported. While Atwood's reported losses in 1992 were much greater than for 1991, its shares rose in value as opposed to the sharp 1991 decline.

J.   The cost method has very little to say for it except conservatism. Income reported under the cost method reflects only actual cash flows (dividends, interest, and realized gains). Reported ROA, however, has very little utility as a measure of what the resources invested actually return.

The equity method has the advantage of including a proportionate share of the operating earnings of the affiliate in the parent's income statement. However, when the affiliate's shares trade, the market value of the investment is a much more useful measure of performance.

Mark to market provides the best information. It tells us the amount of firm resources invested in marketable securities, and thus the "opportunity cost" of those investments. The mark to market return is the actual return earned on the investment portfolio and is not affected by choice of accounting method or management decision. The only disadvantage (lower predictive ability) is that mark to market returns can be volatile, as they track actual market performance.

6. The effect of applying LOCM on an individual basis is that those investments whose carrying amount exceeds market value would be carried at the (lower) market value even though the market value of the total portfolio exceeds its cost. The securities affected would be Banks of Midamerica (1990, 1991) and Weyerhauser (1990).

As the portfolio is noncurrent, the writedowns to market would be recorded as components of stockholders' equity and would not affect reported investment income. Only realized gains and losses are recorded in income for noncurrent portfolios.

Mark to market returns are also unaffected by whether LOCM is applied on a portfolio or individual security basis. Mark to market returns are true market returns and are not affected by the choice of accounting method.

7. A. (All data in $ thousands) The change in carrying cost of equity method affiliates is the net effect of the investor's share of the affiliates' net income (or loss) and the dividends received. The carrying value of Atwood Oceanics declined by $1,664 ($26,341 − $24,677) in 1991, and by $4,957 ($24,677 − $19,720) in 1992. Since Atwood does not pay dividends, these amounts must be the losses (prior to HP's tax provision) for those years. But HP's income statement reports (net-of-tax) losses of $1,540 and $4,585 respectively. The difference must be HP's tax provision:

1991: $1664 − $1540 = $124 $124/$1664 = 7.45%
1992: $4957 − $4585 = $372 $372/$4957 = 7.50%

B. The tax rates computed in part A suggest that HP has assumed that the reinvested earnings of Atwood would eventually be received as dividends qualifying for the dividends-received credit. As HP's other equity method affiliate, Baruch-Foster, was sold in 1991, the dividend assumption (and the resulting lower tax rate) may prove incorrect. If HP sold Atwood it is likely that the taxable profit would exceed the pretax (financial reporting basis) profit.

If HP assumed sale of Atwood, it would have computed deferred taxes using a normal corporate tax rate of 34%. On that basis, after tax losses from Atwood would have been:

1990: .66 x $1664 = $1098
1991: .66 x $4957 = $3272

Note that the deferred tax debits recognized by HP will offset deferred tax credits recognized in earlier years when Atwood was profitable. The sale assumption produces a smaller loss in years of losses but reports lower income during profitable periods.

C.   The differing tax rate (dividends-received versus sale assumption) may be the reason for separate reporting; reporting equity earnings on a pretax basis would result in a distorted effective tax rate.

8.   A.   Exhibit 11S-1 presents the December 31, 1988-89 Balance Sheets for Moore Motors using the equity method of accounting for MMF.

      B.   Exhibit 11S-2 provides Income Statements of Moore Motors for the years ended December 31, 1988-1989 using the equity method for MMF.

      C.   **1989 Ratios:**

	Consolidated	Equity Method	MMF
Receivables turnover*	1.16	6.06	N/A
Interest coverage	1.73	8.02	1.20
Debt/equity	2.55	0.18	11.16
Gross profit margin	14.27	14.27	N/A
ROA	5.93	5.16	6.25
ROE	11.68	11.68	14.76

N/A = Not applicable
*Average trade and finance receivables used in this ratio.

      D.   **Receivables turnover:** Consolidated statements are the most informative (specifically from the perspective of the parent's stockholders) since they include all receivables generated by the firm, unlike the equity method wherein the receivables sold to MMF are excluded from the analysis. Note the large difference in the ratio due to this exclusion.

Interest coverage: Again, the parent's stockholders are best served by the consolidated ratio that reflects the total cost of amounts borrowed whether the debt is reported on MMF's books or those of the parent. The equity method excludes the subsidiary's interest expense as it reports only the parent's share of the net income of its subsidiary. The level and trend of MMF's interest coverage are also useful to examine since the firm's ability to satisfy its debt covenants is an important determinant of its borrowing costs and its ability to borrow in the future.

Debt/equity: The consolidated ratio is the most informative as it reflects the debt of the parent as well as that of its affiliate, MMF. The equity method ratio is misleadingly low as it excludes the debt of MMF. The leverage indicated by the MMF ratio is another useful indicator of its borrowing costs and financial risk. MMF's interest coverage and debt/equity ratios are relevant to the parent's creditors, its stockholders, and MMF's lenders.

Gross profit margin: The consolidated and equity method statements report the same gross profit margin.

Exhibit 11S-1
Moore Motors--Equity Method
($ thousands)
Balance Sheets, December 31, 1988-1989

	1988	1989
Cash and equivalent	$ 6,909	$ 7,070
Accounts receivable--trade	4,541	5,447
--subsidiary	3,515	2,898
Finance receivables	13,246	13,235
Inventories	10,020	10,065
Fixed assets (net)	30,238	32,286
Investment in finance subsidiary	7,271	7,782
Miscellaneous assets	14,908	16,092
Total assets	$ 90,648	$ 94,875
Accounts payable--trade	$ 7,897	$ 7,708
--subsidiary	14,840	14,460
Bank debt	6,255	6,557
Accrued liabilities	21,054	23,847
Accrued income tax	4,930	5,671
Total liabilities	54,976	58,243
Stockholders' equity	35,672	36,632
Total liabilities and equity	$ 90,648	$ 94,875

Exhibit 11S-2
Income Statement, Year Ended December 31, 1989

Sales	$110,448
Equity in finance subsidiary	1,111
Interest income	1,980
Total revenues	$113,539
Cost-of-goods-sold	(94,683)
Selling and administrative	(6,386)
Interest expense	(849)
Depreciation and amortization	(5,664)
Total expenses	(107,582)
Pretax income	5,957
Income tax expense	(1,733)
Net income	$ 4,224

ROA: The ratio based on consolidated statements is the most useful; the equity method ratio is less so because it reports neither the total assets used by the parent and its affiliate nor the total interest expense.

ROE: Because net income and equity are the same under the equity method and consolidation, these methods report the identical ROE. The ratio for MMF indicates how well the affiliate is operated.

ROA and ROE are also useful indicators of the profitability of MMF from the perspective of the parent's lenders, its stockholders and MMF's lenders.

9.   A.   The cash flow consequences of finance or credit receivable transactions are reported as components of investment cash flows. Because MMF's credit receivables are generated by the long-term financing it provides for Moore's customers, i.e., for Moore's essential operating activities, their cash flow consequences should be reported as components of cash flow from operations.

The net cash flow impact of these transactions should be reported as operating cash flows. For the year ended December 31, 1989, the reported operating cash flow of $13,006,000 should be reduced by $5,295,000 (cash inflow of $95,394,000 from liquidation of finance receivables less cash outflow for investment in finance receivables of $100,689,000) for an adjusted operating cash flow of $7,711,000 and adjusted investing cash flow of $9,710,000.

B.   Interest payments of manufacturing and retailing firms should be components of financing cash flows because they reflect firms' leverage choices. The analysis of a firm's ability to generate cash from operations should not be confused by its financing decisions. Interest payments reported by Moore's manufacturing units should therefore be reflected in its financing cash flows. However, interest incurred by MMF is an operating cost and should be considered a component of its operating cash flow.

C.   Exhibit 11S-3 contains the 1989 direct method cash flows of MMF and Moore's manufacturing operations.

D.   Cash flow from MMF to Moore's manufacturing operations $ thousands):

Decrease in intercompany receivables	$(380)
Dividends paid	600
Decrease in intercompany payables	617
Total	$ 837

Note that this computation does not consider the cash flow effects of transactions involving the purchase of and payments for finance receivables. Data required to evaluate these transactions has not been provided in the problem.

E.   The segmentation allows us to separately determine the leverage, profitability, and cash flows generated by the manufacturing unit and the finance operations and to understand the impact of each segment on the consolidated entity. Trends in these critical performance indices can be evaluated in the light of industry and

11-11

Moore Motors--Equity Method
($ thousands)
Statement of Cash Flows, Year Ended December 31, 1989

Indirect Method:

	Moore Motors Finance	Moore Motors (Equity Method)
Net income	$ 1,111	$ 3,713[1]
Depreciation and amortization	1,504	5,664
Δ accounts receivable	---	(906)
Δ inventories	---	(45)
Δ accrued liabilities	(366)	2,793
Δ accrued income taxes	---	741
Δ accounts payable	---	(189)
Δ intercompany receivables	380	(380)
Δ intercompany payables	(617)	617
Miscellaneous operating cash flow	---	(414)
Cash Flow from Operations	$ 2,012	$ 11,594
Net change in fixed assets[2]	(1,645)	(8,065)
Net change in finance receivables[2]	(4,889)	(406)
Cash Flow for Investment	$(6,534)	$ (8,471)
Net change in bank debt[2]	4,993	302
Repurchase of equity	---	(1,474)
New equity issued	---	173
Dividends paid	(600)	(1,963)
Cash Flow for Financing	$ 4,393	$ (2,962)
Net Cash Flow	$ (129)	$ 161

[1]Net income less equity in earnings of finance subsidiary plus dividends received.

[2]Only net entries possible from data provided.

Direct Method:

Sales	$ 110,448	
Δ accounts receivable	(906)	
Cash collections		$ 109,542
Cost-of-goods-sold	(94,683)	
Δ inventories	(45)	
Δ accounts payable	(189)	
Cash inputs		(94,917)
Selling and administrative	(6,386)	
Δ accrued liabilities	2,793	
Cash administration		(3,593)
Interest expense		(849)
Interest income		1,980
Dividend from MMF		600
Miscellaneous operating cash flow		(414)
Income tax expense	(1,733)	
Δ accrued income tax	741	
Income taxes paid		(992)
Δ intercompany receivable		(380)
Δ payables		617
Cash Flow from Operations		$ 11,594

Moore Motors Finance
Direct Method:

Finance Revenues	$ 14,504	
Δ finance receivables	(4,889)	
Cash collections		$ 9,615
Interest expense	(7,908)	
Cash inputs		(7,908)
Net cash collections		$ 1,707
Selling and administrative	(3,540)	
Δ accrued liabilities	(366)	
Cash administration		(3,906)
Income tax expense		(441)
Δ intercompany receivable		380
Δ intercompany payables		(617)
Cash Flow from Operations[1]		$ (2,877)

[1]Cash flow from operations reported under the indirect method is $2,012. The difference of $4,889 [$2,012 - ($2,877)] results from reclassification of the change in finance receivables from investment to operating cash flow.

economic conditions affecting manufacturing operations and those influencing the financing business.

10. A. Given Coke's 49% ownership of Enterprises, the board of directors representation, and the licensor/supplier relationship, clearly Coke is not a passive investor. Purchases from Coke account for nearly 40% of Enterprises' cost-of-goods-sold (Exhibit 11P-3). These close relationships suggest that either full consolidation or proportionate consolidation would be a more appropriate method of accounting, reflecting the effective control by Coke.

The FASB has discussed the use of economic control as the basis for consolidation policy - such a standard would most likely require consolidation of Enterprises by Coke given the extensive operational and managerial influence wielded by Coke. International standards would, in some cases, produce significantly different financial statements, e.g., French GAAP requires consolidation if ownership exceeds 40% and there are no other significant blocks of ownership.

The difference between these two methods is significant. Under consolidation, the financial statements of Coke includes 100% of the assets, liabilities, revenues, expenses, and cash flows of Enterprises. The minority interest account shows the (net) interest in the equity and earnings held by the non-Coke stockholders of Enterprises. Proportionate consolidation, on the other hand, includes only 49% of the assets, liabilities, revenues, expenses, and cash flows of Enterprises in the financial statements of Coke.

Full consolidation may, therefore, overstate the degree to which Coke is responsible for the liabilities of Enterprises. It also overstates the contribution of Enterprises' revenues, expenses, and cash flows to the operations of the total entity. On the other hand, it is unlikely that Coke would allow such an operationally significant affiliate to suffer financial distress.

Proportionate consolidation, on the other hand, may understate the influence of Enterprises. Like other stockholders, Coke is a residual owner. Before it can receive any return on its investment in Enterprises, *all* of the latter company's liabilities must be satisfied. Coke's Statement of Cash Flows reports its proportionate share of the cash flows generated by Enterprises. However, since creditors often have a senior claim on these cash flows, Coke's proportionately consolidated cash flow statement can be misleading.

11. A. [See Exhibits 11S-4 through 11S-6]

Exhibit 11S-4 depicts a proportionate consolidation of the two companies' balance sheet as of December 31, 1990, i.e., 49% of the assets and liabilities of Enterprises have been added to Coke's assets and liabilities.

Two eliminations are required. First, Coke's $667 million investment in Enterprises must be eliminated. This amount is slightly different from 49% of Enterprises' common equity ($675 million), probably due to rounding error, adjustments on Coke's books for deferred taxes, or advances from Coke to Enterprises. As in other consolidations, the net investment is replaced by (in this case 49% of) each asset and liability of the investee company.

11-14

Exhibit 11S-4
Proportionate Consolidation
Coca-Cola/Coca-Cola Enterprises
Balance Sheet, 12-31-90
($ millions)

	Coca-Cola	100% Coca-Cola Enterprises	49% Coca-Cola Enterprises	Elim.	Proportionate Consolidation
Cash + marketable securities	$ 1,492	$ 1	$ 0	$ 0	$ 1,492
Accounts receivable - trade	914	297	145	(10)	1,049
" finance subsidiaries	38	0	0	0	38
Inventories	982	128	63	0	1,045
Prepaids	717	69	34	0	751
Current assets	$ 4,143	$ 495	$ 242	$ (10)	$ 4,375
Investment--Enterprises	667	0	0	(667)	0
--Other bottlers	1,358	0	0	0	1,358
Finance receivables--other	450	106	52	0	502
Property, plant & equip.	2,385	1,373	673	0	3,058
Intangible assets	275	3,047	1,493	0	1,768
Total assets	$ 9,278	$ 5,021	$ 2,460	$ (677)	$11,061
Accounts payable	$ 1,576	$ 457	$ 224	$ 0	$ 1,800
Accounts payable--Coke		21	10	(10)	0
Current debt	2,001	577	283	0	2,284
Accrued taxes	719	0	0	0	719
Current liabilities	$ 4,296	$ 1,055	$ 517	$ (10)	$ 4,803
Long-term debt	536	1,960	960	0	1,496
Deferred taxes	265	335	164	0	429
Other liabilities	332	44	22	0	354
Preferred equity	0	250	122	0	122
Common equity	3,849	1,377	675	(667)	3,857
Total liabilities & equity	$ 9,278	$ 5,021	$ 2,460	$ (677)	$11,061

	Coca-Cola	100% Coca-Cola Enterprises	49% Coca-Cola Enterprises	Elim.	Propor-tionate Consoli-dation
Cash + marketable securities	$ 1,182	$ 10	$ 5	$ 0	$ 1,187
Accounts receivable - trade	768	297	145	(25)	888
" finance subsidiaries	52	0	0	0	52
Inventories	789	128	63	0	852
Prepaids	812	59	29	0	841
Current assets	$ 3,603	$ 494	$ 242	$ (25)	$ 3,820
Investment--Enterprises	695	0	0	(695)	0
--Other bottlers	1,731	73	36	0	1,767
Property, plant & equip.	2,021	1,286	630	0	2,651
Intangible assets	232	2,879	1,411	0	1,643
Total assets	$ 8,282	$ 4,732	$ 2,319	$ (720)	$ 9,881
Accounts payable	$ 1,387	$ 395	$ 194	$ 0	$ 1,581
Accounts payable--Coke	0	52	25	(25)	0
Current debt	1,432	549	269	0	1,701
Accrued taxes	839	0	0	0	839
Current liabilities	$ 3,658	$ 996	$ 488	$ (25)	$ 4,121
Long-term debt	549	1,756	861	0	1,410
Deferred taxes	296	266	130	0	426
Other liabilities	294	34	17	0	311
Preferred equity	0	250	122	0	122
Common equity	3,485	1,430	701	(695)	3,491
Total liabilities & equity	$ 8,282	$ 4,732	$ 2,319	$ (720)	$ 9,881

	Coca-Cola	100% Coca-Cola Enterprises	49% Coca-Cola Enterprises	Elim.	Proportionate Consolidation
Revenues	$ 10,236	$ 4,034	$ 1,977	$ (191) (1,052)	$ 10,970
COGS	(4,209)	(2,359)	(1,156)	1,052	(4,313)
Gross profit	$ 6,027	$ 1,675	$ 821	$ (191)	$ 6,657
Selling & general	(4,076)	(1,349)	(661)	191	(4,546)
Operating income	$ 1,951	$ 326	$ 160	$ 0	$ 2,111
Interest income	170	6	3	0	173
Interest expense	(231)	(207)	(102)	0	(333)
Eqty. in income of affiliates	110	0	0	(38)	72
Other income	14	59	29	0	43
Pretax income	$ 2,014	$ 184	$ 90	$ (38)	$ 2,066
Income tax	(632)	(91)	(44)	0	(676)
Net income	$ 1,382	$ 93	$ 46	$ (38)	$ 1,390
Preferred dividends	(18)	(16)	(8)	0	(26)
Net avail. for common	$ 1,364	$ 77	$ 38	$ (38)	$ 1,364

Second, we must eliminate $10 million (49% of $21 million) of intercompany indebtedness, which can be found in the balance sheet of Enterprises. Coke does not show a receivable from Enterprises; we assume that it is included in accounts receivable--trade.

Exhibit 11S-5 contains a proportionate consolidation of balance sheets as of December 31, 1989. The principles are the same as for 1990. Again we eliminate Coke's $695 million investment in Enterprises and the $25 million (49% of $52 million) payable from Enterprises to Coke.

Exhibit 11S-6 provides an income statement after proportionate consolidation for the year ended December 31, 1990. For each item of revenue and expense, 49% of the Enterprises account is added to the corresponding Coke account.

There are three sets of eliminations. First, we eliminate intercompany revenues and expenses, using data obtained from the footnotes of Enterprises. These are calculated as follows:

Purchases from Coke	$ 920 million
Sales to Coke	132
Total intercompany revenues	$ 1,052 million

This total must be eliminated from consolidated revenues and cost-of-goods-sold, since the revenues (COGS) of Coke are identical to the COGS (revenues) of Enterprises.

Next we must eliminate intercompany payments for marketing and reimbursement of legal costs, as follows:

Marketing payments from Coke	$ 186 million
Reimbursements from Coke	5
Total intercompany payments	$ 191 million

We assume that these amounts are included in and eliminated from the revenue of Enterprises and S,G,&A Expense for Coke. The third elimination is Coke's equity in the earnings of Enterprises. We have now included Coke's share of each revenue and expense line of Enterprises' income statement and have implicitly included Coke's share of the net income. To eliminate double counting we must eliminate Coke's recognition of its share of earnings under the equity method.

B.   **1990 Ratios**

		Equity Method Coca-Cola	Enter-prises	Propor-tionate Consoli-dation
(i)	Debt/equity	.66	1.56	.95
	Debt/tangible equity	.71	NMF	1.71
(ii)	Times interest earned	9.72	1.89	7.20
(iii)	Inventory turnover	4.75	18.43	4.55
(iv)	Receivable turnover	12.17	13.58	11.33
(v)	Gross profit margin	58.9%	41.5%	60.7%
(vi)	Return on sales	13.5%	2.3%	12.7%
(vii)	Return on assets	17.5%	4.7%	15.3%
(viii)	Return on equity	37.7%	5.6%	36.6%

C.   Virtually all of Coke's ratios are adversely affected by the inclusion of Enterprises on a proportionate consolidation basis. Enterprises is much more leveraged and as it has negative tangible equity, the consolidated ratio of funded debt (short and long-term) to tangible equity is especially impacted. Both inventory turnover (COGS/average inventory) and receivable turnover (sales/average trade receivables) are also worse after consolidation despite Enterprises' higher ratios. The elimination of "double counting" explains this surprising result. After eliminations, Enterprises increases proportionately consolidated sales by only 7% but receivables by 15%, thus lowering the turnover ratio.

Enterprises' income based ratios are also greatly inferior to those of Coke. Times interest earned (EBIT/interest expense) is especially low and the consolidated amount is well below that of Coke. Return on total capital (EBIT/average total capital) and return on total equity (net income/average total equity) are also low for Enterprises as compared with Coke. Curiously, on consolidation the impact is relatively small. Because of the elimination entries, Enterprises dilutes Coke's superior return on total capital only modestly. Enterprises' high leverage offsets most of that dilution resulting in return on equity which is virtually the same as Coke under the equity method.

Nonetheless the consolidated statements are less favorable to Coke than those prepared using the equity method.

12.   A.   Full consolidation requires the elimination of all intercompany transactions and the addition of 100% of the assets and liabilities of Enterprises to Coke's balance sheet and 100% of all the revenues and expenses of Enterprises to Coke's income statement. However, since Coke owns only 49% of Enterprises, we must also recognize that 51% of the assets, liabilities, revenues, and expenses are owned by other stockholders.

This is accomplished using "minority interest" accounts on the balance sheet and the income statement. On the former, the minority interest represents the 51% of the net assets of Enterprises owned by non-Coke stockholders. Exhibits 11S-7 and 11S-8 contain the fully consolidated balance sheets for Coke and Enterprises as of December 31, 1990 (1989).

Exhibit 11S-7
Consolidation
Coca-Cola/Coca-Cola Enterprises
Balance Sheet, 12-31-90

($ millions)	Equity Method Coca-Cola	Coca-Cola Enter- prises	Elimina- tions	Consoli- dated
Cash + mrktbl. securities	$ 1,492	$ 1	$ 0	$ 1,493
Accounts receivable - trade	914	297	(21)	1,190
" finance subs.	38	0	0	38
Inventories	982	128	0	1,110
Prepaids	717	69	0	786
Current assets	$ 4,143	$ 495	$ (21)	$ 4,617
Investment--Enterprises	667	0	(667)	0
--Other bottlers	1,358	0	0	1,358
Finance receivables--other	450	106	0	556
Property, plant & equip.	2,385	1,373	0	3,758
Intangible assets	275	3,047	0	3,322
Total assets	$ 9,278	$ 5,021	$ (688)	$13,611
Accounts payable	$ 1,576	$ 457	$ 0	$ 2,033
Accounts payable--Coke	0	21	(21)	0
Current debt	2,001	577	0	2,578
Accrued taxes	719	0	0	719
Current liabilities	$ 4,296	$ 1,055	$ (21)	$ 5,330
Long-term debt	536	1,960	0	2,496
Deferred taxes	265	335	0	600
Other liabilities	332	44	0	376
Minority interest	0	0	710	710
Preferred equity	0	250	0	250
Common equity	3,849	1,377	(1,377)	3,849
Total liab. & equity	$ 9,278	$ 5,021	$ (688)	$13,611

($ millions)	Equity Method Coca-Cola	Coca-Cola Enter-prises	Elimina-tions	Consoli-dated
Cash + mktbl. securities	$ 1,182	$ 10	$ 0	$ 1,192
Accounts receivable - trade	768	297	(52)	1,013
" finance subs.	52	0	0	52
Inventories	789	128	0	917
Prepaids	812	59	0	871
Current assets	$ 3,603	$ 494	$ (52)	$ 4,045
Investment--Enterprises	695	0	(695)	0
--Other bottlers	1,731	73	0	1,804
Property, plant & equip.	2,021	1,286	0	3,307
Intangible assets	232	2,879	0	3,111
Total assets	$ 8,282	$ 4,732	$ (747)	$12,267
Accounts payable	$ 1,387	$ 395	$ 0	$ 1,782
Accounts payable--Coke	0	52	(52)	0
Current debt	1,432	549	0	1,981
Accrued taxes	839	0	0	839
Current liabilities	$ 3,658	$ 996	$ (52)	$ 4,602
Long-term debt	549	1,756	0	2,305
Deferred taxes	296	266	0	562
Other liabilities	294	34	0	328
Minority interest	0	0	735	735
Preferred equity	0	250	0	250
Common equity	3,485	1,430	(1,430)	3,485
Total liab. & equity	$ 8,282	$ 4,732	$ (747)	$12,267

Similarly, "minority interest in income of affiliates" reflects 51% of the net income of Enterprises accruing to its non-Coke owners. Exhibit 11S-9 depicts a fully consolidated income statement for the year ended December 31, 1990.

Exhibit 11S-9
Consolidation
Coca-Cola/Coca-Cola Enterprises
Income Statement, Year Ended 12-31-90
($ millions)

($ millions)	Equity Method Coca-Cola	Coca-Cola Enter-prises	Elimina-tions	Consoli-dated
Revenues	$ 10,236	$ 4,034	$ (191) (1,052)	$ 13,027
COGS	(4,209)	(2,359)	1,052	(5,516)
Gross profit	$ 6,027	$ 1,675	$ (191)	$ 7,511
Selling & general	(4,076)	(1,349)	191	(5,234)
Operating income	$ 1,951	$ 326	$ 0	$ 2,277
Interest income	170	6	0	176
Interest expense	(231)	(207)	0	(438)
Equity in income of affiliates	110	0	(38)	72
Other income	14	59	0	73
Pretax income	$ 2,014	$ 184	$ (38)	$ 2,160
Income tax	(632)	(91)	0	(723)
Net income	$ 1,382	$ 93	$ (38)	$ 1,437
Minority interest	0	0	(39)	(39)
Preferred dividends	(18)	(16)	0	(34)
Net avail. for common	$ 1,364	$ 77	$ (77)	$ 1,364

B.   1990 Ratios

		Coca-Cola	Enter-prises	Full Consoli-dation
(i)	Debt/equity	.66	1.56	1.24
	Debt/tangible equity	.71	NMF	6.57
(ii)	Times interest earned	9.72	1.89	5.93
(iii)	Inventory turnover	4.75	18.43	5.41
(iv)	Receivable turnover	12.17	13.58	11.18
(v)	Gross profit margin	58.9%	41.5%	52.7%
(vi)	Return on sales	13.5%	2.3%	11.0%
(vii)	Return on assets	17.5%	4.7%	13.3%
(viii)	Return on equity [(Net income - minority interest)/ (average equity - minority interest)]	37.7%	5.6%	35.7%
	Return on equity [Net income/average equity (including minority interest)]			30.9%

C.   Full consolidation depicts the impact of all of the debt of
     Enterprises whereas the equity method showed none and proportionate
     consolidation included only 49% of the leverage. The effect can be
     seen clearly in the debt/equity ratio and even more in the
     debt/tangible equity ratio (100% of the intangible assets of
     Enterprises have been deducted from equity). The times interest
     earned ratio is even lower than that under proportionate
     consolidation because 100% of the interest expense is included in
     full consolidation.

     The low inventory carried by Enterprises increases the fully
     consolidated inventory turnover ratio slightly from that of Coke
     alone. On the other hand, its low gross margins dilute the higher
     gross margins shown by Coke. The receivables turnover is marginally
     lower as full consolidation adds relatively more receivables than
     sales. Profitability ratios are also slightly worse off relative to
     proportionate consolidation which showed lower ratios than the
     equity method.

     The lowest ratio (30.9%) is reported when we compare total
     income to total equity, i.e., before deducting minority interest
     from both the numerator and the denominator. The equity method
     presents the profitability in the most favorable light (37.7%)
     followed by proportionate consolidation (36.6%), then a fully
     consolidated ratio based on reported net income (less minority
     interest) divided by equity less minority interest (35.7%).

     In the leverage ratios, the minority interest has not been
     included in either debt or equity. However, since minority holders
     have a residual interest in the firm, it may be considered as a
     component of equity improving the debt/equity ratio to 1.05. The
     minority interest can also be regarded as equivalent to preferred
     stock and as such its inclusion in debt or equity depends on the
     specific objectives of the analysis.

13. A. The absence of current/noncurrent classifications makes all working capital based calculations impossible. It also means that liquidity ratios that depend on components of current liabilities (especially current debt maturities) cannot be calculated.

Another issue is whether ratio norms computed for manufacturing or retailing entities (without finance subsidiaries) have any usefulness when applied to entities with these operations.

B. Times interest earned = EBIT/interest expense

	1991	1990
Consolidated*	$700.7/$450.0 = 1.56	$1022.7/$435.2 = 2.35
Equipment operations	$185.5/$192.7 = 0.96	$603.9/$192.7 = 3.13

*Before restructuring costs

C. The problem with Deere's consolidated times interest earned ratio is that interest is, to a large extent, an operating expense rather than a financing expense. Interest income on customer receivables is balanced by interest expense on debt incurred to finance these receivables. [In reality, it is the spread between the rates received and paid that is important for analysis.]

Given that the purpose of the times interest earned ratio is to measure how well income covers required interest payments, there is a strong argument for excluding both the interest earned on customer receivables and the interest paid to finance them from the calculation of this ratio.

14. A. (All data in $ thousands) Nucor's minority interest rose by $18,607 ($124,048 - $105,441) in 1991. This increase must reflect the minority interest in income and capital contributions or distributions during the year. Given distributions of $7,507, the minority interest in 1991 income must be:

Change in minority interest = 1991 income   - distributions
            $18,607   =   ?   - $7,507

Therefore: ?   = $18,607 + $7,507 = $26,114

This number represents the 49% of the 1991 net income of the joint venture that accrues to the minority shareholder rather than to Nucor.

B. Dividing the data provided by .49 results in 100% of the 1991 net income and 1990 - 1991 equity of the joint venture:

1991 net income = $26,114/.49 = $ 53,294
12-31-90 equity = $105,441/.49 = $215,186
12-31-91 equity = $124,048/.49 = $253,159

1991 return on (average) equity equals:

$53,294/$234,172 = 22.8%

Note that the ROE can also be computed directly from the minority interest data:

$$\$26,114/\$114,744 = 22.8\%$$

C.   This issue mainly depends on how the joint venturers are responsible for the liabilities of the venture. If each party is responsible only for its share of joint venture debt, there is a strong argument for reflecting only that portion of the debt on Nucor's balance sheet (and only its share of the assets as well).

D.   (i)   From the point of view of Nucor management, proportionate consolidation would have two advantages. First, it would hide the profitability of the joint venture, as the analysis is part B would no longer be possible. This may be a competitive advantage. The second advantage is that reported debt and debt based ratios are lower under proportionate consolidation. The only possible disadvantage is that reported sales and assets are also lower under proportionate consolidation.

     (ii) From the point of view of a financial analyst, full consolidation is better in that the analysis in part A can determine the profitability of the joint venture and thus help the analyst understand the source of Nucor earnings.

15. A.   (i)   **Operating profit margin**

	1990	1991	1992
Chemicals	8.7%	11.3%	14.6%
Food	10.0	12.0	12.9
Aerospace	6.0	(0.4)	8.3
Materials	(4.4)	0.8	4.8

     (ii) **Return on assets**

	1990	1991	1992
Chemicals	11.1%	17.0%	23.8%
Food	12.4	12.8	15.1
Aerospace	8.3	(0.4)	8.5
Materials	(4.3)	0.7	4.3

     (iii) **Asset turnover**

	1990	1991	1992
Chemicals	1.28X	1.50X	1.63X
Food	1.25	1.07	1.17
Aerospace	1.38	1.04	1.02
Materials	0.98	0.88	0.90

(iv) **Capital expenditures to depreciation**

	1990	1991	1992
Chemicals	1.60X	1.43X	1.08X
Food	1.26	1.61	1.31
Aerospace	1.16	0.61	0.28
Materials	1.85	1.05	0.62

B.   (i)   Operating profit margins have improved for all segments. However we are also interested in knowing why the improvements took place. Rising volume is clearly not the answer as sales have risen only for chemicals segment. Lower costs/ higher productivity must be responsible. The limited data only give us general trends; management can be questioned to obtain details.

(ii) Return on assets also improved for all segments except aerospace. Declining assets and increasing profitability appear to be responsible. We should be concerned, however, about whether lower assets are the result of better turnover or whether Hercules is skimping on new investment.

(iii) Asset turnover increased only for Chemicals; it has declined for Aerospace. Not surprisingly, sales have increased for Chemicals but have declined sharply (1990-91) for Aerospace. Here again, management should be questioned to understand why these trends occurred and whether they are likely to persist.

(iv) The low (and declining) ratio of capital expenditures to depreciation for the Aerospace segment suggests that Hercules is cutting back this segment. Declining sales confirm a poor trend. Does this represent a declining industry or are firm-specific factors at work? The Materials segment has a similar (but not as low) trend. Management should be asked for explanations.

C.   Segment data suffers from limitations that can be severe:

1.   Acquisitions and divestitures distort the comparison of segment data over time as the segment may gain or lose operational components. This problem is discussed in Chapter 12.

2.   Foreign currency rate changes distort the comparison of segments with foreign operations. It is hard to tell whether sales increases, for example, represent higher unit sales or the effect of a declining parent currency. See Chapter 13.

3.   Companies can change segment definitions, limiting the ability to compare segments over time.

4.   Firms can use different segment definitions, making it difficult to compare similar operations that belong to different firms. Variations in accounting methods also hinder the comparison of similar operations in different firms.

D.   One obvious omission is the level of liabilities. Profitability is more usefully measured against net assets. In addition, the contribution of operating and/or financing leverage helps when evaluating profitability.

It is also important to know whether segment comparisons over time are affected by acquisitions or divestitures, exchange rate effects, writeoffs taken in the segment, or other nonoperating factors. The contribution of unit sales changes versus price changes would also be helpful.

Chapter 12 - Solutions

1. **Balance Sheet at June 30, 1992 ($ millions):**

| | Pooling Method | Purchase Method | |
		Pierson Acquires	Drew Acquires
Current assets	$ 130	$ 135	$ 135
Land	70	70	75
Building	120	120	130
Equipment	110	130	120
Goodwill	0	0	380
Total assets	$ 430	$ 455	$ 840
Current liabilities	$ 140	$ 140	$ 140
Long-term debt	90	95	100
Stockholders' equity	200	220	600
Total liabilities and equity	$ 430	$ 455	$ 840

A. Under the pooling method, the *historical cost* balance sheets of Drew (D) and Pierson (P) are aggregated. There is no recognition of the fair value of the acquired firm's assets and liabilities or of the market value of the shares issued in the merger.

B. When Pierson acquires Drew, Pierson's *historical cost* balance sheet is added to Drew's *fair value* balance sheet. The market value of the shares issued (6 million x $20 = $120 million) is added to the (historical cost) equity of Pierson. The cost of the acquisition ($120 million) is compared with the fair value of the net assets of Drew acquired ($175 - $35 = $140). As the fair value is greater, the write up to market value of Drew's noncurrent assets is limited; they are reported at $40 rather than their fair value of $60. Goodwill would be recognized if the cost of the acquisition exceeded the fair value.

C. This case is the reverse of B. As Drew is the acquirer, its historical cost balance sheet is combined with the fair value balance sheet of Pierson. Once again the value of the shares issued (25 million shares @ $20 = $500 million) is compared with the fair value of the net assets acquired ($330 - $210). The total price paid, $500 million, exceeds the market value of Pierson's assets by $380 million. Thus, all of Pierson's assets are written up to market value and goodwill of $380 million is recognized.

D. Pro Forma Combined Income Statements ($ millions)

Years ended December 31	1991	1992	1993
(i) Pooling of interests method:	P+D	P+D	P+D
Sales	$450	$480	$512
Operating expenses	(375)	(400)	(427)
Interest expense	(9)	(9)	(9)
Pretax income	$ 66	$ 71	$ 76
Income tax expense	(26)	(28)	(30)
Net income	$ 40	$ 43	$ 46
Average shares	31	31	31
Earnings per share	$1.29	$1.39	$1.48

Under pooling, the income statements of Drew and Pierson are aggregated, without adjustment, for both the periods prior to the merger and the periods thereafter. Similarly, the 6 million shares issued to effect the merger are considered outstanding from the beginning of 1991.

	1991	1992	1993
(ii) Pierson acquires Drew:	P	P+.5D	P+D
Sales	$300	$398	$512
Operating expenses	(240)	(329)	(432)
Interest expense	(8)	(8)	(8)
Pretax income	$ 52	$ 61	$ 72
Income tax expense	(20)	(24)	(29)
Net income	$ 32	$ 37	$ 43
Average shares	25	28	31
Earnings per share	$1.28	$1.42	$1.39

Under the purchase method, the results of the acquired firm (Drew) are included only after the merger date. Thus 1991 results are those of Pierson alone; 1992 includes Drew for the period July 1 - December 31; 1993 includes Drew for the entire year. We assume that Drew's 1992 sales and earnings were spread evenly through the year.

In addition, the expenses of Drew must be adjusted to reflect the income statement effects of the purchase method adjustments. These are:

(a) Current assets are $5 million above historical cost; we assume that this reflects inventory. As the written up inventory is sold, COGS will reflect this higher valuation. We assume that $2 million is included in 1992, and the remainder in 1993.

(b) Equipment was written up by $20 million. Assuming a 10 year life, depreciation would increase by $2 million per year ($1 million for the second half of 1992). For a real company we would use the relationship between depreciation and gross carrying value (using schedule V and VI data) to estimate the actual depreciable life of these assets.

(c) Long-term debt was revalued from $10 to $15 million, reflecting current interest rates that were below stated rates. This premium must be amortized over the remaining life of the debt. We assume that amortization subtracts $0.5 million from 1992 interest expense and $1 million from 1992 interest expense.

These adjustments to Drew's income statement increase expenses by $2.5 million (1992) and $4 million (1993) above their amounts assuming no acquisition. These increases are also tax deductible so that income tax expense increases (we assume a 34% tax rate).

Finally, the 6 million shares issued to acquire Drew are assumed outstanding only for the period following the merger. For 1992, they are outstanding only for one-half year.

Years ended December 31	1991	1992	1993
(iii) Drew acquires Pierson:	**D**	**D+.5P**	**D+P**
Sales	$150	$323	$512
Operating expenses	(135)	(286)	(441)
Interest expense	(1)	(5)	(8)
Pretax income	$ 14	$ 32	$ 63
Income tax expense	(6)	(14)	(25)
Net income	$ 8	$ 18	$ 38
Average shares	6	18.5	31
Earnings per share	$1.33	$0.97	$1.23

When Drew acquires Pierson, the latter's operating results are included only for the period following the merger while Drew's results are reported for the entire period. Thus 1991 consists of Drew alone, 1992 of Drew (entire year) plus Pierson for the second half, and 1993 includes both.

Again the purchase method generates income statement effects but now they are based on the fair values of Pierson's assets:

(a)   Again we assume that the current assets adjustment relates to inventories, with the $5 million write up reflected in income in 1992 ($2 million) and 1992 ($3 million).

(b)   For equipment we again assume a ten year life. For buildings we assume a twenty year life. Note that the write up of land does not impact reported income as land is not depreciated. Goodwill is amortized over 40 years.

(c)   Again debt has been revalued upward due to lower interest rates. We assume that amortization is $0.50 million for 1992 and $1.00 million for 1993.

(d)   Tax expense is again affected by the expense adjustments. Note that goodwill amortization is not deductible for taxes.

(e)   Average shares must be adjusted to reflect the 25 million shares issued to acquire Pierson; they are assumed outstanding only for half of 1992. Drew's outstanding shares must be adjusted for all periods to reflect the reverse stock split.

E. Ratios under all three assumptions:

Debt-to-equity at June 30, 1992:
    Pooling of interests $90/$200 = 0.45X
    Pierson acquires Drew $95/$220 = 0.43
    Drew acquires Pierson $100/$600 = 0.17

Book value per share at June 30, 1992:
    Pooling of interests $200/31 = $ 6.45
    Pierson acquires Drew $220/31 = 7.10
    Drew acquires Pierson $600/31 = 19.35

Interest coverage:	1991	1992	1993
Pooling of interests	8.33X	8.89X	9.44X
Pierson acquires Drew*	7.50	8.62	10.00
Drew acquires Pierson*	15.00	7.40	8.87

Return on total capital (June 30, 1992 capital for all years):

	1991	1992	1993
Pooling of interests	25.9%	27.6%	29.3%
Pierson acquires Drew*	33.3	21.9	25.4
Drew acquires Pierson*	13.6	5.3	10.1

Return on equity (June 30, 1992 equity for all years):

	1991	1992	1993
Pooling of interests	20.0%	21.5%	23.0%
Pierson acquires Drew*	32.0	16.8	19.5
Drew acquires Pierson*	8.0	3.0	6.3

*1991 return computed for acquirer only.

F. (i)

	Growth in reported sales	Growth in EPS
Pooling	13.8%	14.7%
Pierson acquires	70.7%	8.6%
Drew acquires	241.3%	(7.5)%

The pooling method reports lower sales growth since it assumes that the two firms had always operated as a single entity even prior to the acquisition. The growth in EPS partly reflects the addition of faster growing Drew. The purchase method distorts the revenue growth rate as it adds the acquired firm only from the acquisition date. When Pierson acquires Drew, reported sales growth increases as 50% of the revenues of Drew is added in 1992 and 100% is added in 1993. The sales growth rate is even higher when we assume that Drew has acquired Pierson because the former is only half the size of Pierson, providing a very low base for the period evaluated.

The purchase method requires the amortization of the excess of fair market value over the historical cost of the acquired firm. Pierson's acquisition of Drew results in a higher EPS than Drew's acquisition of Pierson because it paid less than fair value for Drew and the latter's fixed assets are not written up to their full market value, generating lower amortization costs compared to Drew's acquisition of Pierson. In that scenario, Pierson's assets are written up to their full market value, resulting in higher expenses on the postmerger income statement. The amortization of substantial

12-4

goodwill recognized also lowers reported income and, therefore, results in a significant decline in earnings per share.

(ii) The financial condition of the combined firm is not significantly affected in this case because equity was used rather than debt or cash. The recognition of fair market values improves reported liquidity ratios while reflecting higher risk as the debt has been written up. If Pierson and Drew are diversified, their combination may produce a more stable firm allowing them to improve their financial condition. Given the lower profitability of Drew, equity holders in Pierson are not as well off post-acquisition regardless of the method used.

G. (i) When the pooling of interests method is used, the merger has no reported cash flow effect at the merger date. For accounting purposes there has been no transaction.

Under the purchase method, cash for investment would normally reflect the amount paid for an acquisition. In this case, payment is entirely in common shares, and there is no cash flow to report. The details of the acquisition would be reported elsewhere in the financial statements.

(ii) When the pooling method is used, the cash flow statements of the two firms are combined (with no change) for the periods before and after the merger. Assuming that the merger is tax-free, the cash flow statement is not affected by the merger.

When the purchase method is used, however, the cash flow statement of the acquiring firm includes the cash flows of the acquired firm only following the merger date, similar to the way income statements are combined. Reported cash flows would not be affected by the purchase method adjustments, as these have no cash flow impact except on tax payments. Thus income taxes paid and, therefore, CFO would vary from those reported if there had been no merger.

2. Philip Morris would purchase Kraft for $10.8 billion ($90 x 120 million). This amount would be added to long-term debt, increasing interest expense by $1,188 million (11% x $10.8 billion). The excess purchase price over book value of Kraft would be treated as goodwill, and its amortization over forty years would be:

$$(\$10,800 - \$1,920)/40 = \$222 \text{ million annually.}$$

Interest expense would be tax deductible, reducing taxes paid by $499 million (using Philip Morris' tax rate of 42%). However, goodwill amortization would not reduce taxes paid. Cash flow from operations would be reduced by the additional interest expense less the associated tax reduction ($1188 - $499 = $689 million).

The Merged Company (Pro Forma) data follow ($ millions):

Common shares	234	[Kraft purchased for cash]
Long-term debt	$16,300	[$4700 + $800 + $10,800]
Stockholders' equity	7,394	[Kraft equity eliminated]
EBIT	$ 4,914	[$4340 + $796 − $222]
Interest expense	(1,744)	[$475 + $81 + $1188]
Pretax income	$ 3,170	
Income tax expense	(1,403)	[$1623 + $279 − $499]
Net income	$ 1,767	
Cash from operations	$ 2,892	[$2974 + $607 − $1188 + 499]
Capital expenditures	1,110	[$850 + $260]
Dividends paid	$ 892	[No change]
Earnings per share	$ 7.55	[$1767/234]
Debt to equity	2.20	[$16,300/$7394]
Times interest earned	2.82	[$4914/$1744]

EPS and the debt/equity and TIE ratios have all deteriorated as a result of the acquisition. EPS and TIE are lower because of higher interest expense and the amortization of goodwill. Leverage is increased by the additional debt of $10.8 billion. However, the combined firm generates significant cash flows from operations that mitigate the decline in the other indicators of financial quality.

3. A. Pro Forma Balance Sheet, June 30, 1990

This is a "what if" calculation to show the impact of the merger on the balance sheet.

First, calculate the value of the transaction: GTE issues 201.93 million shares (1.27 x 159) with a market price of $ 33 = $6,664 million.

Second, estimate the *fair market value* of the assets and liabilities of Contel that are being acquired:

Contel Balance Sheet 6/30/90

($ millions)	Historical Cost	Fair Value
Current assets	$ 847	$ 900
Property	4,819	7,228
Investments and other assets	256	256
Goodwill[1]	1,399	---
Total assets	$ 7,321	$ 8,384
Current liabilities	$ 1,432	$ 1,432
Long-term debt	3,240	3,240
Deferred income taxes[2]	607	---
Other NC liabilities	366	366
Total liabilities	$ 5,645	$ 5,038
Net assets acquired	$ 1,676	$ 3,346

[1]Existing goodwill on Contel's balance sheet is eliminated.

[2]Existing deferred taxes on Contel's balance sheet are eliminated under the assumption that the merger is a purchase for both financial reporting and tax purposes, eliminating prior differences in asset basis.

Based on this data compute the *new* goodwill created by the purchase of Contel:

Value of transaction:	$ 6,664 Million
Fair value of assets acquired:	(3,346)
Goodwill required	$ 3,318

We can now prepare the pro forma balance sheet as of June 30, 1990 ($ Millions):

	GTE	Contel	Adjust.	Pro Forma
Current assets	$ 5,554	$ 847	$ 53	$ 6,454
Property	23,882	4,819	2,409	31,110
Investments	2,600	256	---	2,856
Goodwill	131	1,399	3,318	
			(1,399)	3,449
Total assets	$ 32,167	$ 7,321	$ 4,381	$ 43,869
Current liabilities	$ 5,447	$ 1,432	$ ---	$ 6,879
Long-term debt	11,369	3,240	---	14,609
Deferred income tax	3,860	607	(607)	3,860
Other NC liabilities	2,800	366	---	3,166
Total liabilities	$ 23,476	$ 5,645	$ (607)	$ 28,514
S/H equity[3]	8,691	1,676	6,664	
			(1,676)	15,355
Total	$ 32,167	$ 7,321	$ 4,381	$ 43,869

[3]The existing equity of Contel is eliminated, reflecting the retirement of its shares. The market value of the GTE shares issued in the acquisition becomes additional equity.

B.   Pro Forma Income Statement for 1989

    This is a "what if" computation to show the effect of the merger on reported income. We start with pro forma pretax income assuming use of the pooling method:

		($ Millions)
Pretax income	$ 2,339	
Additional depreciation expense[4]	(241)	
Additional goodwill amortization[5]	(83)	
Adjusted pretax income		$ 2,015
Pro forma income tax expense (pooling)	(743)	
Tax effect of additional depreciation[6]	83	
Adjusted income tax expense		660
Adjusted pro forma net income		$ 1,355
Preferred dividends		(47)
Adjusted net income for common shares		$ 1,308

[4]Assumes property depreciated over ten years ($2409/10 = $241)

[5]Assumes goodwill amortized over forty years ($3318/40 = $83)

[6]Assumes 34% tax rate (241 x .34 = 82). Also assumes that elimination of deferred taxes from balance sheet has no impact on income tax expense. As goodwill amortization is not tax deductible, no tax adjustment is made.

C.   **Postmerger statistics:**

		Pooling		**Purchase**	
(i)	Book value per share[7]	$9903/861	= $11.50	$14891/861	= $17.29
(ii)	Tangible book per share	$8373/861	= 9.72	$11442/861	= $13.29
(iii)	Debt-to-equity	$16339/$10367	= 1.58	$16339/$15355	= 1.06
(iv)	Debt-to-tang. equity	$16339/$8837	= 1.85	$16339/$11906	= 1.37
(v)	1989 earnings per share	(given)	$ 1.80	$1308/861	= $ 1.52
(vi)	1989 interest coverage	($2339+$1359)/$1359	= 2.72	($2048+$1359)/$1359	= 2.51
(vii)	Return on assets	$3698/$39488	= 9.4%	$3374/$43869	= 7.7%
(viii)	Return on tangible assets	$3698/$37958	= 9.7	$3374/$40420	= 8.3
(ix)	Return on equity (T)	$1596/$10367	= 15.4	$1355/$15355	= 8.8
	(C)	$1549/$9903	= 15.6	$1308/$14891	= 8.8
(x)	Return on tang. equity (T)	$1596/$8837	= 18.1	$1355/$11906	= 11.4
	(C)	$1549/$8373	= 18.5	$1308/$11442	= 11.4

    [7]Must subtract preferred equity.
    (T) = Total equity   (C) = Common equity

D.   The purchase method makes balance sheet ratios look better because the market value of the equity issued has been recognized. [When property writeup is significant, even ratios based on tangible equity are improved.] Income statement ratios look worse because of higher depreciation and goodwill amortization. When calculating ratios based on shares, it is important to distinguish between actual shares outstanding on a particular date and average shares for an accounting period.

Purchase method requires restatement of assets and liabilities of Contel to fair market value. As a result property is written up, deferred taxes are eliminated, and goodwill is created. Instead of carrying forward the equity of Contel (pooling), the fair market value of the GTE shares issued is reflected. Assets and net worth are higher, liabilities are reduced.

The income statement is also affected, because of the balance sheet impact of the purchase method. Depreciation and goodwill amortization are higher, income tax expense is reduced. Net income is reduced by 15.6% under our assumptions. Different assumptions about depreciation lives and goodwill amortization periods would affect net income (shorter lives = lower net).

No adjustment was made for the inventory writeup of $53 million. If Contel used LIFO, this amount would remain in inventory indefinitely. If not, it would reduce earnings (temporarily) as it flows through cost-of-goods-sold.

E. If the GTE share price was $1 higher, the purchase price would be higher by $202 million. Goodwill and net worth would each be increased by that amount (we assume that goodwill is increased as all other assets have been written up to fair market value). The additional goodwill would reduce net income by $5 million per year ($202/40). The point of this question is that pro forma financial statements issued prior to a merger are estimates and are subject to actual market prices at the date the merger takes place.

4. **1987-1989 (Pre-1989 poolings)**

| | 1987 | | 1988 | | 1989 |
	Original Report	Pooled	Original Report	Pooled	Reported[#]
Revenues	$ 45,894	$86,771	$ 67,804	$125,584	$165,689
Net income	2,667	5,205	5,329	9,877	11,797
ROE[*]	18.3%	29.2%	22.0%	35.3%	27.3%[@]

[#]Pooled and reported amounts are identical in 1989.
[*]Year-end equity used in 1987; average used for 1988 and 1989.
[@]ROE is 26.1% if the average of pooled 1988 and reported 1989 amounts used in equity.

1987-1989 Percent Change

| | 1987-1988 | | 1988-1989 | | 1987-1989 | |
	Original Report	Pooled	Original Report	Pooled	Original Report	Pooled
Revenues	48%	44%	144%	32%	261%	91%
Net income	100%	90%	121%	19%	342%	127%
ROE	20%	21%	24%	(26%)	49%	(11%)

A. Pooling allowed Allwaste to report substantially higher revenues, net income, and return on equity for 1987-1989. However, the rate of increase in revenues and net income from 1987 to 1988 declines when the 1989 acquisitions are pooled. 1988 return on equity increases more under pooling as income increased faster than equity (the acquired firms had very high ROE). The 1987-1989 comparisons also show substantial declines when the pooled data are compared. Note the decline in ROE from 1988 to 1989, and 1989 relative to 1987.

B.   NOTE: If we assume that acquisitions were made at the end of the year, the purchase method would add the assets, liabilities, revenues, and expenses of the acquired companies only as of that date. We have instead assumed that the acquisitions occurred as of the beginning of the year, impacting sales and earnings for that year. Under either assumption, we must first adjust equity to reflect use of the purchase method rather than pooling.

Market value of shares issued for acquisitions	$ 70,000,000
Stockholders' equity of acquired companies[1]	(4,263,000)
Adjustment to stockholders' equity	$ 65,737,000
Reported equity at August 31, 1989 (pooling)	52,359,000
Adjusted equity at August 31, 1989 (purchase)	$118,096,000

[1]Difference in reported equity between equity reported in the restated 1988 balance sheet ($38,077,000) and that reported in the original 1988 balance sheet, ($33,814,000).

The adjustment to stockholders' equity is the excess of purchase price over the book value of the acquired firms (the goodwill recorded by Allwaste) that must be amortized over 40 years for an annual amortization expense of $1,643,000 ($65,737,000/40). Reported net income in 1989 under the purchase method would be $11,797,000 - $1,643,000 = $10,154,000.

C.   **1987-1989 [Pooling versus Purchase]**

	1987		1988		1989	
	Pooled	**Purchase**	**Pooled**	**Purchase**	**Pooled**	**Purchase**
Revenues	$86,771	$45,894	$125,258	$67,804	$165,689	$165,689
Net income	5,205	2,667	9,877	5,329	11,797	10,154
ROE*	29.2%	18.3%	35.3%	22.0%	26.1%	13.5%

*Year-end equity used in 1987; average used for 1988 and 1989.

1987-1989 Percent Change: Pooling versus Purchase

	1988-1989		1987-1989	
	Pooled	**Purchase**	**Pooled**	**Purchase**
Revenues	32%	144%	91%	261%
Net income	19%	90%	127%	281%
ROE*	(26%)	(39%)	(11%)	(26%)

*Year-end equity used in 1987; average used for 1988 and 1989.

Both net income and ROE are lower for 1989 when the purchase method is used as net income is reduced by amortization expense and equity is increased by the excess of the purchase price over book value of the acquired companies. However, the growth rates of sales and net income are significantly increased as amounts for the acquired firms are added only during the year of the acquisition, as compared to the retroactive adjustment of the pooling method.

Because the purchase method recognizes the market value of equity used in the acquisitions, the decline in ROE is substantial. It now shows the cost of acquiring the earnings of other firms.

D. (i)   Annual amortization expense would be $6,574,000 ($65,737,000/10) if a ten-year life were used. Income and ROE would be lower in the periods following the merger.

    (ii) Only half of the sales, net income, and amortization expense would be added to that of Allwaste in the year of the acquisition. The effect would be to "smooth" the reported growth resulting from the acquisitions as the full effect would be seen only in the following year.

E. (i)   EPS increased from $.16/share (1987) to $.27/share (1988) before the 1989 poolings (an increase of 69%). The acquisitions increased EPS retroactively to $.22/share (1987) and $.35/share (1988), a lower growth rate (60%) than reported previously. The rate of increase in EPS was even less in 1989 (after pooling) as EPS rose to $.40/ share.

          We can compute marginal EPS from the acquisitions by dividing the increase in earnings from restatement with the shares issued:

                1987: ($5205 - $2667)/8616 = $0.29 per share
                1988: ($9877 - $5329)/8616 = $0.53 per share

          For each year, the marginal EPS exceeded EPS prior to restatement, thus illustrating the "bootstrapping" technique discussed in the text. The purchase method, by reducing reported earnings from the acquisition and by precluding restatement, makes "bootstrapping" more difficult.

    (ii) If the purchase method is used, 1989 EPS is $.34/share, compared to $.16/share in 1987 and $.27/share in 1988. While the level of EPS is reduced, the reported growth rate is higher.

    (iii) The method changes the level and trend of EPS with the purchase method reporting lower EPS because it adds amortization expense, income, and shares from the date of acquisition as compared with the retroactive adjustment used in pooling.

          Note the level and trend of ROE discussed in part C above. The impact of acquisitions on ROE is greater than the effect on EPS.

F. (i)   The pooling method requires retroactive restatement of the statement of cash flows for all years presented. The acquisition itself does not affect the statement as shares were issued. If cash were used, financing cash flow would be affected.

(ii)   The purchase method would reflect a financing cash flow of $70 million, representing the issuance of equity to obtain the cash needed to purchase the acquired companies.

(iii) Investing cash flow would report the assets acquired. Cash flow from operations would be affected if the firm changed its level of inventories or receivables following the acquisition.

(iv)   Cash flows following the acquisition year are not affected by the accounting method used (ignoring any income tax effects). However reduced working capital needs may overstate reported cash flow from operations.

5. A. **Derivation of Cole balance sheet at acquisition date:**

	Balance Sheet Change	Cash Flow Change	Difference
Cash	$ 15,714	$ 15,714	$ 0
Marketable securities	72,981	72,476	505
Accounts receivable	43,393	39,999	3,394
Prepaid expenses	(5,696)	(7,925)	2,229
Property	43,366	30,701[1]	12,765
Goodwill	1,033	(2,408)[2]	3,441
Total assets	$ 170,891	$ 148,557	$ 22,334
Accounts payable	$ 38,565 }	$ 0	$ 0
Salaries	(5,013) }	34,269	2,231
Claims payable (short-term)	2,648 }	0	0
Income taxes payable	3,080	3,022	58
Dividend payable	1,139	(48,984)	50,123[3]
Deferred income tax	(8,411) }	0	0
Future equipment repairs	2,749 }	(4,984)	4,052
Claims payable (long-term)	4,730 }	0	0
Total liabilities	$ 39,787	$ (16,677)	$ 56,464
Additional capital	19,121 }	0	0
Treasury stock	14,699 }	18,693	15,127
Retained earnings	97,284	147,407	(50,123)
Total equities	$ 170,891	$ 149,423	$ 21,468
Assets less equities	0	(866)	(866)

[1]Reconciliation of property account:

    Net purchases $201,011   [$211,073 - $10,062]
    Depreciation   (170,287)   [$172,695 - $2,408 goodwill amort.]
    Loss on sale   (23)   [cash flow statement]
    Net change $ 30,701

[2]Reconciliation of goodwill account:

    Goodwill purchased $ 3,441   [Given]
    Balance sheet change   (1,033)
    Amortization $ 2,408

[3]Note that change in dividends payable = discrepancy in retained earnings.

        As the cash flow statement provides balance sheet changes that exclude the effects of the acquisition of Cole, the differences between the balance sheet changes and cash flow changes must be due to the acquisition.

        The differences tell us that Roadway acquired:
             Assets of Cole $ 22,334
             Liabilities of Cole   (6,341)
             Net assets acquired $ 15,993

        Roadway paid for Cole with:
             Cash $ 866
             Roadway shares valued at 15,127
             Total payment $ 15,993

Note that the cash paid for Cole is equal to the net cash flow change.

B.

Ratios	Cole	Roadway
Fixed asset turnover	1.49	3.73
Accounts receivable turnover	5.60	12.17
Equity to assets	0.72	0.60

C. Roadway's fixed asset and accounts receivable ratios are more than twice those of Cole. The higher ratios may be due to the advantages of size or to better management. In that case we would expect the differences to disappear as Cole is integrated into Roadway. The cash flow implications would be positive as higher turnover would reduce the investment in fixed assets and accounts receivable.

There are other possible explanations. Cole's fixed assets were revalued upwards, decreasing reported turnover. Cole's fixed assets may be newer than Roadway's, understating the turnover ratio. Again this would imply lower future investment. Roadway's higher accounts receivable turnover might be due to the sale of receivables. This is a form of financing (see Chapter 10). If this practice were ended, the future *reported* cash flow of Roadway would be reduced.

D. If Roadway had significant foreign operations, the differences between balance sheet changes and cash flow changes could be due to changes in exchange rates. For this reason the methodology in part A could not be used to derive the balance sheet of Cole with a high degree of accuracy. See Chapter 13 for more on this issue.

E. Roadway purchased Cole for almost $16 million. The future earnings of Cole should be used to compute the return on this investment.

6. A. Using only the data in Exhibit 12P-6A, we are limited to computations of net sales and operating income ($ thousands):

	1989	1990	1991
Coors (excluding ACX):			
Sales	$1,366,108	$1,477,271	$1,530,347
Operating income	71,081	100,662*	59,126
*Excluding special charge			
ACX Technologies:			
Sales	$ 324,595	$ 361,295	$ 387,075
Operating income	(25,906)	20,187	(19,463)

These data exclude corporate expenses as there is no basis upon which to allocate them between the two companies. Also excluded are interest expense, "other income," and income tax expense. To prepare more accurate pro forma income statements we would also need data regarding intercorporate transactions (especially purchases of aluminum and packaging by the beer business from the other segments) and the additional cost of having a second public company.

B. Using the data in Exhibit 12P-6B, we can compute ratios before and after the exclusion of ACX:

			Originally Reported	ACX	Pro forma
(i)	Long-term	1989	.00	.07	.00
	debt-to-equity	1990	.10	.45	.10
		1991	.20	.63	.20
(ii)	Times interest	1989	19.9X	5.0X	NMF*
	earned	1990	200.5	3.4	NMF*
		1991	36.8	1.0	NMF*
(iii)	Return on sales	1989	0.8%	1.1%	0.7%
		1990	2.1	0.7	2.7
		1991	1.2	0.2	1.6
(iv)	Return on equity	1989	1.2%	1.8%	1.0%
		1990	3.6	1.2	4.4
		1991	2.2	0.5	2.8
(v)	Book value	1989	$28.75	$7.77	$20.98
	per share	1990	29.12	7.86	21.26
		1991	29.33	7.86	21.47
(vi)	Asset turnover	1989	1.10X	1.10X	1.10X
		1990	1.04	0.90	1.11
		1991	0.97	0.85	1.02
(vii)	Working capital	1989	$193.6	$78.9	$114.7
	($ millions)	1990	201.0	124.4	76.7
		1991	110.4	101.0	9.4
(viii)	1989-1991 growth:				
	Sales		13.4%	16.4%	12.2%
	Operating income		(35.7)	(40.2)	(32.2)
	Net income		82.1	(73.2)	178.7

*This computation is not meaningful due to lack of information regarding intercorporate borrowings, short-term debt, and the capitalization of interest. Using data from Coors' 1992 annual report, in which ACX is treated as a discontinued operation, times interest earned is 20.4 (1990) and 2.3 (1991), much lower than the ratios originally reported. The ratios are even lower (less than 1.0 for 1991) if interest costs (before capitalization) are used in the denominator.

C. Pro forma data are subject to a number of limitations. Most important, they assume that the same operating decisions (and results) would have occurred under different managements. Second, they rely on sometimes arbitrary cost allocations and assumptions regarding intersegment pricing. Third, the ratios are based on incomplete data; for example short term debt is not reported.

D. (i) The segment data for the non-beer segments could be aggregated, resulting in approximate balance sheet and income statement data for ACX.

(ii)   To complete the estimate, we would require details of the balance sheet (e.g. fixed assets, inventories, accounts payable) and income statement (COGS).

(iii)   Historic segment data, while useful indicators of how ACX performed during the periods shown, have limited usefulness as predictors of future results. The segment data refers to asset writedowns, for example, but details must be obtained from elsewhere in the financial statements to estimate operating earnings. We would also need to know about past capital expenditures, research and development spending, and any changes in operations made by the post-spinoff management.

E.   (i)   ACX may have been viewed as a "turnaround" company. While past returns on sales and equity have been nominal, future returns may be higher. The segment data reveal substantial capital expenditures in the non-beer segments, especially aluminum, over the 1989-1991 period. There is often some delay before new facilities become profitable, and investors may have seen the possibility of substantial profit gains. In addition, they may have believed that ACX would fare better as a separate company than as part of a major beer producer.

(ii)   The efficient market hypothesis suggests that the value of a firm should not be affected by its division into two parts. The value of the firm should be equal to the sum of the value of each part.

        In reality, however, spinoffs may change investor expectations about one or both parts. While segment data provides an indication of how each segment performs, those data are highly summarized. When detailed information about a segment is released, that data may help investors to understand the firm operations. This is especially true when the spinoff is a small part of the firm.

        Small segments are frequently "lost" in a big firm. Investors focus only on the prospects for the major business; the results of that business dominate the results of the pre-spinoff firm. When the smaller segment is separated, its operating results become significant to investors in the spinoff.

        In addition, investors who had no interest in the beer business may have been attracted to the aluminum, packaging, and/or ceramics businesses. ACX shares, which initially sold at a price well below book value, may also have attracted investors who use book value (rather than reported earnings) to select investments.

        While the performance of spinoffs appears to violate the EMH, there are some costs involved. Investors must spend time studying the spinoff firm's financial statements, interviewing management, etc. In addition the cost of preparing these data, and maintaining a second public company, reduce the profitability of the spinoff firm as compared to the period when it did not bear these costs.

F. If Coors had sold ACX (either to another company or through an initial public offering) it would have recognized a gain or loss measured as the difference between the equity of ACX and the proceeds of sale. Given the poor profitability of ACX, it seems likely that the assets would have been sold for less than their book value, resulting in a loss, and reducing the reported earnings of Coors. By spinning off ACX, no loss was recognized.

In addition, a buyer of ACX may have been unwilling to shoulder that company's large debt load. By spinning off ACX, Coors was able to eliminate virtually all of its long-term debt from its balance sheet.

Finally, Coors management may have anticipated that investors would be interested in ACX at its post-spinoff "bargain" price. They may have believed (based on their examination of other spinoffs) that their shareholders would benefit by having shares in two companies rather than one.

7. The data in Exhibit 12P-7 can be used to calculate return on (ending) equity for each company:

	1981	1991
CONCO	16.1%	17.0%
NECCO	22.1	3.0

These data are, however, only the beginning of our analysis. To understand why ROE declined for NECCO while showing little change for CONCO, we must disaggregate ROE into its components:

ROE   = profitability x asset utilization   x leverage

$$\frac{\text{Net income}}{\text{equity}} = \frac{\text{net income}}{\text{sales}} \quad x \quad \frac{\text{sales}}{\text{assets}} \quad x \quad \frac{\text{assets}}{\text{equity}}$$

CONCO
1981:
16.1% = .093 [$115/$1293] x 1.156 [$1243/$1075] x 1.503 [$1075/$715]

1991:
17.0% = .101 [$306/$3044] x 1.032 [$3044/$2950] x 1.639 [$2950/$1800]

NECCO
1981:
22.1% = .127 [$21/$165] x 1.179 [$165/$140] x 1.474 [$140/$95]

1991:
3.0% = .008 [$6/$710]   x .607 [$710/$1170] x 5.850 [$1170/$200]

CONCO's ratios changed little over the ten year period. Small increases in profitability and leverage were partially offset by a small decline in asset utilization (turnover). The result was a small increase in ROE.

In the case of NECCO, however, the changes were much more significant. While leverage increased by a factor of four, profitability and utilization both declined sharply. The ratio changes were partly due to real operational factors and partly due to the 1988 LBO. We examine each ratio in turn.

12-17

Profitability declined because of:

(i)   High interest expense due to the LBO debt.

(ii)   Depreciation of asset writeups and amortization of goodwill resulting from use of the purchase method of accounting at the time of the LBO.

(iii) Lower gross margins.

The decline in NECCO's asset utilization may also be largely due to the asset writeups and goodwill created by the LBO. Without more data we cannot tell whether this factor accounted for all of the decline in utilization.

The increased leverage of NECCO was primarily the result of the substitution of debt for equity at the time of the LBO. The purchase method adjustments would also have increased this ratio by increasing reported assets.

The decline in NECCO's ROE, therefore, was largely due to the economic (increase in debt) and accounting (writeup of assets) effects of the LBO. These effects compounded the decline in operating profitability, producing the sharp drop in ROE.

8.   A.   The first table was prepared from the U.S. GAAP data in Exhibit 12P-8:

Hanson Industries Goodwill (£ millions):

	1988	1989	1990	1991
Opening balance	£2,041	£1,811	£3,724	£3,550
Amortization	(50)	(56)	(97)	(95)
Disp. goodwill	(180)	(92)	(171)	(46)
New goodwill[1]	0	2,061	94	29
Closing balance	£1,811	£3,724	£3,550	£3,438

[1]Deduced; assumed to be zero for 1988 as opening balance not provided.

Notice that the amortization period appears to be in the range of 35 years in accordance with U.S GAAP requirements.

The second table was prepared assuming a ten year amortization period for goodwill and that new goodwill and disposal goodwill are accounted for halfway through each year.

Hanson Industries Adjusted Goodwill (£ millions):

	1988	1989	1990	1991
Opening balance	£2,041	£1,666	£3,370	£2,960
Amortization[2]	(195)	(265)	(333)	(295)
Dis. goodwill	(180)	(92)	(171)	(46)
New goodwill[3]	0	2,061	94	29
Closing balance	£1,666	£3,370	£2,960	£2,648

[2](Opening balance + (new - disposal)/2)/10.

[3]Same as previous table; new goodwill depends on acquisitions made and is unaffected by amortization method or period.

Note that disposal goodwill is unchanged. However faster amortization would reduce the remaining balance of goodwill at disposal. For simplification we omit this complex calculation; extra credit should be awarded to the reader who sees its necessity.

The effect of these adjustments on U.S. GAAP net income and stockholders' equity follows:

Net income[1] £(145)	£(209)	£(236)	£(200)
Stockholders' equity[2] (145)	(354)	(590)	(790)

[1]The increase in amortization reduces net income.

[2]The cumulative net income effects.

Adjusted net income and stockholders' equity (U.S. GAAP) are:

Net income £ 735	£ 718	£ 714	£ 756
Stockholders' equity 3816	4471	6042	6303

B. Now compute return on (ending) equity under all three methods:

U.K. GAAP	51.1%	105.3%	35.3%	33.3%
U.S. GAAP	22.2	19.2	14.3	13.5
U.S. GAAP Adjusted	19.3	16.1	11.8	12.0

Net income is fairly constant under each of the three accounting methods. However the level is lower under U.S. GAAP (mainly due to goodwill adjustments) than under U.K. GAAP, and even lower when goodwill is amortized over a (shorter) ten year period.

Return on equity is vastly different depending on the method used. Under U.K. GAAP, with goodwill written off immediately, ROE appears very high, exceeding 100% for 1989. Under U.S. GAAP, with income reduce and equity increased, ROE is not particularly high, and decreases sharply from 1989-1992. After adjustment to a shorter amortization period, the level of ROE declines further. Note however that it increases in 1992 reflecting the reduced level of equity after several years of rapid goodwill amortization.

C. Profits on disposal are reduced when the associated goodwill is written off. Adjusted disposal profits are:

Unadjusted profit				
(U.K. GAAP)	£ 445	£ 288	£ 168	£ 115
Disposal goodwill	(180)	(92)	(171)	(46)
Adjusted profit				
(U.S. GAAP)	£ 265	£ 196	£ (3)	£ 69

Over the four year period, recognition of disposal goodwill reduces reported disposal profits by 48% (from £1016 to £527), For 1990 the adjustment creates a reported loss on disposal.

D. The adjustments in part C (already reflected in the U.S. GAAP data) are one factor in the lower level of earnings and ROE (both before and after the adjustment for rapid amortization). As goodwill is already written off under U.K. GAAP, there is no effect on the ROE denominator; the reduction of reported earnings thus reduces ROE.

9. A.

[$ Millions]	Prior	Following
Debt	$ 800	$ 11,600
Equity	1,920	100[1]
Total capital	$ 2,720	$ 11,700
EBIT	796	574
Interest expense	81	1,269
Net income	436	(475)
(i) Debt-to-equity	.42	116.00
(ii) Return on total capital (EBIT/total capital)	.29	.05
(iii) Interest coverage ratio	9.83	0.45

(iv) Net profit margin is clearly negative when the purchase method adjustments are pushed down into Kraft.

[1]We assume that Philip Morris put a nominal amount of equity capital into new Kraft. A different amount would not change the analysis meaningfully.

B. The comparison of Kraft data before and after the merger is affected by the economic effects (higher debt and interest expense) and the accounting effects (asset writeups and income statement amortization) of the merger. While the business is unchanged, the financial statements and all ratios derived from them are radically different. While one can argue that the economic effects are "real" the accounting effects are less so.

C. The comparability of Kraft financial data with that of firms that have not been acquired is also affected by the problems discussed in B. The accounting adjustments, in particular, make it difficult to tell whether interfirm differences are real or the result of accounting variations alone.

D. The push down adjustments replace the historical cost of Kraft's assets and liabilities with their fair value at the merger date. To the extent that certain assets and liabilities are not adjusted, we can infer that fair value does not exceed cost. The creation of goodwill implies that all assets have been written up to fair value and that Kraft has no "undervalued" assets following the merger.

In addition, the amortization periods may be an indication of the useful life that management ascribes to assets acquired.

E.   The advantage of push-down accounting is that Kraft's financial statements fully reflect the merger transaction, including a writeup of assets and liabilities to fair market value. The disadvantage is that push-down limits the comparability of Kraft financial statements with those prior to the merger and with those of other companies.

Chapter 13 - Solutions

1. (i)   No effect; reported sales are translated at the average rate regardless of the choice of functional currency.

    (ii) No effect; cash flow from operations is translated from local currency cash flows using the average rate for the period.

    (iii) When the local currency is the functional currency, translation gains and losses are based on the net investment in each local currency.

          When the dollar is the functional currency, translation gains and losses are based on net monetary assets or liabilities in each local currency.

    (iv) When the local currency is the functional currency, translation gains and losses are accumulated in the cumulative translation adjustment component of stockholders' equity and do not affect reported income except when a subsidiary is sold or the decline in the currency is deemed permanent.

          When the dollar is the functional currency, translation gains and losses are included in reported net income for each accounting period.

2. A.   Subtracting U.S. income of E&O, Erzi's income statement in dollars follows:

($ millions)	19X0	19X2	19X3
Revenues	$ 50.0	$ 60.0	$ 70.0
Operating expenses	25.0	27.0	29.0
Income taxes	7.0	9.4	11.8
Net income	$ 18.0	$ 23.6	$ 29.2
% Change:			
Sales		20%	17%
Net income		31%	24%

     To remove the impact of exchange rate changes we convert the income statement to LC's (using the *average* exchange rate for each year):

	19X0	19X2	19X3
Exchange rate	1	1.5	0.75
Revenues	LC50.0	LC40.0	LC93.3
Operating expenses	25.0	18.0	38.7
Income taxes	7.0	6.3	15.7
Net income	LC18.0	·LC15.7	LC38.9
% Change--operations:			
Sales		(20%)	133%
Net income		(13%)	147%

These data give the operating results of Erzi; year 2 operating performance declined whereas year 3 was a "boom" year.

Looking at the consolidated results of E&O, we can now disaggregate the effect of Erzi's operations and that of exchange rate changes for the 19X0-19X2 period:

	Sales	Net income
Erzi's operations[1]	$ 43.3	$ 20.9
Exchange rate effects[2]	(23.3)	(9.7)
Net change	$ 20.0	$ 11.2

[1]The dollar change in sales and income assuming that the exchange rate remained at the 19X0 level of 1.0.
[2]The effect of the decline in the LC on reported sales and net income (19X2 amounts x .25).

B. Sales were unaffected by the choice of functional currency as they were translated at the average rate for the year regardless of that choice.

Net income was affected by the functional currency choice. If the LC was the functional currency, translation adjustments did not affect net income; if the dollar was the functional currency, translation gains and losses were included in the determination of net income.

3. A. With dollar as the functional currency, FI is translated using the temporal method (SFAS 8).

	Ponts (Millions)	Exchange Rate (Ponts/$)	Dollars (Millions)
Balance Sheet:			
Cash	82	4.0	$ 20.50
Accounts receivable	700	4.0	175.00
Inventory	455	4.0	113.75
Fixed assets (net)	360	4.0	90.00
Total assets	1,597		$ 399.25
Accounts payable	532	4.0	$ 133.00
Capital stock	600	3.0	200.00
Retained earnings	465		132.86
Translation adjustment	---		(66.61)*
Total liabilities and equities	1,597		$ 399.25
Income Statement:			
Sales	3,500	3.5	$ 1,000.00
Cost of sales	(2,345)	3.5	(670.00)
Depreciation expense	(60)	3.5	(17.14)
Selling expense	(630)	3.5	(180.00)
Net income	465		$ 132.86

*Translation Adjustment $= 600 \left(\dfrac{1}{3} - \dfrac{1}{4} \right) = 600 \, (1/12) = \$(50.00)$

$\qquad\qquad\qquad\quad + 465 \left(\dfrac{1}{3.5} - \dfrac{1}{4} \right) = 465 \, (1/28) = \underline{(16.61)}$

$\qquad\qquad\qquad\qquad\qquad\qquad\qquad\qquad\qquad\quad \$(66.61)$

B. (i) **Dollar:** Inventory and fixed assets translated at historical rates.

   Pont: All assets and liabilities translated at current exchange rates.

   Dollar: Translation gain (loss) computed on the basis of net monetary assets.

   Pont: Translation gain (loss) computed on the basis of net investment (all assets and liabilities).

   (ii) **Dollar:** All revenues and other expenses are translated at the average rate for the period; cost of sales and depreciation expense translated at historical rate.

   Pont: All revenues and expenses translated at average rates for the period.

   Dollar: Translation gain(loss) included in net income (volatility increased).

   Pont: Translation gain(loss) reported in separate component of stockholders, equity. Net income is less volatile.

(iii) **Dollar:** Financial statement ratios skewed by translation effects.

Pont: Ratios in dollars are similar to ratios in ponts.

4.   A.   IP states that translation adjustments are included as cumulative translation adjustments in stockholders' equity; from this we infer that IP uses the local currencies as functional currencies for all of its non-U.S. operations.

As a result, reported income excludes translation adjustments, making it more stable. Stockholders' equity includes the CTA. Cash flow from operations is unaffected as local currency cash flows must be translated at the average rate regardless of the choice of functional currency.

B.   Sales of IP's European segment more than doubled from 1989-1991. U.S. sales were erratic over this period, increasing by 2% in 1990 and declining by 3% in 1991. Four possible explanations for the increase in European sales are:

Real sales growth (in local currencies)

Rising prices (in local currencies)

Rising exchange rates against the dollar

Acquisitions

C.   The choice of functional currency had no effect on reported sales growth as sales are translated at the average rate regardless of the functional currency choice.

5.   (i)   Monetary loss of $27: translation loss based on net monetary liabilities; included in reported income under SFAS 8.

(ii)   Nonmonetary realized gain of $12; difference between net income (before translation loss):

$136 (SFAS 8) − $124 (SFAS 52) = $12

Corresponds to differences in depreciation ($6) + COGS ($6)

Under SFAS 52 these amounts are included in the cumulative translation adjustment.

(iii) Nonmonetary unrealized gain of $102: difference in total assets:

$1790 (SFAS 52) − $1688 (SFAS 8) = $102

Corresponds to differences in inventory ($16) + fixed assets ($86).

(iv)   All gains and losses of $87: the SFAS 52 cumulative translation adjustment in balance sheet.

(v)   All gains and losses except realized monetary loss of $(15); the difference in net income under the two methods:

$$\$109 \text{ (SFAS 8)} - \$124 \text{ (SFAS 52)} = \$(15)$$

Under SFAS 52 these amounts are included in the cumulative translation adjustment.

6.   (ii) **Nonmonetary realized gain of $12:**

Income prior to translation adjustment:

        Remeasurement (SFAS 8) = $136
        Translation (SFAS 52)   = $124

Difference of $12 consists of realized holding gains ($11.76) on nonmonetary assets (see below) that are included in operating income under remeasurement (temporal method).

Realized gain on nonmonetary assets:

Inventory[1]   LC175.00 x [1/1.02 - 1/1.06] = $ 6.47
Fixed assets[2]   LC143.00 x [1/1.02 - 1/1.06] =   5.29
   Total gain $ 11.76

[1]Opening inventory of LC 175 sold ("realized"), under the FIFO assumption, at an average exchange rate of 1.02.

[2]Depreciation expense of LC 210 must be divided into LC 143, depreciation of fixed assets held on 12/31/90 (LC 860 of a total fixed assets of LC 1260) and LC 67, for fixed assets acquired during 1991 (LC 400 of a total fixed assets of LC 1260). Therefore, as depreciation is "realized" (included in income), the related holding gain on LC 143 of fixed assets is realized during 1991.

(iii) Nonmonetary unrealized gain of $102:

Difference of $102 consists of unrealized gain on nonmonetary assets ignored in remeasurement but included under translation. It is computed as follows:

Inventory acquired during 1991[1]
        LC220 x [1/0.95 - 1/1.02]   = $ 15.89
Fixed assets held entire year[2]
        567 x [1/0.95 - 1/1.06]   =   61.94
Fixed assets acquired during year[3]
        333 x [1/0.95 - 1/1.02]   =   24.06
   Total $ 101.89

[1]Ending inventory purchased at an average exchange rate of 1.02 and held to year-end when the exchange rate was 0.95.

[2]The remaining fixed assets of LC 567 (710 - 143) were held for the whole year.

[3]The net increase in fixed assets during 1991 was LC 333 (purchases of LC 400 less depreciation of LC 67); unrealized gains are based on the net increase of LC 333.

(iv)   All gains and losses of $87:

Realized gain on nonmonetary assets [see (ii)]	$ 11.76
Unrealized gain on nonmonetary assets [see (iii)]	101.89
Loss on net monetary position (see Exhibit 13-4)	(26.54)
Total gains and losses (cumulative translation adjustment)	$ 87.11

(v)   Net income: remeasurement (SFAS 8) $109
                 : translation (SFAS 52) $124

Difference of $(15) stems from items included in the income statement when remeasurement is used but not under translation.

Realized gain on nonmonetary assets [see (ii)]	$ 11.76
Loss on net monetary assets (Exhibit 13-4)	(26.54)
Net translation loss	$ (14.78)

7.   (i)   Monetary loss of $43: translation loss included in reported income under SFAS 8.

(ii)   Nonmonetary realized gain of $58:

Difference between net income (before translation loss)

$222 (SFAS 8) - $164 (SFAS 52) = $58

Corresponds to difference in depreciation ($29) + COGS ($29).

For SFAS 52 these amounts are included in the cumulative translation adjustment.

(iii) Nonmonetary unrealized gain of $99 is difference in total assets less amount "unrealized" in previous years

$2586 (SFAS 52) - $2385 (SFAS 8)	=	$ 201
Less 1991 portion [see 5(iii)]	=	102
Net amount		$ 99

Corresponds to differences in inventory and fixed assets

(iv)   All gains and losses of $114 is the change in the SFAS 52 cumulative translation adjustment ($201 - $87) in the balance sheet.

(v)   All gains and losses except realized monetary of $15 is the difference in net income under the two methods:

$179 (SFAS 8) - $164 (SFAS 52) = $15

Under SFAS 52 this amount is included in the cumulative translation adjustment.

8.   (ii) Income prior to Translation Adjustment:

$$
\begin{array}{ll}
\text{Remeasurement (SFAS 8)} & = \$222 \\
\text{Translation (SFAS 52)} & = \$164
\end{array}
$$

Difference of $58 consists of realized holding gains ($57.81) on nonmonetary assets that are included in operating income under remeasurement (temporal method):

Realized Gain on Non-Monetary Assets

Inventory[1]	LC220.00 x [1/0.90 - 1/1.02] =	$ 28.76
Fixed assets[2]	127.22 x [1/0.90 - 1/1.06] =	21.34
	59.17 x [1/0.90 - 1/1.02] =	7.73
		$ 57.83

[1]Opening inventory of LC 220 sold ("realized"), under the FIFO assumption, at an average exchange rate of 0.90.

[2]Depreciation expense of LC 250 must be divided among LC 127 for fixed assets purchased in 1990 (LC 860 of total fixed assets of LC 1690), LC 59 for assets acquired in 1991 (LC 400), and LC 63 for fixed assets acquired during 1992 (LC 430 of total fixed assets of LC 1690). Therefore, as depreciation is "realized" (included in income), the holding gain on LC 127 and LC 59 of fixed assets is realized during 1992.

(iii) Net Income plus Change in Cumulative Translation Adjustment:

Remeasurement (SFAS 8)		$ 179
Translation (SFAS 52)	$164 + $114 =	278
Difference		$ 99

Difference consists of unrealized gain on nonmonetary assets ignored in remeasurement but included under translation:

Unrealized gains on net nonmonetary assets:

Inventory[1]:		
Acquired during the year		
LC310 x [1/0.85 - 1/0.90]	= $	20.27
Fixed assets[2]:		
Held entire year		
LC440 x [1/0.85 - 1/1.06]	=	102.55
Held entire year		
LC274 x [1/0.85 - 1/1.02]	=	53.72
Acquired during the year[3]		
LC366 x [1/0.85 - 1/0.90]	=	23.92
Subtotal		$ 200.46
Less amount recognized in 1991		(101.67)
Net amount recognized in 1992		$ 98.79

[1]Ending inventory purchased at an average exchange rate of 0.90 and held to year-end when the exchange rate was 0.85.

[2]Of the 1990 (and prior years) purchases, the remaining fixed assets of LC 440 (710 - 143 - 127) were held for the whole year. Similarly, from the 1991 acquisitions, assets costing LC 274 (400 - 67 - 59) were held for all of 1992.

[3]The net increase in fixed assets acquired during 1992 was LC 366 (purchases of LC 430 less depreciation of LC 64); unrealized gains are based on the net increase of LC 366.

(iv) All gains and losses of $114

Realized gain on nonmonetary assets [see (ii)]	$ 57.83
Unrealized gain on nonmonetary assets [see (iii)]	98.79
Loss on net monetary position (see Exhibit 13-4)	(42.65)
Total gains and losses (cumulative translation adjustment)	$113.97

(v) Net income: remeasurement (SFAS 8) $ 179
           translation (SFAS 52)   164
    Difference $ 15

This difference stems from items included in the income statement under remeasurement but not under translation:

Realized gain on nonmonetary assets [see (ii)]	$ 57.83
Loss on net monetary assets (Exhibit 13-4)	(42.65)
Net translation gain	$ 15.18

9. **Computation of Effect of Exchange Rate Changes on Cash**

1991

Beginning cash balance: LC   34
Effect of change in exchange rate[1] $\dfrac{34}{1.06} - \dfrac{34}{.95}$ = $ 3.71

Effect on operating activities:
Cash flow from operations (CFO)   LC 216
Effect of change in exchange rate[2] $\dfrac{216}{1.02} - \dfrac{216}{.95}$ = 15.60

Effect on investing activities:
Cash flow from investing activities   LC(400)
Effect of change in exchange rate[2] $\left(\dfrac{400}{1.02}\right) - \left(\dfrac{400}{.95}\right)$ = (28.90)

Effect on financing activities:
Cash flow from financing activities   LC 320
Effect of change in exchange rate[2] $\dfrac{320}{1.02} - \dfrac{320}{.95}$ = 23.12

Total effect of exchange rate changes on cash: $13.53

[1]The revaluation of the LC cash balance to reflect the change in exchange rate during the year.
[2]The difference between the amount shown on the cash flow statement (translated at the average rate for the year) and the U.S. dollar equivalent of that cash flow at the year end rate.

10. For exchange rate information use the data provided in Exhibit 13-13:

	1989	1990
Year-end rate	.937	.837
Average rate	.986	.891

A. Balance sheet translated at *year-end rate*
   (millions of $US and LC)

	1989		1990	
	$US	**LC**	**$US**	**LC**
Cash (5% of CA)	$ 1018	LC 954	$ 1217	LC 1019
Other current assets	19343	18124	23120	19351
Current liabilities	(12124)	(11360)	(15917)	(13323)
Net working capital	$ 8237	LC 7718	$ 8420	LC 7047
Net property	9879	9257	11628	9733
Investments	6822	6392	9077	7597
Total assets	$ 24938	LC 23367	$ 29125	LC 24377
Long-term debt	$ 3358	LC 3146	$ 5060	LC 4235
Other liabilities	2607	2443	2699	2259
Deferred taxes	1814	1700	2381	1993
Total liabilities	$ 7779	LC 7289	$ 10140	LC 8487
Net assets (equity)	17159	16078	18985	15890
Total equities	$ 24938	LC 23367	$ 29125	LC 24377

B. Income statement translated at *average rate* for year
   (millions of $US and LC)

	$US	LC
Revenues	$ 41886	LC 37320
Earnings before tax	7844	6989
Income tax expense	(3270)	(2914)
Net income	$ 4754	LC 4075

C.

Net assets at December 31, 1989	LC 16078
Net income for 1990	4075
Subtotal	LC 20153
Net assets at December 31, 1990	(15890)
Discrepancy	LC 4263

There must be dividends paid and/or share redemptions by IBM's foreign subsidiaries during 1990. It is possible that a small portion of the discrepancy is the result of valuation allowances included in equity.

D. Investments translated at *average rate* for the year.

	$US	LC
Investment in property	$ 3020	LC 2691

Net property at December 31, 1989	LC 9257
Investment for 1990	2691
Subtotal	LC 11948
Net property at December 31, 1990	(9733)
Difference	LC 2215

This difference reflects depreciation expense for the year. We assume (lacking data) that there were no acquisitions or divestitures and no property dispositions during the year.

E. See Exhibit 13S-1

E. Use the transactional analysis method (LC millions):

	Income Statement	Balance Sheet			Cash Effect	
		12/31/89	12/31/90	Change	+	−
Earnings before tax	6989				6989	
Other current assets		18124	19351	1226		1226
Current liabilities		11360	13323	1963	1963	
Other liabilities		2443	2259	(184)		184
Depreciation expense*	2215				2215	
Income tax expense	(2914)					2914
Deferred taxes		1700	1993	293	293	
Cash from operations						7136
Depreciation expense	(2215)					2215
Net property		9257	9733	476		476
Investments		6392	7597	1205		1205
Cash for investment						(3896)
Long-term debt		3146	4235	1089	1089	
Dividends paid (part C)						4263
Cash from financing						(3174)
Net cash flow	4075]					66
[Net income						

*As depreciation expense can be assumed to be included in the computed earnings before tax, it must be reclassified to properly compute the components of cash flow.
Net cash flow should equal the change in cash, providing a check on our calculations.
Net income is checked against the sum of all income statement items to ensure that none have been omitted.

F. Translation of LC cash flow components to $US at *average rate* for 1990 of .891 (data in millions):

	LC	$US
Cash from operations	7136	8008
Cash for investment	(3896)	(4373)
Cash for financing	(3174)	(3562)
Net cash flow	66	73

G. Percentage of consolidated cash flow obtained from non-U.S. operations ($ millions):

		Consoli-dated	Non-U.S.	Percent-age
i.	Cash from operations	$7472	$8008	107%
ii.	Cash from debt financing	2958	1222	41
iii.	Cash for investment	(7144)	(4373)	61

iv. It appears that IBM's 1990 operating cash flow was derived *entirely* from its non-U.S. operations. These operations accounted for 61% of investment cash flow, similar to their proportion of operations (measured by revenues or assets). This suggests that IBM's U.S. operations had significant liquidity problems.

IBM's foreign operations were able to generate more than $4 billion in cash for the parent company (part C).

The debt financing ratio (ii.) may not be meaningful. Much of IBM's debt is short-term and the short-term debt of the non-U.S. operations is not broken out. This problem also affects the computation of CFO. If the short-term debt (included in current liabilities) of IBM's non-U.S. operations rose, CFO has been overstated.

More analysis would be needed to understand whether these conditions were temporary or reflected longer term trends.

It must also be remembered that these conclusions are based on summarized data and simplifying assumptions. It is possible that more detailed data would modify these conclusions.

In sum, the data derived suggest that IBM's non-U.S. operations in 1990 were much healthier that domestic operations. The data could have been used to question management about these conditions.

H. The effect of exchange rates on cash and cash equivalents:

	LC	Multi-plier*	$ Effect
Beginning cash balance	LC 954	.1275	$ 122
Effects on:			
Cash from operations	7136	.0724	517
Cash for investment	(3896)	.0724	(282)
Cash for financing	(3174)	.0724	(230)
Net effect			$ 127
Actual effect			$ 131
(Exhibit 13-11)			

*The beginning cash balance was translated at the rate of .937 at December 31, 1989 but is now translated at the rate of .837. The effect on LC cash is [(1/.937)-(1/.837)] = .1275.
Cash flows during 1990 are assumed to have originated at the average rate of .891 but are now translated at the year-end rate of .837. The effect on 1990 cash flows is therefore [(1/.837)-(1/.891)] = .0724.

Alternative method:

Cash balance at December 31, 1989: LC954/.937	$ 1018
1990 increase in cash (net cash flow): LC65/.891	73
Subtotal	$ 1091
Cash balance at December 31, 1990: LC1019/.837	(1217)
Effect of exchange rates on cash	$ (126)

The difference between the computed and the actual effect is quite small, suggesting that our assumption that non-U.S. cash is 5% of current assets was approximately correct. Even if it were exactly correct, differences in the distribution by currency would introduce an element of error. Another possible source of error is the assumption that 100% of IBM's foreign operations uses local functional currencies.

The point of this exercise is that non-U.S. cash and cash equivalents can be estimated by estimating cash flows and reversing this process. Subtracting the effect of rate changes on cash flows from the total effect provides the impact on the beginning cash balance. As we know the exchange rate, we can estimate the beginning cash balance. Thus the actual effect, provided in the consolidated cash flow statement, provides the answer; the question is the amount of non-U.S. cash and cash equivalents.

11. A. From Note 4 we can conclude that Bristol-Myers (BMY) uses local currencies as functional currencies except for operations in highly inflationary economies. The existence of the currency translation adjustment (CTA) in the equity section of BMY's balance sheet confirms this inference.

For operations in highly inflationary economies (such as Brazil), BMY uses the $ US as the functional currency as required by SFAS 52. These operations generate large losses (see footnote 4) that are included in reported income, confirming that they result from remeasurement of local currency results into the $ US.

B.   From the Geographic Areas segment disclosure, net sales outside the
      United States (before inter-area eliminations as we lack the data to
      allocate them) were:

                    1988: $3,448 Million
                    1989: 3,685   (+ 6.9%)
                    1990: 4,421   (+20.0%)

*Note: We include all foreign sales regardless of functional currency
as sales are always translated at the average exchange rate for the
period.*

     It appears that the growth rate of foreign sales in 1990 was
far greater than in 1989. But the question is whether currency
changes affected the trend.

     The discussion of "Net Sales and Earnings" reveals that
currency translation increased 1990 sales by approximately 2% but
reduced 1989 sales by 2% as compared with the prior year. These
percentages are assumed to apply to total sales:

          1989 effect: (.02) x $8,558 = $(171) million
          1990 effect: .02 x $9,189 =   184 million

     These amounts can be used to adjust non-US sales for currency
effects, resulting in adjusted sales as follows:

                    1988: $3,448 million
                    1989: 3,856   (+ 11.8%)
                    1990: 4,237   (+ 9.9%)

     While these calculations are crude, it appears that BMY's
foreign net sales grew less rapidly in 1990 than in 1989, the
opposite of what the unadjusted data report.

C.   (i)   The cash flow statement shows an increase of $168 million in
             inventories for 1990; the balance sheet shows an increase of
             $227 million. As the dollar weakened in 1990, foreign
             inventories would translate into more $US, resulting in an
             increase in $US dollar inventories. As BMY made no
             acquisitions in 1990, that other possible explanation is
             excluded.

      (ii)   The CTA showed a positive change of $88 million or 9.2% of 12-
             31-89 net foreign assets of $ 957 million. Net foreign assets
             were 18.8% ($957/$5084) of total net assets on that date.
             Applying these percentages to 12-31-89 inventory:

                  .092 x .188 x $1,139 = $ 20 million, or one-third of the
             discrepancy between the balance sheet change and cash flow.
             This calculation assumes that inventories were distributed
             evenly (by currency) throughout the company. This assumption
             appears not to hold; it appears that BMY's inventories were
             concentrated in currencies that appreciated against the
             dollar.

             *NOTE: an alternative computation would use the data from
             Exhibit 13-13. However it is better to use firm-specific data.*

D. (i)   BMY must have substantially increased its non-$US liabilities
          during the year, reducing net assets despite the increase in
          total (gross) assets. Net assets may also have been affected
          by differential effects of currency changes on assets and
          liabilities, but this effect is unlikely to be large.

    (ii) An increase in liabilities reduces net assets, decreasing the
          company's exposure to currency changes when the local currency
          is the functional currency. Depending on the nature of the
          assets and liabilities (monetary or nonmonetary), the exposure
          for (hyperinflationary) operations where the $US is the
          functional currency may also change.

    (iii) Given the decline of the dollar, it appears that BMY would
          have been better off with larger foreign currency exposure.
          However, we do not know the exposure by currency. It is
          possible that the company reduced its exposure to depreciating
          currencies while maintaining or increasing its exposure to
          strong currencies.

              Additionally, it is possible that the reduced exposure
          was effected early in 1989, BMY would have benefitted in that
          year as the dollar rose in value. Note that the 1990 CTA
          increase was about 2.5 times the 1989 CTA decrease.

              The data provided do not, therefore, provide a
          definitive answer to this question. However the analysis does
          supply data permitting the analyst to intelligently query the
          company and gain insight into the firm's strategy regarding
          foreign currency exposure.

              Note that the firm took a charge for "integrating
          operations" in 1989. Management confirmed to one of the
          authors that this charge included a writeoff of assets in
          foreign subsidiaries. That writeoff contributed to the
          decrease in net foreign assets.

E. Note 11 contains data (required by SFAS 105) regarding BMY's
    financial instrument exposure. Note the large increase in foreign
    exchange contracts in 1989. Depending on the nature and timing of
    these contracts, they may have protected the company against the
    effects of the 1989 rise of the dollar on its non-dollar exposures.
    As in the case of D (iii), the data provide raw material for
    questions rather than definitive answers.

F. (i)   Data in $ millions

          Foreign net assets:

December 31	Reported	Change
1988	$1,563	---
1989	957	$(606)
1990	1186	229

          Cumulative Translation Adjustments:

December 31	Reported	Change
1988	$ (114)	---
1989	(149)	$ (35)
1990	(61)	88

"Real" change in net assets:

Year	Reported	–	Change in CTA	=	Real
1989	$ (606)	–	$(35)	=	$(571)
1990	229	–	88	=	141

The reported 1989 decline in foreign net assets was exaggerated slightly by exchange rate changes; the 1990 increase was significantly affected by translation. Note that the decline in 1989 net assets includes the effects of the charge for integrating operations.

In part B of this problem we showed that, contrary to the unadjusted reported data, BMY's foreign net sales grew at a lower rate in 1990 (9.9%) than 1989 (11.8%). BMY's U.S. sales increased by 7.7% in 1989 and 8.3% in 1990. Thus, sales growth declined in its foreign operations but increased moderately in the U.S. Within the foreign regions reported separately, the Europe, etc. area reported the highest unadjusted growth rate. However, in the absence of exchange rate data by region, this inference must be used with caution.

The operating profit data are quite different:

Geographic Area	1990	1989	1989
United States	$ 1,747	$ 1,259	$ 1,462
Change	38.8%	-13.8%	---
Foreign	$ 921	$ 387	$ 573
Change	138%	-32.5%	---

The translation effect on operating profits is the same as that on sales, an increase (decrease) of 2% (2%) for 1990 (1989), the adjusted changes in foreign profits would be a decline of 11.8% in 1989 and an increase of 136% in 1990.

(ii) Looking at year-end assets by geographic segment (note that these are total assets, not net assets) BMY appears to be investing most heavily in the U.S. and the European region. Year-end assets of the European region grew by 36% (from $1172 to $1590) and by 22% in the U.S. Note that the foreign amounts have not been adjusted for the effects of changes in exchange rates. As indicated in part D, foreign net assets declined in 1989 due to a charge for integrating operations. However, BMY has not disclosed the region for which this charge was taken.

This pattern of investment suggests that higher sales and income growth should occur in those two regions. It would be helpful if capital expenditure data were available by region, as such data would suggest growth in operating capacity (an indicator of future sales growth) rather than increases in working capital (that may relate only to past growth).

G.   Reported segment data is affected by changes in exchange rates in different geographic areas, as already discussed. These data also reflect the impact of real sales growth, price changes, and acquisitions and divestitures, all of which affect local currency operating results.

12. A. The Swiss Franc (or another non-dollar currency) must have been the functional currency for the Swiss subsidiary. Use of the dollar as the functional currency for that unit would have reported translation adjustments as part of income, rather than accumulating them in the stockholders' equity account.

B. The deferred translation gains of $3,213,000 reflect appreciation of the functional currency of the Swiss subsidiary against the dollar; net assets of that subsidiary were translated into an increased dollar amount.

C. (i) The gain on liquidation did not result from operating activities but from the recognition of previously deferred exchange rate effects.

(ii) The gain should not be considered 1991 income as it was generated over the life of the subsidiary and recognized in 1991 only because management chose to liquidate in that year.

D. Change in cumulative translation adjustment:

1991 $ (6,405,000)   [The $3,213,000 reduction in the CTA due to the liquidation must be excluded.]
1990   13,246,000
1989   (3,607,000)

Because the liquidation of the inactive subsidiary was completed in the first quarter of 1991, the effect of exchange rate changes is captured by the decline of $6,405,000 on foreign net assets of $96,933,000 (net assets on October 31, 1990 of $100,146,000 less the $3,213,000 of deferred gains relating to the Swiss subsidiary):

$$\frac{\$(6,405,000)}{\$96,933,000} = (6.61\%)$$

Thus, the functional currencies used by the firm declined by 6.61% against the dollar in 1991. The actual decline may be higher since the net assets of the Swiss unit should be deducted from the net assets, resulting in a lower denominator. However, that information is not available.

E. The cash flow statement reports that the 1991 effect of exchange rate changes on cash was $(2,075) million. Using the result of part D, the estimated cash balance in nondollar functional currencies at October 31, 1990 was:

$(2.075)/.0661 = $31.392 million.

NOTE: This calculation ignores the effect of exchange rate changes on the increase in cash balances during 1991.

Commercial Intertech's total balance of cash and cash equivalents at October 31, 1990 was $12,049 million, making the estimate clearly wrong. We can conclude that the company kept cash balances in foreign currencies that depreciated by more than the functional currency average computed in part D. Given the size of the loss, an analyst might have questioned management about it.

F.   First we must estimate inventories in nondollar functional currencies. One estimate would compare 1991 foreign sales to total sales (in $ millions):

$229/$437 = 52.4%

The comparison of total foreign assets at October 31, 1990 to total assets would result in a 44.6% estimate.

Either of these percentages can be applied to total inventories at October 31, 1990 of $59,762 million to estimate foreign inventories. The result is then multiplied by the adjustment factor computed in part D to obtain the estimated effect of exchange rates on inventories in nondollar functional currencies:

.524 x $59,972 x .0661 = $2.07 million
or   .446 x $59,972 x .0661 = $1.77 million

The actual effect can be estimated by comparing the balance sheet change in inventories with the cash flow change (data not provided in problem). This method, which assumes no acquisition or divestiture activity for the year, results in an estimate of $2.76 million.

As this estimate is somewhat higher than that arrived at by using the geographic segment data, it appears that the company has higher inventories relative to sales (lower inventory turnover) in its foreign subsidiaries. An alternative explanation would be higher inventories in weaker currencies (similar to part E).

G.   Reported foreign net assets:

1991	$ 94,709,000
1990	100,146,000
Decrease	$ 5,479,000

The net decrease of $5,479,000 was reported after a total decline in the CTA of $9,618,000 of which $6,405,000 was due to exchange rate changes and $3,213,000 stemmed from the liquidation of the Swiss subsidiary. Thus, the firm must have *increased* its local currency investments in its foreign subsidiaries.

H.   (i)   The percentage decline in foreign sales is significantly below the decline factor computed in part D. However the part D factor is based on comparison of exchange rates at fiscal year-ends. The effect on sales is based on average rates for the fiscal years, which might be quite different.

Therefore, while the sales decline probably reflects weak foreign currencies, and should not surprise us, more data is needed to estimate the exchange rate impact on reported sales.

(ii)   The data needed would be average exchange rates for the fiscal year, preferably weighted by Commercial Intertech's sales in each foreign currency.

(iii)   Year to year sales comparisons are also affected by volume changes, price changes (in local currencies), and acquisition and divestiture activities. Removing exchange rate changes from the sales trend may permit better focus on these other effects.

13.   A.   Functional currency = hib means that local financial statements are prepared in hib and then translated into dollars.

First in First Out	Last in First Out
Cost of goods sold: Opening inventory hib 6,000 becomes COGS; translate at rate when sold ($1 = 6 hib) makes COGS $1,000	Purchases during the year of hib 7,500 becomes COGS; translate at rate when sold ($1 = 6 hib) makes COGS $1,250
Ending inventory: Purchases during the year of hib 7,500 translated at closing rate of $1 = 6 hib makes inventory $1,250	Opening inventory of hib 6,000 remains in inventory; when translated at the closing rate makes inventory $1,000

NOTE: COGS and ending inventory must total hib 13,500, the sum of opening inventory and purchases, regardless of inventory method.

B.   Functional currency = dollar means that calculations are made using dollars; rules of SFAS 8 apply.

First in First Out	Last in First Out
Cost of goods sold: Opening inventory of $1,500 (hib 6,000/4) becomes COGS	Purchases during the year of $1,500 (hib 7,500/5) become COGS
Ending inventory: Purchases during the year of $1,500 remain in inventory	Opening inventory of $1,500 remains in inventory

NOTE: COGS and ending inventory must total $3,000, the sum of opening inventory and purchases.

C.   The essence of LIFO is that (with rising prices) higher priced purchases become COGS, whereas lower priced goods remain in inventory; FIFO is the reverse, resulting in higher income (lower COGS) and higher inventory valuation.

The choice of functional currency interacts with the choice of inventory method. When the functional currency is the hib (local

13-18

currency), the normal LIFO/FIFO effects are directly transmitted to the parent company financial statements. This accords with the objective of SFAS 52 of having parent results replicate subsidiary results.

However, SFAS 8 applies when the dollar (the parent or reporting currency) is used as the functional currency. Price changes are measured in dollars rather than hibs. In this case, the unit price in dollars has not changed. Purchases are at $15 (hib 75/5) which is unchanged from the cost of opening inventory (hib 60/4). Thus, in dollars there is no price change and LIFO = FIFO.

Generalizing, the choice of functional currency determines whether the effects of changing prices are determined in the local currency or the reporting currency. Depending on the interplay between price changes and currency exchange rates, the impact of LIFO versus FIFO can be quite different depending on the choice of functional currency.

14. A. Tooling costs decrease Swedish equity, perhaps reflecting more rapid writeoff than under U.S. GAAP.

Interest costs also decrease Swedish equity, suggesting that interest is not capitalized under Swedish GAAP.

Business combinations reduce equity under Swedish GAAP as well. That may be due to different treatment of goodwill or varying standards for use of the pooling and purchase methods.

Leasing reduces equity under U.S. GAAP, suggesting that some capital leases are treated as operating leases under Swedish GAAP.

Income taxes have the largest effect of all, sharply reducing equity under U.S. GAAP. Apparently Swedish GAAP does not require deferred taxes.

B. The effect of income tax accounting on net income varies from year to year depending upon the relationship between pretax income and taxable income. Deferred tax effects for an individual year can be positive or negative.

C. Reported net income (millions of SEK)

	1988	1989	1990	1991
Swedish GAAP	3329	5128	(1020)	682
U.S. GAAP	4953	5400	(23)	816

Net income under Swedish GAAP appears to be more volatile than under U.S. GAAP. This may be due to the absence of deferred tax accounting which often smooths variations in reported income.

D. There is no simple answer to this question; a good answer requires additional data. For example, income taxes account for the largest share of the difference in both equity and net income. Which set of figures is better depends on the likelihood that deferred taxes will require cash outflows in the near future (see Chapter 7 for discussion). Similarly, the choice of depreciation methods and lives should reflect economic depreciation rather than arbitrary standards.

The benefit of the reconciliation is that it presents net income and equity under two sets of accounting principles, permitting the analyst to gain insight into the key determinants of the amounts reported in financial statements.

15. A. 1. Publishing rights, titles, and television licenses are not required to be amortized.

2. Assets can be revalued above historic cost.

3. Redeemable preference shares and minority interest are considered to be equity.

4. Refinancing costs are charged to earnings immediately.

5. The equity method of accounting is not allowed.

B. Net income ($A millions):

	1990	1991	1992
Australian GAAP	A$343	A$(393)	A$502
U.S. GAAP	270	(305)	241
Operating earnings*	365	(240)	432

*Australian GAAP net income plus adjustments for equity method, interest on convertible notes, startup and refinancing costs. Amortization of intangibles, valuation adjustments, and other nonoperating items are excluded.

U.S. GAAP earnings are less volatile than Australian GAAP net income and (over the three year period) 54% lower due primarily to the amortization items. Operating earnings are higher still, due to the absence of nonoperating items as well as amortization. Operating earnings are also less volatile than Australian net income.

Chapter 14 - Solutions

1.
Total shareholders' equity (reported)	$ 8498 million
Less: liquidation preference of preferred stock	(6256)
Equals: Book value of common stock	$ 2242

Number of common shares outstanding: 92.6 million

Book value per common share = $2242/92.6 = $24.21

2.
Total shareholders' equity (reported)	$45,000,000
Less: liquidating value of preferred shares[1]	(19,000,000)
Less: preferred dividends in arrears[2]	(1,260,000)
Equals: Book value of common stock	$24,740,000

Number of common shares outstanding: 300,000

Book value per common share = $24,740,000/300,000 = $82.47

> [1]200,000 @ $95 per share liquidating value. The call price of $105 would be used when it is expected that the preferred shares would be called.
> [2]1991 dividends must eventually be paid because of cumulative feature: 7% x $90 par value = $6.30 per share x 200,000 shares

3. The equity value screen has apparently computed the long-term debt/total long-term capital ratio as follows:

> long-term debt/(long-term debt + minority interest + common equity)
> = $675/ ($675 + $100 + $2050)
> = $675/$2825
> = 23.9%

    A.   (i)   Joint venture: add the amount of the debt to both long-term debt and fixed assets. Under the equity method, subsidiary debt is excluded from the parent company balance sheet yet the parent is indirectly liable for the debt. The guarantee by Lubbock is another reason to show the debt on its balance sheet.

         (ii)   Inventories: add $200 million to both inventories and equity to show inventories at current cost.

         (iii) Leases: add the $750 million present value of the operating lease payments to both plant and equipment and debt. Long-term leases should be capitalized even when they do not meet the definition of capital leases (see Chapter 8).

Total result of these adjustments is that debt is increased by $1000 million ($250 + $750) while equity is increased by $200 million. The adjusted long-term debt to total capital ratio is:

($675 + $1000)/($2825 + $1000 + $200)
= $1675/$4025
= 41.6%

B.   There is no tax impact of the first adjustment as it represents principal payments. The LIFO reserve would be taxable if it were liquidated. Under some circumstances the aftertax reserve should be used. The leases are taxed as operating leases whether or not they are capitalized for reporting purposes. The difference gives rise to temporary differences that are eliminated by the end of the lease term. If leases are capitalized for analysis purposes, deferred taxes related to the temporary differences should be recognized in theory; in practice they are small enough to ignore in most cases.

C.   (i)   Prior to the adoption of SFAS 115, marketable equity securities were carried at the lower of cost or market as either current or noncurrent assets; debt securities were usually carried at amortized cost. Realized gains and losses were included in reported income, along with some valuation changes on current portfolios.

Under SFAS 115 marketable debt and equity securities are divided into three categories (basis for carrying amount in parentheses):

1.   Held for investment (amortized cost)
2.   Held for sale (market value)
3.   Trading (market value)

Both realized and unrealized gains and losses for securities in the third category (trading), and realized gains and losses for the first two categories, are recognized in reported income. (For category 2, unrealized gains and losses are charged directly to equity.)

Thus, differences in the categorization of investment portfolios and in whether unrealized gains and losses are realized affect both the balance sheet and reported income. For purposes of analysis, all securities should be marked to market, with income and equity adjusted for the difference between cost and market value.

(ii)   Starting in 1993, all firms must use SFAS 109 to account for income taxes. Under that standard, the following differences among companies should be noted:

1.   Valuation allowances on deferred tax assets
2.   Recognition of deferred taxes on foreign subsidiaries and joint ventures.
3.   Recognition of deferred taxes on pre-1993 earnings of domestic joint ventures.

The analyst must also consider how to treat deferred tax assets and liabilities (see Chapter 7 for discussion).

(iii) Capitalization policy: interest, computer software, R&D, and so forth. All affect reported income and, therefore, net worth.

(iv) Convertible securities and other hybrids must be considered for appropriate classification between debt and equity.

(v) Postretirement benefits; under SFAS 87 (pensions) and SFAS 106 (other postretirement benefits), gains and losses and other events are subject to smoothed recognition. Both debt and equity may have to be adjusted for unrecognized items.

(vi) Choice of functional currency for foreign operations will affect the translated balance sheet as well as the disposition of translation gains and losses. Both factors can change equity.

D. SFAS 106 requires that postemployment benefits be accounted for on the accrual basis. Firms offering such benefits were required to either recognize the transition liability at the time of adopting the new standard or amortize that liability over a twenty year period. The choice of transition method and the choice of actuarial assumptions may significantly affect reported debt and equity.

SFAS 109 replaced both SFAS 96 and APB 11. The new standard may affect reported equity by permitting recognition of deferred tax assets, by requiring restatement of purchase method acquisitions, and by restating deferred tax assets and liabilities for changes in tax rates.

4. (1) The excess of the PBO over plan assets is $160,000 ($585,000 – $425,000). While SFAS 87 permits only gradual recognition of this difference in many cases, the entire difference should be recognized for analysis. The difference should be considered debt with an offset to equity. This would raise Jersey's leverage ratios. The interest coverage ratio would not be affected.

(2) The adoption of SFAS 106 will result in either a large one time charge (transition liability) or recognition of that liability over a twenty year period. Annual expense will also rise. The transition liability should be considered debt. Recognition of the liability would reduce equity. Leverage ratios would be increased. Times interest earned is not affected.

(3) $150 million should be added to Jersey's debt and assets, increasing leverage ratios. The annual interest of $15 million (at 10% interest rate) would reduce the interest coverage ratio.

(4) Eighty ($80) million should be added to assets and equity to report all inventories at current cost. This adjustment would lower (improve) Jersey's leverage ratios.

(5) The present value of these operating leases should be added to assets and debt; the times interest earned ratio should be adjusted as well. The present value of the leases (at 10%) is $180 million. The 1993 interest expense is $18 million (at 10%). Leverage ratios rise and the interest coverage ratio falls.

- All of the adjustments together would:

- Increase debt as a result of adjustments 1, 2, 3, and 5.

- Increase equity as a result of adjustment 4.

- Decrease equity as result of adjustment 1 and 2.

- Increase assets as a result of adjustment 3, 4 and 5.

- Increase interest expense as a result of adjustments 3 and 5.

The adjusted times interest earned ratio can be calculated:

Reported ratio = 3.5;
EBIT = $350 million;
therefore interest expense must be $100 million.

Adjustment (3) increases both EBIT and interest expense by $15 million. Adjustment (5) increases interest expense by $18 million and will increase EBIT by the difference between lease expense and depreciation. If lease expense is $36 million and depreciation is $9 million ($180 million/20 years), then EBIT rises by $27 million.

Adjusted ratio
= ($350 + $15 + $27)/($100 + $15 + $18)
= $392/$133
= 2.95.

To complete the leverage calculations, we require:

(i) Amount of transition obligation under SFAS 106

(ii) Reported levels of debt and equity.

5. A.

	Before Kraft	Consolidated
Pretax interest coverage[1]	10.64X	3.76X
Long-term debt/total capital[2]	28.11%	61.99%
Cash flow/total debt[3]	71.14%	23.14%

[1]   ($4820+$500)/$500   ($4420+$1600)/$1600

[2] $3883/($3883+$9931) $15778/($15778+$9675)

[3] ($2820+$750+$100-$125)   ($2564+$1235+$390-$125)
    ($3883 + $1100)   ($15,778 + $ 1783)

B. Pretax interest coverage moves from the AA range to the BBB range. Long-term debt/total capital shifts from A to less than B. Cash flow/total debt declines from between A and AA to BB.

C.   Prior to the merger, Philip Morris debt would have a strong A rating based on these criteria. After the Kraft merger, BB would be appropriate based on these same criteria.

6.   *NOTE: The answers given below concern the effect of the merger on the probability of bankruptcy as predicted by Altman's models. It is not clear that ratio changes caused by external events (such as an acquisition) have the same predictive ability as those resulting from normal operations.*

The variables used in Altman's two models (see Exhibit 14-15) are listed below by category:

	(1977 model)	*(1968 model)*
Activity		Sales to total assets
Liquidity	Current ratio	Working capital to total assets
Leverage and Solvency	Equity (market) to debt	Equity (market) to capital
	Times interest earned	
Profitability	Return on assets	Return on assets
	Retained earnings to total assets	Retained earnings to total assets
Earnings Variability	Standard error of ROA	
Size	Total assets	

Activity

(1968 model) Sales to total assets

Sales increased by $11,610 (approximately 33%) from $33,080 to $44,690 as a result of the merger. Although Exhibit 14P-2 does not provide the data directly, we can infer from the data available that the increase in assets would be greater.

Debt plus equity increased[1] by $12,322. When we consider that current operating liabilities and other (nondebt) liabilities also increased as a result of the merger, we can infer that total assets grew by *at least* $12,322.

[1]Total debt + equity (pre merger) = $1100 + $3883 + $9931 = $14,914
                    (post merger) = $1783 + $15778 + $9675 = 27,236
        Increase   =   = $12,322

If, prior to the merger, the asset turnover ratio was greater than 1, then adding a given amount ($11,610) to the numerator and a larger amount to the denominator would reduce the ratio, increasing the likelihood of bankruptcy.

If, on the other hand, prior to the merger, the asset turnover ratio was less than 1, then more information about actual asset levels is needed to determine the effect on this ratio.

Liquidity

(1977 model) Current ratio
(1968 model) Working capital to total assets

The information in Exhibit 14P-2 is insufficient to assess the impact of the merger on working capital and the current ratio.

Leverage and Solvency

(1977 model) Market value of equity to debt
(1968 model) Market value of equity to capital

Before the merger, Philip Morris' total debt was $4,983 million ($1,100+$3,883). As a result of the merger, total debt increased more than threefold to $17,561 million ($1,783+$15,778). Unless the market value of equity increased by the same proportion [Philip Morris' market value actually *decreased* following the merger announcement] the equity to debt (capital) ratio would be reduced considerably, increasing the likelihood of bankruptcy.

(1977 model) Times interest earned

From problem 5, we have

	Before Kraft	Consolidated
Pretax interest coverage	10.64X	3.76X

Based on the (1977) model, the reduction in the coverage ratio would increase the likelihood of bankruptcy.

Profitability

(Both Models) Return on assets

Philip Morris' EBIT rose from $5320 million ($4820+$500) to $6020 million ($4420+$1600). As a percent of sales, EBIT decreased from 16% ($5320/$33080) to 13.5% ($6020/$44690). The impact on ROA depends on the asset turnover (discussed earlier). However, unless asset turnover increased by (at least) 18.5%, the net effect would be a reduction in ROA.

(Both Models) Retained earnings to total assets

Since the merger is accounted for under the purchase method, Kraft's retained earnings are eliminated. As total assets increase, this ratio would be greatly reduced. The reported ratio results in prediction by the model of a greater likelihood of bankruptcy.

Earnings Variability

(1977 model) Standard deviation of ROA

Similar to portfolio diversification, the variance of return measures such as ROA should decline following the merger, reducing the likelihood of bankruptcy.

Size

(1977 model) Total assets

As total assets increase as a result of the merger, the model predicts a smaller likelihood of bankruptcy.

7. The theoretical as well as empirical models (Exhibit 14-17), indicate that beta risk is a function of both the operating (unleveraged beta) and financial (leveraged) risk of the company. As Philip Morris' debt increased by approximately $12 billion as a result of the merger without a commensurate increase in equity the firm's financial leverage increased. Ceteris paribus, this should result in an increase in financial risk and beta.

    The effect on operating risk depends on how Kraft's cost structure compares with that of Philip Morris, that is, on the mix between fixed and variable costs. The impact on beta would depend on the answer to this question.

8. A. 1. KO has better short-term liquidity as its current and acid test ratios are higher. Note its large cash balance. Accounts receivable turnover is the same for both firms. CCE has a much higher inventory turnover ratio, however.

        2. KO's ratio of long-term debt to equity is far lower than CCE's. However, KO has substantial short-term debt; the total debt to equity ratio, while still higher for CCE, is less disparate. CCE's debt burden and low profitability result in an interest coverage ratio that is far below that of KO.

        3. KO's property and total asset turnover ratios are superior to those of CCE; the latter is more capital intensive.

        4. KO is more profitable than CCE by all measures. Higher gross margins are carried down to net income. Given its lower capital requirement, KO's return ratios are also higher.

    B. and C. 1. Adjustment of inventories to current cost mainly affects KO. Effect is to reinforce KO's superior current and debt ratios. On the other hand, it reduces KO's turnover ratios.

        2. Adjustment of KO investments from carrying amount to market value ($291 million). Effect is to reduce leverage but also turnover ratios and return ratios.

        3. Recognize off-balance sheet obligations. Larger effect for KO ($133 million guarantee) than for CCE (operating leases). Recognition increases relative leverage of KO, decreases return and turnover ratios.

        4. Remove nonrecurring items from income statement of CCE: pretax gain on debt repurchase, restructuring provision, and gain on sale of operations. Net gain is $85.5

million ($104+$8.5-$27). Removal reduces profitability of CCE further relative to KO.

5. Remove purchased goodwill from balance sheets; major impact on CCE as equity is now negative. The low profitability of CCE suggests that this is accounting goodwill with no economic justification. Elimination sharply raises leverage ratios but improves asset turnover and return ratios. The last two ratios also benefit from the elimination of goodwill amortization from the income statement.

9. A. (i) **Fiscal 1991 ratios**

	Deere Ratio	Rating Category
Pretax interest coverage[1]	1.35X	BB/B
Pretax fixed charge coverage[1]	1.35X	BB
Pretax funds flow interest coverage[2]	1.75X	B
Funds from operations/total debt[3]	5.67%	CCC
Free operating cash flow/total debt[4]	(13.49%)	CCC
Pretax return on permanent capital[5]	5.49%	CCC
Operating income/sales[6]	8.59%	B
Long-term debt/capitalization[7]	43.75%	BB
Total debt/capitalization[8]	66.69%	B
Total debt/capitalization[8] (including leases)	66.69%	BB

NOTES: *Calculations exclude restructuring costs from income.*
Data for income, restructuring costs, interest expense, CFO, and cash for investments obtained from Deere financial statements (Appendix 1-B).
Data for debt and capitalization summarized in Exhibit 14-3.

[1](Pretax income + restructuring + interest expense)/interest = (-$26+$182+$450)/$450
[2](FFO + interest expense)/interest = ($338+$450)/$450
[3]FFO/total debt = $338/$5677
[4]Free operating cash flow for Deere = CFO less cash for investment = $613-$1379; debt = $5677
[5]Permanent capital for Deere defined as common equity = $2836; Pretax return = -$26+$182
[6]Operating income = -$26+$450+$182; total revenues = $7055
[7]Long-term debt/capitalization = $2206/($2206+$2836)
[8]Total debt/capitalization = $5677/$8513

(ii) Based on the ratios in A (i), it appears that Deere debt should be rated B.

B. (i) Using Exhibits 14-1 and 14-3, the following adjusted ratios can be computed for fiscal 1991:

	Deere Ratio	Rating Category
Long-term debt/capitalization [$2241/($2241+$2075)]	51.92%	BB-
Total debt/capitalization [$5959/$8034]	74.17%	B
Total debt/capitalization [$5959/$8034] (including leases)	74.17%	B

Additional ratios can be adjusted using the cash flow analysis in Exhibit 14-13:

Funds from operations/total debt [-$29/$5959]	(0.49)%	CCC-
Free cash flow/total debt [-$391/$5959]	(6.56)%	CCC

(ii) The adjusted ratios suggest that even a B rating may be too high.

(iii) and (iv) Bond ratings act as a "surrogate" measure of the probability of a firm defaulting on its interest or principal payments. Thus, in assessing Deere's default risk, knowledge of these adjustments should increase the probability of default. However, it may not lead to a change in the bond rating. Similar adjustments may be made for other firms and the bond rating agency may have already incorporated these adjustments in their rating classification. Unless the adjustments for Deere are much different than for other firms, adjustment to current cost will not change the *relative* rating of firms.

(v) On a univariate basis, an early study by Beaver found that the best predictor of bankruptcy was the CFO/total liabilities ratio. The importance of CFO in avoiding Type I errors was further confirmed by the results of the Casey and Bartczak study. For the multivariate models listed in Exhibit 14-15, leverage was found to be an important variable for each model. As the adjustments made increase reported debt and reduce reported CFO, the overall effect would be to increase the probability of bankruptcy.

C. The unrecognized transition obligation means that many of Deere's ratios are worse than they appear. Thus, *the existence* of the transition liability should increase the probability of default and/or bankruptcy. However, as many other firms may also have large unrecognized transition obligations, the relative ranking of Deere and hence its rating classification may not differ after this factor is taken into account.

10. A. The following ratios can be computed from the data in Exhibit 14P-5:

	1991	1992
Debt/total capital	0.42	0.58
Operating income/sales	0.05	(0.01)
Interest coverage	1.96	(0.25)
CFO/total debt	0.21	(0.05)
Pretax ROE	0.05	(0.09)

The 1992 data in Exhibit 14P-5 show marked deterioration. Using 1991 data, only debt/capital justified a BBB rating. Interest coverage and CFO/debt were BB while the other ratios were poor. In 1992, only the debt/capital ratio justified a BB rating; the others were below CCC. Given these ratios, the S&P decision seems unsurprising.

B. Abbreviated data are not sufficient to evaluate a firm's credit rating. Full financial statements and footnotes are required to assess the quality of a firm's assets. Attention should be paid to whether off-balance sheet or other "window dressing" transactions were engaged in during 1992. Detailed cash flow analysis would also be helpful.

C. The difficulty with this comparison is that 1992 was a year of serious recession in the paper industry; 1988-1990, while not boom years, were not poor ones either. In any case, the sample of firms used to compile Exhibit 14-22 may not be comparable to James River.

11. A. The following ratios can be computed from the data provided:

	1991	1992
Debt/total capital	0.37	0.38
Operating income/sales	0.14	0.13
Interest coverage	3.26	3.02
CFO/total debt	0.34	0.33
Pretax ROE	0.13	0.12

Despite some deterioration in 1992, most of Westvaco's ratios would justify a BBB rating. The debt/total capital ratio alone would justify an A rating.

B. Based on the long-term debt/capital ratio, Westvaco should be BBB rated while James River and Union Camp are BB. The 1991 interest coverage ratio for James River falls into the BB range while the other firms justify a BBB rating.

Thus all three firms would appear to be candidates for the downgrading of their debt.

C. and D. The data in Exhibit 14P-7 show the effect of the recession on three paper companies. The comparison shows that all three firms should be downgraded based on 1991 data alone. Given a longer term perspective, however, rating agencies should be willing to tolerate poor performance during recessions as long as operating results (and ratios) are at acceptable levels over the entire business cycle. Thus, it is not as clear that a downgrading is required, especially for Westvaco, whose 1992 ratios held up relatively well.

12. A.   Book value per share (£), September 30,

		1990	1991
(i)	U.K. GAAP (2834/4796; 3325/4808)	£0.59	£0.69
(ii)	U.S. GAAP (6632/4796; 7093/4808)	1.38	1.48

Method of calculation: stockholders' equity/shares outstanding

B.   Book value under U.S. GAAP is more than two times that under U.K. GAAP. The major difference is goodwill as it is included in book value under U.S. GAAP but has been written off under U.K. GAAP. As accounting goodwill bears little relationship to economic goodwill, U.K. book value is a better starting point.

This amount should, however, be adjusted for such items as postemployment benefits, the market value of assets, and income taxes. Footnote data and information from outside the financial statements may be needed to estimate current cost book value per share, which is the best representation of the Hanson's financial status.

C.   The executive options should be considered as exercised as the option price is well below market.

The first set of warrants should also be included as their exercise price in Sterling ($3.60/1.75 = £2.06) is also below market.

The second set of warrants should be excluded as their exercise price is well above market.

Hanson's convertible bonds should also be excluded; their conversion price is above market.

Interestingly, assuming exercise of any of these equity linked securities would increase book value per share (especially that under U.K. GAAP).* U.S. accounting principles for computing earnings per share (see Appendix 3-C) require that anti-dilutive securities be excluded. However, given the relationship of exercise prices to Hanson's market prices, it seems logical to assume exercise when it appears highly likely that exercise will take place.

*Because the exercise price exceeds the current book value.

13. A.   Book value per share (A$), June 30,

		1991	1992
(i)	Australian GAAP (9707/268; 11699/384)	A$36.22	A$30.47
(ii)	U.S. GAAP (2952/268; 4232/384)	11.01	11.02

Note that book value per share under Australian GAAP is approximately three times that under U.S. GAAP. Because asset revaluations are spread over more shares, 1992 book value per share is lower than the 1991 figure despite significant net income in 1992. Book value per share under U.S. GAAP is virtually unchanged.

B.   The advantage of including the revalued carrying amounts of publishing rights, book titles, and television licenses is that book value is more representative of the value of equity and the resources at management's disposal.

The disadvantage is that the amount and timing of revaluations are inherently subjective and can misstate the true values of these assets.

14.   A.   Book value per common share, Atlas Copco Group
SEK (rounded):

		1990	1991
(i)	Swedish GAAP	SEK 177	SEK 181
(ii)	U.S. GAAP	192	196
(iii)	IASC GAAP	169	173

B.   1.   Revaluation, given rising prices over time, should result in higher book values under Swedish GAAP.

2.   The equity method tends to increase book value as reported income includes the reinvested earnings of affiliates. Thus Swedish GAAP book value should be lowered.

3.   With declining corporate tax rates (especially in the U.S.), adjusting deferred tax liabilities for changing tax rates reduces their amount, with a corresponding increase in equity. Thus IASC GAAP book value should be lower.

4.   In most European countries dividends are first *proposed* by management but must be approved by shareholders. In that sense, they differ from dividends *declared* by the board of directors (shareholders' representatives). Under US GAAP, proposed dividends are not recognized. They must be declared before they are recognized. When proposed dividends are charged to equity, that figure is reduced. This factor should depress IASC GAAP book value.

IASC GAAP book value is lowest, presumably reflecting factors three and four. U.S. GAAP book value is highest, presumably reflecting use of the equity method. As Swedish GAAP book value is lower than that under U.S. GAAP, it appears that Atlas Copco has not used revaluation extensively.

C.   A current cost book value per share would include asset revaluations, use of the equity method (unless market value is available), and recognition of tax rate changes. Until a dividend is payable, it should be included in book value. Other adjustments could be made for inventories, marketable securities, employee benefit plans, and contingencies. Thus all of the GAAP book values, as well as other available data, can be used to compute an improved measure of book value per share.

Chapter 15 - Solutions

1. The models should give identical results. Using 1993 expected dividends of $4.50, a discount rate r of 20%, and growth rate g of 15%, we find that:

$$P = \frac{D}{r-g} = \frac{\$4.50}{.20-.15} = \$90$$

The dividend payout ratio for both 1992 ($4.05/$10.03 = 40.4%) and 1993 ($4.50/$11.40 = 39.5%) is approximately 40%. The long term growth rates for earnings and dividends differ. This is possible only if the payout rate will change over time. Thus, in an earnings based model using the earnings growth rate of 14%, we must use another (higher than 40%) estimate for the payout ratio. A payout ratio of 47.5% would result in the same valuation:

$$P = \frac{kE}{r-g} = \frac{(.475)(\$11.40)}{.20-.14} = \$90$$

Based on these models, Emfil shares are not attractive at a price of $115, and should not be added to the portfolio.

2. A. The P/E ratio with a dividend payout of k, discount rate of r and growth rate equal to g can be derived as:

$$P = \frac{kE(1+g)}{r-g} \text{ and } \frac{P}{E} = \frac{k(1+g)}{r-g}$$

For the Lo Company:

$$\frac{P}{E} = \frac{.2(\$1+.04)}{.10-.04} = 3.467$$

B. Hi's P/E ratio must be identical to that of Lo (3.467) as both firms have the same market value and earnings.

C.   Lo Company

	1988	1989	1990	1991	1992
1) Earnings per share	$1.00	$1.04	$1.08	$1.12	$1.17
2) Number of shares	1000	1000	1000	1000	1000
3) Net income	$1000	$1040	$1082	$1125	$1170
4) Dividends paid	200	208	216	225	234
5) New investment	800	832	865	900	936
6) Firm value at period end	3467	3605	3750	3900	4056
7) Price per share	3.47	3.61	3.75	3.90	4.06
8) P/E ratio	3.467	3.467	3.467	3.467	3.467

Calculations:
Item
1)   Given
2)   Since no new financing and no stock dividends or splits; shares must remain constant over time.
3)   Earnings per share x number of shares
4)   Dividends per share (given) x number of shares
5)   Net income - dividends paid
6)   (.2 x next year's income)/(.10-.04); 1992 value assumes that net income continues to grow at 4% rate.
7)   Firm value/number of shares
8)   Firm value/current year net income

Hi Company

	1988	1989	1990	1991	1992
1) Earnings per share	$1.00	$0.80	$0.64	$0.51	$0.41
2) Number of shares	1000	1300	1690	2197	2856
3) Net income	$1000	$1040	$1082	$1125	$1170
4) Dividends paid	1000	1040	1082	1125	1170
5) New investment	800	832	865	900	936
6) New financing	800	832	865	900	936
7) Firm value at period end	3467	3605	3750	3900	4056
8) Price/share before new issue	3.47	2.77	2.22	1.77	1.42
9) P/E ratio	3.467	3.467	3.467	3.467	3.467
10) Shares issued	300	390	507	659	857
11) Price/share at new issue	$2.67	$2.13	$1.71	$1.37	$1.09

Calculations based on issuance of shares at end of year:
Item
1)   Given
2)   1988 given; From 1989 on, previous year shares plus new shares issued
3)   Earnings per share x number of shares
4)   Dividends per share (given) x number of shares
5)   Identical in amount to that computed for Lo Company
6)   Equal to (5)
7)   Identical to Lo Company [(.2 x next year's income)/(.10-.04)]; 1992 value assumes that net income continues to grow at 4% rate.
8)   Firm value/number of shares
9)   Firm value/current year net income

10) and 11)   Since (number of shares + shares issued) x price per share at
               new issue = firm value and shares issued x price per share at
               new issue = new financing, therefore:
    10)   shares issued = new financing/price per share at new issue
    11)   price per share at new issue = (firm value - new financing)/
           number of shares (item 2)

D.   The growth rate is 4% for net income, dividends, and firm value. For
      the Lo Company, EPS also grows at 4% since the number of shares is
      constant. The Hi Company, on the other hand, keeps issuing new
      shares. Therefore, although net income is growing, earnings per
      share declines. This problem demonstrates the effect of dividend
      policy on reported growth rates.

      The company's return on new investments is 5%.

      Using the formula for growth,
          g = (1-k) x ROE,

      with k = 20% and g =4%, ROE = 5%.

          Alternatively, using 1989 as an example, on the additional
      investment of $800 the company's income increases by $40 or 5%.

          This return is lower than the required rate of return of 10%.
      Hence, the low P/E ratio. Both companies would be better off paying
      out all earnings as dividends and not making any new investments.

          Firm value would then equal $1000/.10 = $10,000

3.   A.   Cash flow before interest payments (i.e., free cash flow to the
            firm) is the same regardless of which bond is issued:

(in $ million)	Conventional		Zero Coupon	
	19X1	19X2	19X1	19X2
EBIT	$ 20	$ 20	$ 20	$ 20
Taxes	6	6	6	6
Free cash flow	$ 14	$ 14	$ 14	$ 14

            However cash flows reported in accordance with SFAS 95 differ:

(in $ million)	Conventional		Zero Coupon	
	19X1	19X2	19X1	19X2
Cash flow before interest	$ 14.0	$ 14.0	$ 14.0	$ 14.00
Interest paid	(1.0)	(1.0)	---	----
Tax benefit	0.3	0.3	0.3	0.33
	$ 13.3	$ 13.3	$ 14.3	$ 14.33

          The venture receives a tax benefit of 30% of interest expense
      in both cases because of the deductibility of interest expense.

15-3

B. For the conventional bond, bondholders will receive $1 million annually. The zero coupon bondholders will receive no cash interest. The after-tax interest paid by the firm is $0.7 million for the conventional bond, but a $0.3 million *inflow* for the zero coupon bond.

C. and D. The answers to parts A and B imply that the amount available for dividends is based on reported cash flows that depend on the form of the bond. This implication is incorrect. The "fallacy" is that, on January 1, 19X3 the conventional bond will require a debt repayment of $10 million. The zero coupon bond, however, will require payment of $12.1 million. The extra $2.1 million* precludes the use of the "extra" cash flow for dividends. Focusing on the free cash flows, however, indicates that firm values are identical as long as their WACCs are equivalent**.

*$1 million for two years   = $ 2.0 million
10% interest on first year's $1 million =   .1
Total accrued interest at 1-1-X3 $ 2.1 million

**The relative WACCs are also a consideration as, after 19X1, the zero coupon bond will result in higher debt. In most cases, the debt/equity ratio will rise.

4. A.

$$P = \frac{E}{r}$$

$$\frac{P}{E} = \frac{1}{r}$$

$$r = \frac{1}{P/E}$$

For a firm with a P/E ratio of 12

$r = 8.25\%$

B. (i) The increase of $3 is transitory. The market is saying that the price/earnings ratio should reflect only the "normal" earnings of $10 per share.

(ii) The increase of $3 is permanent and earnings in the future are expected to remain at $13. The market value is based on $13 per share of normal earnings.

(iii) The increase of $3 implies not only permanence but growth as future earnings are expected to increase above the present level of $13.

5. A. g = (1 - dividend payout) x ROE

12% = (1-k) x 20%

1-k = .6

 k = .4

Dividend payout ratio is 40%

B. With a dividend payout ratio of 40 %, new investment (from equity) must be .6 x $30,000 = $18,000

Current interest expense of $5000 at an interest rate of 10% implies debt of $50,000. At a growth rate of 12%; new investment from debt will equal .12 x $50,000 = $6000. [Alternate calculation: interest expense used to calculate debt level; $5600/.10 = $56,000.]

Total investment:

Replacement (depreciation)	=	$ 8,000
New investment	=	24,000 ($18,000 + $6,000)
Total		$ 32,000

C. **Cash Flow Statement**

	Current	Forecast
Net income	$30,000	$33,600
Depreciation	8,000	8,960
Cash from operations	$38,000	$42,560
Cash for investment	(32,000)	(35,840)
Cash for financing:		
New debt	6,000	6,720
Dividends paid	(12,000)	(13,440)
	$(6,000)	$ (6,720)
Change in Cash	0	0

NOTE: *this cash flow statement assumes no change in working capital accounts.*

D. **Free Cash Flow Calculation**

	Current	Forecast
Operating income	$ 35,000	$ 39,200
Depreciation	8,000	8,960
	$ 43,000	$ 48,160
Investment	(32,000)	(35,840)
Free cash flow	**$ 11,000**	**$ 12,320**
Financing cash flows:		
New debt	6,000	6,720
Interest paid	(5,000)	(5,600)
	1,000	1,120
Dividends paid	(12,000)	(13,440)
Financing cash flow*	$(11,000)	$(12,320)

*Remember that interest paid must be reclassified from operating to financing cash flow for purposes of valuation.

E.   The value of the debt is:

      ($50,000 + $6,000)   = $ 56,000

The value of the equity is:

$$\frac{\$12,000 \times (1.12)}{.15 - .12} = \frac{\$13,440}{.03} = \underline{\$448,000}$$

Value of the firm is: $504,000

Check:

WACC = ($56000/$504000)(.10) + ($448000/$504000)(.15)
     = .14444

[FCF(1+g)]/(WACC-g) = [$11000(1.12)]/(.14444-.12)
                        = $12320/.02444
                        = $504000

6.   A.   From problem 5 we have $6,000 of new investment financed by debt. The present value factor for 5 years at 10% is 3.79 yielding lease payments of:

$$\frac{\$6000}{3.79} = \$1583 \text{ per year}$$

B.   The difference between the two forecast statements is in the selling and interest expense categories. We begin by disaggregating these items from the current and forecast income statements of problem 5:

Selling Expense:

	Current	12% Increase	Forecast
Depreciation	$ 8,000	$ 960	$ 8,960
Other	17,000	2,040	19,040
Total	$25,000	$ 3,000	$28,000

| Interest Expense | $ 5,000 | $ 600 | $ 5,600 |

    The new investment of $24,000 increases depreciation by $960. With $6,000 of the new investment as a lease, the additional depreciation (on the remaining $18,000) is only $720.

Reconciliation for operating lease:

Selling Expense:

	Current	Increase	Forecast
Depreciation	$ 8,000	$ 720	$ 8,720
Other	17,000	2,040	19,040
Rent expense			1,583
Total			$29,343

The difference of $1343 ($29,343 - $28,000) between selling expense for the operating lease method and that for Problem 5 is due to $1583 rent expense replacing $240 of depreciation.

Interest Expense: The $600 difference between the two methods represents the interest expense on the leased asset. Under the operating expense all payments are included in selling expense.

Reconciliation for capital lease:

Selling Expense:

	Current	Increase	Forecast
Depreciation	$ 8,000	$ 720	$ 8,720
Other	17,000	2,040	19,040
Amortization of leased asset			1,200
Total			$28,960

The $1200 amortization of leased assets replaces $240 of depreciation, increasing selling expense by $960 ($28,960 - $28,000) as compared with the problem 5 forecast. Note that amortization is not equal to depreciation because the leased assets must be amortized over the (5 year) lease term unless there is a bargain purchase option.

Interest Expense: is the same as interest on the capital lease equals interest on the debt that it replaces.

C. Before presenting the cash flow statements, we must note the cash flow consequences of the lease.

Increased cash outflow to lessors: The lease requires annual outlays of $1583, all charged to cash from operations for the operating lease. [$600 is interest and the remaining $983 is principal repayment for the capital lease]. In the problem 5 scenario, only $600 in interest is paid.

Decrease in replacement cost: Our example assumes that depreciation equals replacement cost for acquired assets. When some assets are leased, this equality no longer holds as depreciation is reduced by $240. However, leased assets "used up" must still be replaced. We assume that such replacement is effected through additional leases.

To maintain similar levels of debt and equity the company must obtain additional cash of $743 ($983-$240) each year by borrowing.

Cash Flow Statement, Operating Lease:

	Current	*Forecast*
Net income	$30,000	$32,857
Depreciation	8,000	8,720
Cash from operations	$38,000	$41,577
Cash for investment	(26,000)	(28,880)
Cash for financing:		
Dividends paid	(12,000)	(13,440)
New debt	---	743
Total	(12,000)	(12,697)
Change in cash	0	0

Lease payments are included in cash from operations. The "acquisition" of the leased asset, however, is ignored in the statement of cash flows.

D.   **Cash Flow Statement, Capital Lease:**

	Current	Forecast
Net income	$ 30,000	$ 32,640
Depreciation/amortization	8,000	9,920
Cash from operations	$ 38,000	$ 42,560
Cash for investment	(26,000)	(28,880)
Cash for financing:		
Dividends paid	(12,000)	(13,440)
Debt repayment (lease)		(983)
New debt	---	743
Total	$(12,000)	$(13,680)
Change in cash	0	0

Principal payments for the leased assets are included in cash for financing but the interest payment is part of cash from operations. The actual acquisition of the leased assets is not shown directly in the cash flow statement. Rather, it is disclosed as a "significant noncash investment and financing activity".

E.   **Free Cash Flow Calculation**

Based on reported cash flows alone, free cash flow (after removing interest) appears to be:

		Forecast Year	
	Current	Operating	Capital
Operating income	$35,000	$37,857	$38,240
Depreciation	8,000	8,720	9,920
Cash from operations	$43,000	$46,577	$48,160
Cash for investment	(26,000)	(28,880)	(28,880)
"Reported free cash flow"	$17,000	$17,697	$19,280

However economically, these cases are identical to the problem 5 case, where free cash flow is $12,320 (5-D). The only difference from that case is that the LZ company has leased assets rather than purchasing them, and two different accounting methods are used to account for the leases.

To obtain this result we must adjust reported free cash flow by treating leases as investment and financing activities:

		Forecast Year	
	Current	Operating	Capital
"Reported free cash flow"	$17,000	$17,697	$19,280
Rent expense	---	1,583	---
Acquisition of leased assets	(6,000)	(6,960)	(6,960)
Free cash flow	$11,000	$12,320	$12,320

For the forecast year, leased assets acquired = $6720 + $240. The first component is 12% above the current year amount, reflecting the assumed 12% growth rate. The second component is required to replace "used up" assets (see Part C).

Free cash flows are now identical to those found in problem 5.

F.   The solutions will be identical to problem 5E as the leases are another form of investment and debt and should be so treated in any valuation context.

G.   Leases should not affect a valuation model as long as appropriate analytic adjustments are made. Leases are a form of investment and debt and their substitution should not affect valuation.

7.   *NOTE: The FAB example illustrates the difficulty of applying theoretical valuation models to an actual company and the sensitivity of the results to the assumptions made.*

The data available is as of September 1, 1989, well into that year. Thus, in the valuation analysis, although 1989 data is forecast, in many cases we treat 1989 as the "current" year.

A.   FAB's 1988 book value is $26.62 per share; the 1989 forecast is $28.95. The market value of $36 per share is well above these amounts. This suggests that FAB has some economic goodwill.

Alternative explanations may be that the historical value of its inventories and/or fixed costs are below market values. The LIFO valuation basis gives some credence to this viewpoint. Also see Exhibit 14-1 (page 1020) for other possible adjustments to book value.

B.   (i)   **Implicit Growth Rate**

	1985	1986	1987	1988	1989
All per share:					
Earnings	$2.39	$2.95	$2.94	$2.62	$3.20
Dividends	0.50	0.60	0.60	0.70	0.80
Book value	19.52	21.86	24.70	26.62	28.95
Payout ratio	20.9%	20.3%	20.4%	26.7%	25.0%
ROE = $\frac{EPS}{Ave.\ BPS^*}$	12.9%	14.3%	12.6%	10.2%	11.5%
Estimated growth**	10.2%	11.4%	10.1%	7.5%	8.6%

*1984 BPS approximated as 1985 BPS - 1985 EPS + 1985 DPS
**Implicit growth rate = (1 - payout ratio) x ROE

Historical Growth Rate (from prior year)

	1985	1986	1987	1988	1989
Earnings per share: Arithmetic Average: 8.5% Geometric Average: 7.6%	---	23%	0%	(11%)	22%
Dividends per share: Arithmetic Average: 10.0% Geometric average: 12.5%	---	20%	0%	16%	14%

Value Line Forecast Growth Rates
     Earnings per share: 10%
     Dividends per share: 9.5%

The implicit growth rate has been erratic and declined over the period to about 8.00%. This is in line with the historical growth rate for earnings but considerably less than the historical growth rate for dividends. Value Line's forecast growth rates seem to be "compromise" estimates. They have estimated a higher growth rate for EPS, implicitly assuming a recovery in ROE but lowered the rate for DPS, assuming that the payout ratio will return to the lower level of earlier years.

The implicit growth rate estimates have the advantage of being derived from the actual operating results of FAB and, therefore, showing the declining trends of ROE and the implicit growth rate. Using this estimate for forecast purposes requires assumptions about whether these trends will continue.

The historical growth rates are very erratic, limiting their usefulness for forecasting. Using averages solves the variability problem but gives little insight into trends.

The Value Line estimates have the advantage of reflecting some informed judgment about the company and may also reflect "guidance" from management. On the other hand, these estimates are only as good as the analyst making the forecast. Comparisons of companies followed by different analysts may suffer from differing forecast methods and biases.

(ii)   Historical growth rates of per share data may be distorted as FAB has repurchased shares, distorting the data in two ways:

   (1)   since the number of shares has changed the per share growth pattern may differ from the pattern in total dollars.

   (2)   in the context of valuation models, share repurchases should be treated as dividends.

   We can estimate the amount of repurchases by converting the per share data into total dollars (multiplying by the number of shares). The resulting data can be used to calculate adjusted historical growth rates:

(data in millions)	1985	1986	1987	1988	1989
Number of shares[*]	3.63	3.63	3.53	3.43	3.28

[*]This is the number of shares at year end. EPS and DPS should be multiplied by the *average* number of shares outstanding. Using the year end shares understates dollar earnings and dividends when shares outstanding are declining.

($ millions)	1985	1986	1987	1988	1989
Earnings	$ 8.68	$10.71	$10.38	$ 8.99	$10.50
Dividends	1.82	2.18	2.12	2.40	2.62
Book value	70.90	79.40	87.20	91.30	95.00
Implied book value[1]		79.40	87.66	93.79	99.18
Repurchases		$ 0	$ .46	$ 2.49	$ 4.18
Total dividends[2]		2.18	2.58	4.89	6.80

[1]Implied book value can be calculated by adding earnings and subtracting dividends from the prior year's book value.
[2]Actual dividends plus share repurchases

	1986	1987	1988	1989
Implicit Growth Rate				
Adjusted payout ratio	20.3%	24.9%	54.4%	64.8%
Adjusted ROE	14.3%	12.5%	10.1%	11.3%
Adjusted implicit growth	11.4%	9.4%	4.3%	4.0%
Historical Growth Rate				
Earnings	23.0%	(3.1%)	(13.4%)	16.8%
Arithmetic average: 5.8%				
Geometric average: 4.9%				
Dividends (ignoring repurchases)	19.8%	(2.8%)	13.2%	9.2%
Arithmetic average: 9.8%				
Geometric average: 9.5%				
Dividends (including repurchases)	19.8%	18.3%	89.5%	39.1%
Arithmetic average: 41.7%				
Geometric average: 43.1%				

C.   Using the CAPM allows us to estimate FAB's cost of equity as:

$$r = R_f + B(R_m - R_f) = .08 + .8(.06) =   12.8\%$$

As we shall see, valuation is sensitive to the estimates used for the relevant parameters.

Dividend discount model

For this model, as well as the other models, we must forecast the future level of dividends. Is the starting point $2.62 million (ignoring repurchases) or $6.80 (including repurchases)? That is, which level is more indicative of future payments to shareholders? Will management continue to make share repurchases?

With current dividends of $2.62 million (ignoring repurchases) as the appropriate starting point, we use a 9.5% growth rate. This rate is the Value Line forecast and is consistent with historical growth rates. Thus:

$$P = \frac{D(1+g)}{r-g} = \frac{(\$2.62)(1.095)}{.128-.095} = \$86.94 \; million$$

The value of $86.94 million translates to $26.51/share ($86.94/3.28), approximately 25% less than the market price of $36/share. The sensitivity of the model to the assumed growth rate can be illustrated by increasing the growth rate by 0.5% to 10%. The model now yields a value of $31.40 per share, an increase of close to 20%.

With dividends of $6.80 million (including share repurchases) as the appropriate starting point, the choice of growth rate is more difficult. The historical growth rate of 40% for dividends (including repurchases) seems untenable in the long run. At the other extreme is the 4% implicit rate. The following table shows the per share value of Fab with varying growth rates:

Growth rate	Per share value
5%	$27.91
8%	$46.65
10%	$81.45

Given the 1989 payout ratio of 64.8% and the declining ROE, 5% seems like a maximum expectation. Yet a growth rate of approximately 6.3% is required to predict the market price of $36 per share.

Earnings Based Model

Earnings growth rates are considerably more volatile and, on average, below that of dividends. The historical growth rate as well as the implicit rate [g = (1−k)ROE], imply a growth rate of 4 to 5% when the dividend payout includes the repurchase of stock. When the dividend payout excludes repurchases, the growth rate is 7.5 to 8.5%.

Value Line's growth rate forecast of 10% seems high as it is based on per share data that, as we have shown, may be distorted by the repurchases. We use a growth rate of 8% and assume a dividend payout of 40%, allowing for continued stock repurchases.

$$P = \frac{kE(1+g)}{r-g} = \frac{(.40)(\$10.50)(1.08)}{.128-.08} = \$94.50 \; million$$

or $28.81 per share ($94.50/3.28), approximately 20% below the market price of $36/share.

Similar to the dividend model, the following table shows the sensitivity of the valuations to assumed growth rates and payout ratios:

FAB price per share
Effect of payout ratios and growth assumptions

Growth Rates	Payout Ratios				
	20%	**25%**	**40%**	**50%**	**60%**
5%	8.6	10.8	17.2	21.6	25.9
8%	14.4	18.0	28.8	36.0	43.2
10%	25.2	31.4	50.3	63.0	75.5

Interestingly, at a payout ratio of 50% (consistent with the repurchase program) and a growth rate of 8%, the predicted price is identical to the market price.

Free Cash Flows

Based on the data available, free cash flows can only be approximated. On a per share basis, they are:

	1985	1986	1987	1988	1989
"Cash flow"	$3.18	$3.87	$4.13	$4.02	$4.70
Capital spending	1.04	1.71	2.47	0.95	1.15

Converting to millions of dollars by multiplying by the number of shares:

	1985	1986	1987	1988	1989
"Cash flow"	$11.54	$14.05	$14.58	$13.79	$15.42
Capital spending	3.78	6.21	8.72	3.26	3.77
"Free cash flow"	$ 7.76	$ 7.84	$ 5.86	$10.53	$11.65

These amounts are not actual free cash flows as they do not include changes in operating working capital. However, in the absence of better data, we use them to estimate the growth rate:

	1986	1987	1988	1989
Change from prior year	1%	(25.3%)	79.6%	10.6%

  Arithmetic average: 16.5%
  Geometric average: 10%

The changes are very erratic and we use Value Line's forecast of 9.5%

For the changes in operating accounts we have one year's data (Part C of Exhibit 15P-1). These data show increased receivables of $3 million, increased inventory of 0.1, and decreased accounts payable of 1.1. [The increase in cash of .9 is assumed not to be required for operations (See part D).] These amounts reduce cash flows by $4.2 million ($3.0 + $0.1 + $1.1), bringing our 1989 estimate of free cash flows to $11.65 - $4.2 = $7.45 million. Ignoring any effect that the changes in operating accounts may have on growth rates, the free cash flow forecast becomes:

$$P = \frac{FCF(1+g)}{r-g} = \frac{(\$7.45)(1.095)}{.128-.095} = \$247.20 \; million$$

The value is $75 per share ($247.20/3.28), more than twice the market price of $36/share. This should not surprise us. As dividends are paid in the long run from free cash flow, a dividend growth rate of perhaps 5% and a free cash flow growth rate of 9.5% are not consistent. Growth rates should be examined for consistency; they cannot be used mechanically.

If we accept the market price as the benchmark, then the models do not do very well. However, even if the actual price is ignored, the results are troublesome. The dividend and earnings models yield valuations that are far below those of the free cash flow model. As suggested in the previous paragraph, more attention to the growth rates used is required. It is also possible that earnings and/or free cash flow (and the growth rates derived from their historical amounts) require adjustment because of accounting methods or other transactions that distort reported amounts.

D.   Dividend and earnings based DCF models assume that cash generated is used either for dividends or for new investment. When cash is "hoarded", the results of the models are distorted as both dividend payments and new investments become subject to management discretion. [This problem also exists for the free cash flow model to the extent any change in cash is treated as a working capital "requirement".]

Thus, the discrepancy between the dividend/earnings models and the free cash flow model may result from the fact that the free cash flow model "correctly" accounts for this "excess" cash. Hence its higher value for FAB.

One method of adjusting the earnings/dividend models is to consider FAB's cash position of more than $10/share. If these funds are not needed for operations then $10/share should be added to the valuations generated by the DCF models. This adjustment would have the effect of raising the dividend and earnings model valuations above the current market price. This adjustment still leaves values below that computed by the free cash flow model. The adjustment has valued only the excess cash arising from past operations and excludes the effect of excess cash to be generated in future periods.

On this basis, all models now indicate (to varying degrees) that FAB was underpriced. *It is interesting to note that over the next eighteen months FAB's stock price increased by approximately 100% to over $70/share.*

E.   We use Value Line's forecasts (after adjusting to dollars) for 1990 and 1992-1994 as follows:

1990	Given
1991	Average of 1991 and 1992-1994
1992-1994	Base level for future

We assume a growth rate of 9.5%.

	1990	1991	1992 and later
Dividends	$2.93	$3.17	$3.41

$$Value = \frac{\$2.93}{1.128} + \frac{\$3.17}{(1.128)^2} + \left[\frac{1}{(1.128)^2} x \frac{\$3.41}{(.128-.095)}\right] = \$86.30 \; million$$

or $26.31 per share ($86.30/3.28)

Earnings

Using the payout ratios forecast by Value Line, the earnings based model will be identical to the dividend model.

Free Cash Flows ($ millions)

	1990	1991	1992
"Cash flow"	$16.58	$19.07	$21.55
Capital spending	4.55	5.77	6.98
"Free cash flow"	$12.03	$13.30	$14.57

For the free cash flow model we need the changes in working capital. We will make the assumption that operating working capital (accounts receivable + inventory - accounts payable) increases by 10%/year. Since in 1989 these components totalled $43.9 million ($28.5 + $23.8 -$8.4), the requirement for 1990 and succeeding years will be:

Working capital change	4.39	4.83	5.31
Free cash flows	$7.64	$8.47	$9.26

where the last line is free cash flow as generally used in the chapter. Therefore:

$$Value = \frac{\$7.64}{1.128} + \frac{\$8.47}{(1.128)^2} + \left[\frac{1}{(1.128)^2} x \frac{\$9.26}{(.128-.095)}\right] = \$233.96 \; million$$

or $71.33 per share ($233.96/3.28)

The results are very similar to those calculated in part C.

F. In Part B, an estimate of r^*, ROE, was calculated at approximately 11-12%. Based on these values, r is approximately = r^* and reinvestment should not make a difference.

Using the 1990 level of earnings (in $ millions) of $11.375 ($3.50 x 3.25), a no reinvestment, no growth policy would yield:

Value = $11.375/.128 = $88.87 million or $27.09 per share ($88.87/3.28)

which is comparable to the estimates derived using reinvestment and growth.

8. The first step is to convert per share amounts to dollars by multiplying by the number of shares outstanding (as in problem 7, we should use *average* shares):

$ millions	1990	1991	1992
Earnings	$10.11	$15.57	$16.32
Dividends	2.50	3.09	3.08
"Cash flow"	15.35	20.39	22.48
Capital spending	6.80	3.03	7.39
"Free cash flow"	$ 8.55	$17.36	$15.09

Assuming a growth rate of 9.5% after 1992 yields, for the dividend model:

$$Value = \frac{\$2.50}{1.128} + \frac{\$3.09}{(1.128)^2} + [\frac{1}{(1.128)^2} \times \frac{\$3.08}{(.128-.095)}] = \$77.99 \ million$$

or $23.71 per share ($77.99/3.28)

For the earnings model, unless we alter the growth assumption, the results are identical.

It should, however, be noted that these calculations ignore share repurchases—a form of dividends. For 1990, if we treat repurchases as dividends, they would be ($ millions):

Book value at 1989 year end	$ 95.81	(3.29 x $29.12)
1990 earnings	10.11	
Cash dividends	(2.50)	
"Implicit" net worth	$103.42	
Actual net worth	97.72	(3.12 x $31.32)
Implied repurchases	$ 5.70	

This result can be approximated as follows:

Reduction in shares	.17 million (3.29 - 3.12)
Current price (1990)	$36

Approximate repurchase $6.1 million (.17 million x $36)

It appears that FAB bought shares at an average price below $36.

Including stock repurchases triples the 1990 dividend. In later years the repurchase amounts were lower, although that it appears that the firm continued to generate "excess" cash. (The firm may not have continued repurchases because of the higher stock price in later years.) By using the free cash flow model, the effects of dividend and repurchase policy can be mitigated if we assume that the company has enough cash for its operations.

As in question 7, we assume that operating working capital needs increase by 10% annually. Thus free cash flows are ($millions):

	1990	1991	1992
"Cash flow"	$15.35	$20.39	$22.48
Capital spending	6.80	3.03	7.39
"Free cash flow"	$ 8.55	$17.36	$15.09
Working capital change	4.39	4.83	5.31
Free cash flow	$ 4.16	$12.53	$ 9.78

Therefore:

$$Value=\frac{\$4.16}{1.128} + \frac{\$12.53}{(1.128)^2} + [\frac{1}{(1.128)^2} x \frac{\$9.78}{(.128-.095)}] = \$246.43 \text{ million}$$

or $75.13 per share ($246.43/3.28)

9. *NOTE: FAB's cost of equity of 12.8% (computed in 7-C) is based on its current beta of 0.8. As noted in Chapter 14, the beta of a leveraged firm differs from that of an unlevered firm. Consequently, the appropriate return on equity would also differ. For this example we have ignored the adjustment as it would change by an immaterial amount (0.2%).*

A. The problem can be solved readily if we assume that FAB maintains a constant debt to equity ratio. In that case, we can estimate 1990 free cash flow as follows:

FCF (1989) = $7.45 million (computed in 7-C)
FCF (1990) = $8.16 million, assuming a 9.5% growth rate

Interest (net of taxes) on the current debt of $50 million: (1-.34) x 11% x $50 million = $3.63 million.

To maintain the constant debt/equity ratio, debt must grow at the same 9.5% rate. New debt = $50 x 9.5% = $4.75 million.

Thus free cash flow available for equity holders equals unlevered FCF less interest expense + new debt:

$8.158 - $3.63 + $4.75 = $9.278 million

and the value of equity = $\frac{\$ 9.278}{(.128-.095)}$ = $281.15 million

B. Adding the value of equity to the value of debt:

Value of equity $281.15 million
Value of debt   50.00
Value of firm $331.15 million

Alternatively, the WACC can be computed as follows:

$$(\frac{\$281.15}{\$331.15} x .128) + (\frac{\$50}{\$331.15} x (.11 x (1-.34))) = .1196$$

Using 1990 unlevered FCF yields the value of the firm:

$$Value = \frac{FCF(1+g)}{r-g} = \frac{(\$7.45)(1.095)}{.1196-.095} = \$331.15 \text{ million}$$

10. A. **Statement of Cash Flows**

Net income	$19,200
Depreciation	8,500
	$27,700
Changes in operating accounts:	
Account receivable	(500)
Accounts payable	500
Cash from operations	$27,700
Cash for investment:	
Fixed assets	(9,000)
Cash for financing:	
Dividends paid	(16,700)
Change in cash	$ 2,000

To estimate free cash flow we assume that the increase in cash of $2000 is needed for operations, not held as "excess" cash by the firm. After reclassifying interest expense (after tax) from cash from operations to cash for financing:

Operating income (net of tax)	$21,000	
Depreciation	8,500	
Funds from operations		$ 29,500
Changes in operating accounts:		
Cash	$(2000)	
Accounts receivable	(500)	
Accounts payable	500	
		(2,000)
Adjusted cash from operations		$ 27,500
Cash for investment:		(9,000)
Free cash flow		**$ 18,500**
Cash for financing:		
Interest (net of tax)	(1,800)	
Dividends paid	(16,700)	
Total		$(18,500)

B. Begin by estimating the fixed and variable cost components of the income statement. We use the method shown in Appendix 3-A and the equation:

Fixed costs = total costs - (variable cost % x sales)

COGS: Increase in cost of $3,000 for sales increase of $10,000 implies variable cost percentage of 30% and fixed costs of $20,000.

Selling and General: Increase of $2,000 for sales increase of $10,000 implies variable cost percentage of 20% and fixed selling and general costs of 0.

If fixed selling costs are 0, $8,500 of depreciation must be included in cost of goods sold. To complete the forecast of operating income we must forecast depreciation expense.

Estimating Fixed Asset Investments and Depreciation:

The average fixed asset turnover ratio for 19X1 and 19X2 is

Using gross assets	1.06
Using net assets	1.70

Our forecast should maintain these ratios and also be consistent with depreciation expense of 8%-9% of gross fixed assets (implying an average life of about 12 years). That forecast is:

	19X3	19X4	19X5
Sales	$150,000	$180,000	$200,000
Fixed assets (gross)	140,000	170,000	190,000
Accumulated depreciation	(52,500)	(66,500)	(81,500)
Fixed assets (net)	$ 87,500	$103,500	$108,500

As 19X2 accumulated depreciation was (41,000), we can derive depreciation expense from the annual change in accumulated depreciation (assuming no retirement of fixed assets):

	19X3	19X4	19X5
Depreciation expense	$ 11,500	$ 14,000	$ 15,000

These estimates yield the following turnover ratios (consistent with the historical pattern):

	19X3	19X4	19X5
Fixed assets (gross)	1.07	1.06	1.05
Fixed assets (net)	1.71	1.74	1.84
and depreciation rates of	8.2%	8.2%	7.9%

These estimates allow us to forecast (pre and posttax) operating income:

	19X3	19X4	19X5
Sales	$150,000	$180,000	$ 200,000
Cost of goods sold	(68,000)	(79,500)	(86,500)
Selling and general	(30,000)	(36,000)	(40,000)
Operating income	$ 52,000	$ 64,500	$ 73,500
Operating income (after 40% tax)	$ 31,200	$ 38,700	$ 44,100

To complete the income statement we need to estimate the firm's interest expense.

Forecast of borrowing needs and interest expense:

Turnover ratios for current operating accounts are:

Cash	10
Accounts receivable	12
Inventory	8.5
Accounts payable	6

These turnover ratios imply the following working capital accounts, based on the sales and cost of goods sold figures determined earlier:

	19X3	19X4	19X5
Cash	$ 15,000	$ 18,000	$ 20,000
Accounts receivable	12,500	14,500	16,500
Inventory	7,500	9,000	10,000
Accounts payable	(11,500)	(13,500)	(14,500)
Operating working capital	$ 23,500	$ 28,000	$ 32,000

To estimate the company's borrowing needs, we need some additional assumptions:

(1) The present level of dividends ($16,700) will be maintained as funds are needed to finance expansion.

(2) Any cash needed will be borrowed. Excess cash will be used to repay debt.

(3) Although borrowing would most likely be done throughout the year, for simplification we assume that borrowings occur at year end.(This will also be relevant for valuation purposes.)

	19X3	19X4	19X5
Opening balance of debt	$ 30,000	$ 49,300	$ 50,758
Interest expense (10%) Net of tax (60%)	3,000 1,800	4,930 2,958	5,076 3,046
Operating income after tax Depreciation expense Change in operating w.c. Cash from operations [before interest exp.]	31,200 11,500 (6,500) $ 36,200	38,700 14,000 (4,500) $ 48,200	44,100 15,000 (4,000) $ 55,100

Cash for investment and
financing:
  Increased fixed assets
    (gross)
  Dividends paid
  Interest (net of tax)
    Subtotal
	(37,000)
	(16,700)
	(1,800)
	$(55,500)
		(30,000)
		(16,700)
		(2,958)
		$(49,658)
			(20,000)
			(16,700)
			(3,046)
			$(39,746)

Borrowing (repayment) [Cash from operations less cash for investment and financing]	19,300	1,458	(15,354)
Closing balance of debt [Opening balance plus borrowing (less repayment)]	$ 49,300	$ 50,758	$ 35,404

Income statements and balance sheets follow:

	19X3	19X4	19X5
Income Statement:			
Sales	$150,000	$180,000	$200,000
Cost of goods sold	(68,000)	(79,500)	(86,500)
Selling and general	(30,000)	(36,000)	(40,000)
Operating income	$ 52,000	$ 64,500	$ 73,500
Interest expense	(3,000)	(4,930)	(5,076)
Pretax income	$ 49,000	$ 59,570	$ 68,424
Tax expense	(19,600)	(23,828)	(27,370)
Net income	$ 29,400	$ 35,742	$ 41,054
Balance Sheet:			
Cash	$ 15,000	$ 18,000	$ 20,000
Accoaunts receivable	12,500	14,500	16,500
Inventory	7,500	9,000	10,000
Current assets	$ 35,000	$ 41,500	$ 46,500
Fixed assets (gross)	$140,000	$170,000	$190,000
Accumulated depreciation	(52,500)	(66,500)	(81,500)
Fixed assets (net)	$ 87,500	$103,500	$108,500
Total assets	$122,500	$145,000	$155,000
Accounts payable	$ 11,500	$ 13,500	$14,500
Debt	49,300	50,758	35,404
Stockholders' equity	61,700	80,742	105,096
Total liabilities & equity	$122,500	$145,000	$155,000

C.   Estimate of free cash flow:

	19X3	19X4	19X5
Operating income after tax	$ 31,200	$ 38,700	$ 44,100
Depreciation	11,500	14,000	15,000
Change in operating w.c.	(6,500)	(4,500)	(4,000)
	$ 36,200	$ 48,200	$ 55,100
Increased fixed assets	(37,000)	(30,000)	(20,000)
Free cash flow	$ (800)	$ 18,200	$ 35,100
Cash for financing:			
Interest (net of tax)	(1,800)	(2,958)	(3,046)
Borrowing (repayment)	19,300	1,458	(15,354)
Dividends paid	(16,700)	(16,700)	(16,700)
Total	$ 800	$(18,200)	$(35,100)

D.   After 19X5, the company will reach "steady state" and maintain operations equal to that year. At that point, it will not need new investments in fixed assets or working capital. Cash for investments will be required only for replacement. If we assume that depreciation approximates replacement of assets we have the following forecast:

	19X6 and later
Operating income after tax	$44,100
Depreciation	15,000
Change in operating working capital	0
Cash from operations	$59,100
Increase in fixed assets	(15,000)
Free cash flow	$44,100

If we assume that all free cash flows are used to pay interest and dividends:

Cash for financing:	
Interest (net of tax)	$ (2,025)
Dividends paid	(42,075)
Total	$(44,100)

Dividends to equity shareholders are ($ thousands):

	19X3	19X4	19X5	19X6 and later
Dividends	16.7	16.7	16.7	42.1

$$\text{Value of equity at end of 19X5} = \frac{\$42.1}{.15} = \$280.7$$

$$\text{Value at end of 19X2} = \frac{\$16.7}{(1.15)} + \frac{\$16.7}{(1.15)^2} + \frac{\$16.7 + \$280.7}{(1.15)^3}$$

$$= \$222.7$$

As value of equity	= $222.7
and value of debt	= 30.0
Value of firm	$252.7

Alternatively, the value of the firm can be determined using free cash flows:

	19X3	19X4	19X5	19X6 and later
($ thousands)				
Free cash flows	(.8)	18.2	35.1	44.1

We must first estimate WACC. As the after tax cost of debt = .06:

$$WACC = \frac{\$222}{\$252} \times .15 + \frac{\$30}{\$252} \times .06 = .139$$

$$\text{Value of firm at end of 19X5} = \frac{\$44.1}{.139} = \$316.6$$

$$\text{Value of firm at end of 19X2} = \frac{\$(.8)}{(1.139)} + \frac{\$18.2}{(1.139)^2} + \frac{\$35.1 + \$316.6}{(1.139)^3}$$

$$= \$251.3$$

The slight discrepancy between the two answers ($252.2 and $251.3) is due mainly to rounding. In addition, since the amount of debt (relative to the value of equity) changes from period to period, the WACC changes also. We have ignored this refinement and used a constant WACC as the changes from period to period are slight.

11. A. Assuming that the market value of Kraft prior to the merger was "appropriate" the amount by which Philip Morris "overpaid" can be calculated (in $ millions) as:

Market value of Kraft prior to merger ($65 x 120)	$ 7,800
Amount paid for acquisition of Kraft ($90 x 12)	(10,800)
"Overpayment"	$(3,000)

On a per share basis, the overpayment should have decreased the market price of Philip Morris shares by:

$$\frac{\$3,000}{234} = \$12.80 \text{ per share}$$

The actual market price decrease of $4.50 was considerably less than the amount determined by the asset based approach.

B. The smaller decline in the price of Philip Morris shares suggests that the market expected synergistic effects from the merger that partly offset the "overpayment". Investors in Philip Morris may have believed that Kraft was "undermanaged" and that its profitability would be improved by Philip Morris management.

C. The problem in using any of the DCF models is predicting the effect of the acquisition on the parameters of the model.

1. For example, the acquisition of Kraft would be expected to have no immediate effect on dividends paid to Philip Morris shareholders. The need to service the debt incurred to buy Kraft, however, might reduce the future growth rate of dividend payments, reducing their present value. The higher leverage of Philip Morris following the merger would also increase the required discount rate, further decreasing the stock price.

2. For an earnings-based model, the effect on current earnings (dilution) as well as the effect on the growth rate and discount rate, must be considered.

3. The Kraft acquisition reduces the free cash flow of Philip Morris initially. After tax interest expense of $770 million [11% x $10,800 x (1-.35) exceeds the free cash flow of Kraft (estimated as CFO + interest - capital expenditures = $607 + $81 - $260). As in the other cases, the effect on the growth rate and discount rate must also be considered.

   The advantage of the dividend model is that there is no effect on the current level of dividends; thus only the growth rate and discount rate effects must be estimated.

12. A. Free cash flow is calculated for Deere in Exhibit 14-13. The definition of free cash flow, however, differs from that used in the free cash valuation model in Chapter 15; we must remove interest expense (net of taxes) ($ millions):

	1989	1990	1991
Free Cash Flow:			
Operating cash flow	$ (238)	$ (468)	$ (29)
Increase in marketable securities	(60)	(74)	(64)
Capital expenditures	(181)	(292)	(298)
Free cash flow (Exhibit 14-13)	$ (479)	$ (834)	$ (391)
Interest expense (Exhibit 1B-2)	407	435	450
Tax effect (34% tax rate)	(138)	(148)	(153)
Free cash flow	$ (210)	$ (547)	$ (104)

B. Market value of equity = 76.231 x $56   = $ 4,269 million
    Total debt (Exhibit 14-3)   5,959
        Total market value $10,228 million

C. Given the (negative) free cash flows found in part A, the free cash flow valuation model breaks down for Deere. The implied discount rate is negative, a nonsensical result.

    Assuming that the free cash flow discount model is valid, the market must be assuming positive free cash flows in future years.

13. Deere's cost of capital is:

$$r = .05 + 1.3 \times .06 = .128$$

Dividend model:

    From the statement of cash flows in Exhibit 1B-2, we find that Deere has steadily increased its dividend payments:

    1989 $86.2 million
    1990   140.3
    1991   152.3

The growth rate from 1989 - 1990 was 62%; from 1990 to 1991 it was 8.8%. As the table below indicates, the market seemed to be using the more recent rate. Deere's current dividend rate was $2.00/share. Using the valuation formula of:

$$\frac{\$2.00 \times (1+g)}{.128 - g}$$

we find for various estimates of g:

g	Value	
5%	$27	
7%	$37	
8%	$45	
9%	$57	(approximates market value of $56)
10%	$79	

15-25

Earnings model:

Exhibit 15-7 shows normalized earnings of:

1988	$241 million
1989	378
1990	390
1991	6

The last year is clearly an aberration due to the recession. If we assume that 1990 was a normal earnings year, we can use $390 million as an estimate of normal earnings for 1992.

From Exhibit 15-3 (ignoring 1991), Deere's ROE averages 14.7%. The dividend payout ratio for those years (excluding 1991) averages 26%. As the payout ratio has increased, we estimate a payout ratio of 30%.

The implied growth rate is approximately 10% [(1-.3) x .147].

Our estimated market value is
$$\frac{.3 \times \$390}{.128-.10} = \$4,179 \text{ million}$$

As the average number of shares outstanding is 76.231 million, this implies a per share price of $54.82 ($4179/76.231) that is very close to the actual price of $56/share.

Free cash flows: See solution to problem 12-C.

14. From a theoretical perspective there are a number of problems with the price to cash flow ratio suggested by the article.

1. The measure used, net income + depreciation + amortization, is equal to funds from operations (FFO), an incomplete measure of cash flow. It does not reflect changes in operating working capital accounts or other adjustments required to calculate CFO as defined by SFAS 95. FFO has been shown to have little or no explanatory power beyond that provided by net income.

2. The theoretical basis for a price to cash flow ratio is based on a free cash flow model. As noted in the chapter, free cash flow is considerably different from CFO, and is even more distant from FFO.

Notwithstanding the above, the price to cash flow ratio may be a useful "filter," similar to the price to earnings ratio (PER). As noted in the chapter, the PER itself is predicated on the assumption that earnings is a useful surrogate for or predictor of cash flows to investors. Thus, the efficacy of both ratios depends to some extent on how well they can predict relevant variables of interest.

In this respect CFO may be more useful than earnings as it is less subject to manipulation by the selection of accounting principles. On the other hand, CFO suffers from a conceptual limitation relevant to valuation in that it does not reflect the cost of asset replacement (whereas the depreciation component of earnings may approximate this cost). This limitation may be overcome if replacement cost is a constant proportion of cash flow. In this case, it will be imbedded in the price to cash flow ratio.

Ultimately, however, the usefulness of the ratio should be tested empirically.

15.   A.   IIMR headline earnings attempts to take on some of the characteristics of each of the four definitions of income. However, ultimately it is not identical to any of them.

Although, headline earnings excludes capital items (e.g. sale of assets) it differs from operating income as it includes interest income/expense. By including items that are abnormal in nature and size, as well as discontinued operations, headline earnings differs from both permanent and sustainable income. Finally, it is not equivalent to economic income as it excludes capital items and valuation adjustments that are part of economic earnings.

B.   The purpose of IIMR earnings appears to be the desire to have a reported income amount that is relatively free from capital gains and losses and other nonoperating adjustments. This measure should be less affected by the timing of asset sales and such extraneous items as prior period adjustments.

Towards that end, IIMR headline earnings would exclude gains or losses from the sale of net assets, the disposal of operating segments, and acquisitions. Prior period adjustments would also be excluded. Finally, income tax expense would be adjusted for any components of net income excluded from IIMR headline earnings.

The result would be a normalized earnings amount. However the operating results of discontinued operations as well as many nonrecurring items, would remain within the IIMR earnings report. The proposal appears to leave further adjustment for these items to the individual analyst rather than permitting management to make those judgements.

C.   To Whom It May Concern:

My major concern is related to the three reasons given for the delineation of earnings. They suffer from two faults: (1) the reason itself is not compelling; and (2) the reason contradicts one of the other reasons.

The first reason given is that "in evaluating a company the stock market must order published information in some useful way. If this so, ... information should ... be ordered in that way...." Since we do not know the manner in which the markets order the information, or even whether or not markets do so, how can we attempt to order the information in this "unknown" manner?

The second reason relates to those who do not have any expertise in "distilling" information contained in the accounts. While one may be sympathetic to their plight, it is not clear that these investors actually influence the market (see discussion in Chapter 4). Even if they do, why should we assume that headline earnings is the appropriate input for their use? In addition, this reason contradicts the previous one, that is geared to providing a number that will satisfy the manner in which the markets "order published information in some useful way". That implies a sophisticated level of information processing.

Finally, there is the argument that there is a need for an unambiguous reference point. That may be true. It does not however point to headline earnings. Any agreed upon number will do.